Edward Bujak is Associate Professor of History at Harlaxton College, the British campus of the University of Evansville, Indiana. He is the author of *England's Rural Realms: Landholding and the Agricultural Revolution* (I.B.Tauris, 2008).

'*Reckless Fellows* is a most welcome addition to the historiography of air power in World War I; it is immaculately researched and provides a fascinating insight into the world of the operational aircrew.'

– Peter Gray, Senior Research Fellow in Air Power Studies, University of Birmingham

'*Reckless Fellows* makes a welcome contribution to the growing interest in pilot studies that is both scholarly and readable. Edward Bujak's insights into changes in the training programme and the social make up of the Royal Flying Corps skilfully connects local and social history with the wider experience of airmen in World War I.'

– Maryam Philpott, author of *Air and Sea Power in World War I*

'In spite of the celebrity of individual air aces, we still know surprisingly little about British pilots in World War I. *Reckless Fellows* is therefore a welcome addition to the literature, and will undoubtedly stimulate debate.'

– Gary Sheffield, Professor of War Studies, University of Wolverhampton

RECKLESS FELLOWS

THE GENTLEMEN OF THE ROYAL FLYING CORPS

EDWARD BUJAK

In memory of
ALBERT STANTON CURTIS
(1892–1985)
Sergeant, Air-Gunner/Observer, Royal Flying Corps, 1916–18

Published in 2015 by
I.B.Tauris and Co. Ltd
London • New York

BRIDGEND LIB & INFO SERVICE	
3 8030 60136 358 6	
Askews & Holts	4835196
940.44941	£20.00
	OVA

The right of E ... been asserted by the aut ... Act 1988.
All rights r ... or any part thereof, ma ... l system, or transmitted ... otocopying, recording ... publisher.
Every attempt ... s in this book.

References to websites were correct at the time of writing.

ISBN: 978 1 78453 442 4
eISBN: 978 0 85773 952 0

A full CIP record for this book is available from the British Library
A full CIP record is available from the Library of Congress

Library of Congress Catalog Card Number: available

Typeset by Fakenham Prepress Solutions, Fakenham, Norfolk NR21 8NN
Printed and bound in Sweden by ScandBook AB

Contents

List of Illustrations vi
Acknowledgements xi

Introduction 1

Chapter 1: Poor Bloody Observers and Aerial Reconnaissance 15

Chapter 2: Reckless Fellows and Aerial Superiority 32

Chapter 3: Young Icarus and Flight Training 47

Chapter 4: Gosport and the Flight Instructor 63

Chapter 5: Airmen and their American Mechanics 81

Chapter 6: An Australian Odyssey from Egypt to England 100

Chapter 7: The Aerodrome and the Armistice 118

Conclusion 134

Appendix I: RFC/RAF Harlaxton (Training Squadron Station and Training Depot Station) Roll of Honour, 1917–18   146

Appendix II: The Last Parade, 1919 152

Notes 163
Bibliography 195
Index 205

List of Illustrations

1. Harlaxton, vertical photograph, 11 June 1917. Aerial view 013. PC94/132/013. Reproduced with the kind permission of the Trustees of the Royal Air Force Museum.   2

2. Harlaxton Manor. T608051-116. Harlaxton-Russia Prints. Reproduced with the kind permission of the Trustees of the Royal Air Force Museum.   8

3. Denton Manor. T608051-137. Harlaxton-Russia Prints. Reproduced with the kind permission of the Trustees of the Royal Air Force Museum.   13

4. BE2e (A2847), Harlaxton, 1917. JMB/GSL/01677. Photograph reproduced with the kind permission of the Fleet Air Arm Museum.   16

5. Harlaxton Photographic Section. T608051-190. Harlaxton-Russia Prints. Reproduced with the kind permission of the Trustees of the Royal Air Force Museum.   22

6. Trenches, Harlaxton Park. T608051-076. Harlaxton-Russia Prints. Reproduced with the kind permission of the Trustees of the Royal Air Force Museum.   22

7. Machine Gun Lecture Room, Harlaxton, © Imperial War Museum (2004-11-53). Collection: Klynes A.H. (Flying Officer).   26

8. Royal Flying Corps pilots at Mess, Harlaxton, 1917. Source: Library and Archives Canada/Credit: William John Dalziel/William John Dalziel Collection/C-028097.   28

9. Billiard Room, Officers' Mess, Harlaxton, © Imperial War Museum (2004-11-53). Collection: Klynes A.H. (Flying Officer).   31

LIST OF ILLUSTRATIONS

10 2nd Lieutenant Stanley Arthur Rutledge, RFC. Reproduced with the kind permission of Queen's University Archive, Canada. 39

11 Royal Flying Corps pilots from Canada, Harlaxton, 1917. Source: Library and Archives Canada/Credit: William John Dalziel/William John Dalziel Collection/C-028091. 41

12 'Waiting for a bus': RFC pilots under training, Harlaxton, 1917. Source: Library and Archives Canada/Credit: William John Dalziel/William John Dalziel Collection/C-0028044. 44

13 Belvoir Castle. T608051-056. Harlaxton-Russia Prints. Reproduced with the kind permission of the Trustees of the Royal Air Force Museum. 46

14 Aerial view. T608051-164. Harlaxton-Russia Prints. Reproduced with the kind permission of the Trustees of the Royal Air Force Museum. 48

15 Hangar construction. X002-9372. Papers of AVM Arthur Stanley Gould Lee. Reproduced with the kind permission of the Trustees of the Royal Air Force Museum. 49

16 Harlaxton, interior of hangar, 13 April 1917. PC94/132/12. Reproduced with the kind permission of the Trustees of the Royal Air Force Museum. 49

17 Group photograph of flight cadets of No. 40 Training Depot Station, Harlaxton. Papers of Air Mechanic, 3rd Class, William Frederick Leedham, X003-2951. Reproduced with the kind permission of the Trustees of the Royal Air Force Museum. 52

18 Aerial view. T608051-186. Harlaxton-Russia Prints. Reproduced with the kind permission of the Trustees of the Royal Air Force Museum. 54

19 'A bad landing', in a Maurice Farman Shorthorn, © Imperial War Museum (2004-11-53). Collection: Klynes A.H. (Flying Officer). 57

20 Lieutenant W.J. Dalziel, Wapella, Sask., in a BE2e aircraft prior to his first solo flight, Harlaxton, 11 December 1917. Source: Library and Archives Canada/Credit: William John Dalziel/William John Dalziel Collection/C-028067. 59

LIST OF ILLUSTRATIONS

21 Sopwith two-seater crash, © Imperial War Museum (2004-11-53). Collection: Klynes A.H. (Flying Officer). 70

22 'Practice aerial scrap, 10,000ft. A.W. Bus.' Photograph of an Armstrong Whitworth FK8 in flight. Papers of Air Mechanic, 3rd Class, William Frederick Leedham, X003-2951. Reproduced with the kind permission of the Trustees of the Royal Air Force Museum. 72

23 Clay pigeon shooting, Harlaxton, © Imperial War Museum (2004-11-53). Collection: Klynes A.H. (Flying Officer). 73

24 Officers and air mechanics in front of an RE8, Harlaxton. X006-7310E. Reproduced with the kind permission of the Trustees of the Royal Air Force Museum. 74

25 Harlaxton crash – Avro 504. PC75/5. Photograph album of pre-war and war-time aviation, 1899–1919. Reproduced with the kind permission of the Trustees of the Royal Air Force Museum. 76

26 'DH6 makes an attempt for the hangar'. Papers of Air Mechanic, 3rd Class, William Frederick Leedham, X003–2951. Reproduced with the kind permission of the Trustees of the Royal Air Force Museum. 82

27 'Captain Saint and pupil killed, August 1918'. Papers of Air Mechanic, 3rd Class, William Frederick Leedham, X003-2951. Reproduced with the kind permission of the Trustees of the Royal Air Force Museum. 82

28 'Flight Cadet Iddon, killed, RE8, Harlaxton'. Papers of Air Mechanic, 3rd Class, William Frederick Leedham, X003-2951. Reproduced with the kind permission of the Trustees of the Royal Air Force Museum. 89

29 Harlaxton 1917. PC75/5. Photograph album of pre-war and war-time aviation, 1899–1919. Reproduced with the kind permission of the Trustees of the Royal Air Force Museum. 90

30 The 50th Aero Squadron, US Army Aviation Service, at Harlaxton, 1918. Reproduced from the personal papers of Alfred C. Beardslee with the kind permission of his granddaughters. 93

LIST OF ILLUSTRATIONS

31 Eleven officers and sixteen other ranks sitting and standing outside a tented hangar at Harlaxton, X006–7310A. Reproduced with the kind permission of the Trustees of the Royal Air Force Museum.   96

32 BE2c with US Mechanics. X004-6770. Collection of photographs compiled by Frank M. Tobin during his RAF service in England and Belgium, 1918–19. Reproduced with the kind permission of the Trustees of the Royal Air Force Museum.   97

33 'Yanks and Limeys'. Reproduced from the personal papers of Alfred C. Beardslee with the kind permission of his granddaughters.   98

34 'Lt Mather. Killed Harlaxton, 1918, RE8'. Papers of Air Mechanic, 3rd Class, William Frederick Leedham, X003-2951. Reproduced with the kind permission of the Trustees of the Royal Air Force Museum.   99

35 'De Havilland 5, crash', © Imperial War Museum (2004-11-53). Collection: Klynes A.H. (Flying Officer).   101

36 Group portrait of officers and ground staff of No. 68 Squadron, Australian Flying Corps (later known as No. 2 Squadron), arriving at Harlaxton aerodrome, 1917. CO1854, Australian War Memorial.   104

37 Major Watt OC 68th Squadron (AFC) and Major Jenkins, OC 44th Squadron RFC, Harlaxton, June 1917, © Imperial War Museum (2004-11-53). Collection: Klynes A.H. (Flying Officer).   106

38 Capt. Muir, MC, AFC, with squadron mascot, Brrr, the monkey, © Imperial War Museum (2004-11-53). Collection: Klynes A.H. (Flying Officer).   109

39 Group portrait of pilots from 68 Squadron, Australian Flying Corps (later known as No. 2 Squadron), posed in front of a De Havilland DH5 aircraft at Harlaxton aerodrome, 1917. CO1852, Australian War Memorial.   117

40 Harlaxton aerodrome, Grantham, 1918–19. Papers of Air Mechanic, 3rd Class, William Frederick Leedham, X003-2951. Reproduced with the kind permission of the Trustees of the Royal Air Force Museum.   119

LIST OF ILLUSTRATIONS

41 'Three South African boys', © Imperial War Museum (2004-11-53). Capt. Frost, 2nd Lt Nicholson and 2nd Lt Van der Riet. Collection: Klynes A.H. (Flying Officer).   126

42 'Season's Greetings'. RFC Christmas card, including monochrome portrait, RAF Harlaxton, *c.* 1914–19. T203914. Reproduced with the kind permission of the Trustees of the Royal Air Force Museum.   128

43 Hangar, tender and DH4, Harlaxton X002-9372. Papers of AVM Arthur Stanley Gould Lee. Reproduced with the kind permission of the Trustees of the Royal Air Force Museum.   131

44 'Off duty', Klynes at the wheel of a sports car, © Imperial War Museum (2004-11-53). Collection: Klynes A.H. (Flying Officer).   133

45 Aerial view, sports day, Harlaxton. T608051-195. Harlaxton-Russia Prints. Reproduced with the kind permission of the Trustees of the Royal Air Force Museum.   139

46 Invitation to Harlaxton Sports Day. Papers of Air Mechanic, 3rd Class, William Frederick Leedham, X003-2951. Reproduced with the kind permission of the Trustees of the Royal Air Force Museum.   141

Acknowledgements

Grateful thanks to: Roger Bragger, Joanne Bujak, Phyllis E. Bujak, Mick Davis, Linda Dawes, Andrew Dennis, Priscilla Engeman, Dr Caroline Magennis, Peter McNab and the McNab family, Dr Danielle O'Donovan, Dr Gerald Seaman, Dr Helen Snow, Peggy Woods, the Australian War Memorial, the Fleet Air Arm Museum, the Imperial War Museum, the Library and Archives Canada, the Trustees of the Liddell Hart Centre for Military Archives, Queen's University Archives and the Royal Air Force Museum.

Introduction

This book tells the story of the pilots who learned to fly with the various training squadrons of the Royal Flying Corps (RFC) stationed at Harlaxton aerodrome between 1916 and 1918. It examines how the training programme being pioneered in England at this time came to mirror the tactics and techniques being developed by pilots in France. It also considers the expansion of the RFC into an imperial air service with pilots from across the Empire arriving in rural England for their training. After the war, Australia, Canada, New Zealand and South Africa would establish their own air services. In so doing, the memory of this imperial air service dissipated, but there was to be one last coming together of this force at Harlaxton Manor, in 1919, when the aerodrome became a repatriation camp for the pilots waiting for a ship home. In 1919, they would have all belonged to the new Royal Air Force (RAF) which had replaced the RFC in April 1918. In this last gathering together of RAF pilots from across the Empire we can also glimpse a group of individuals who had refashioned themselves into a new air-officer elite during their earlier training amidst the country house estates of rural England.

The conjoined experiences of training and combat transformed the self-identity of pilots, whose masculinity was expressed through their symbiotic relationship with flying ever more powerful and faster aeroplanes. As a result, the pilots of the First World War came to have an almost mythological status as the ultimate embodiment of manliness.[1] But what of their social status? Throughout the war flying was consistently compared to riding a horse. The original officers of the RFC were cavalrymen and fox-hunting country gentlemen who belonged to the social elite of Edwardian England. By 1917 and 1918, the social exclusivity of the RFC had been eroded and the RAF pilot officer belonged to a new technocracy of highly proficient pilots from all over the world and from all classes, not just the aristocracy. But in 1918, when strafing the enemy, these pilots were exhibiting the same recklessness as the Edwardian cavalry officer and fox-hunter hedge-hopping over the farms and fields of rural England in 1912. In 1918, Ernst von Hoeppner, the commander of the German *Luftstreitkräfte*, and himself an ex-cavalry officer, complimented the pilots of the RFC on their 'sporting audacity'.[2] Was this because the pilots of 1917 and 1918 were transforming themselves into officers and gentlemen, in training, in the same social context that had produced the original cadre of flying officers?

In late 1916, when the RFC's new training aerodrome was opened at Harlaxton Manor, the Corps was only four years old. The RFC was formally constituted by a Royal Warrant issued on 13 April 1912. This was accompanied by a Special Army Order issued two days later. Two years later, in 1914, when the British Expeditionary Force (BEF) was sent to France, every available pilot and aeroplane in the Corps went too, to supplement the reconnaissance work of the cavalry. However, once the Germans opted to dig in, wherever possible on the high ground, cavalry reconnaissance became redundant. This was the moment when the RFC came into its own and, in so doing, superseded

Figure 1. Harlaxton, vertical photograph, 11 June 1917. Aerial view showing both Harlaxton aerodrome and Harlaxton Manor.

the elite cavalry regiments in one of their primary roles: reconnaissance. The British needed to see what was going on beyond the heavily defended ridges and the only way to do so was through aerial reconnaissance. Naturally, the Germans were equally determined to prevent the RFC from flying over their entrenchments. These countermeasures overturned the unarmed reconnaissance role envisaged for what was, in 1912, the Military Wing of the RFC. This was now an air war in which the pilots and observers of the RFC had to fight to gather the information needed by the Army (see Chapter 1) and especially the Royal Field Artillery (RFA); the latter beginning to work ever more closely with the RFC when targeting its batteries of heavy guns.[3] The development of this artillery cooperation role required the RFC to adopt new tactics and technology, including signalling using wireless transmitters, using cameras for photographic reconnaissance and operating specialist fighting machines to defend this work. These tactical and technological developments were, in turn, shaped by the new strategic doctrine of establishing air-superiority or air supremacy over the German air service.

These new tactics and technologies were developed during the war, amidst what Yeats so brilliantly described as the 'tumult of the clouds'.[4] Throughout the First World War, the primary objective of the RFC remained the supply of information to the artillery and infantry. In 1916, Sir Hugh Trenchard, the General Officer Commanding the RFC in the field (from August 1915 to January 1918) sought to attain and secure aerial ascendancy over the Germans through offensive patrols spearheaded by specialist fighting squadrons committed to 'attacking and continuing to attack'.[5] This policy was an extension of the RFC's primary objective, in that this relentless and incessant offensive provided a protective screen for the work of the reconnaissance and artillery-spotting machines. The machines needed for the latter were designed for steady, level flight to provide a stable aerial platform from which the enemy could be photographed. Similarly, level, stable flight allowed observers to 'spot' targets for the artillery, which was now the key weapon in a war where the British were effectively besieging the Germans on their ridgelines. Seen from the optimistic pre-war perspective of flying on reconnaissance, free of interference, pilots needed only to be taught the rudiments of flying in a straight, level pattern, rather than 'jinking', 'stunting' or 'show' flying. Indeed, this type of flying was originally looked upon somewhat contemptuously by the Corps.[6] Pre-war flying theory was, however, confronted by the military realities of 1914 and 1915 where RFC pilots were flying reconnaissance patrols in an increasingly contested space, epitomised by the appearance of new German 'fighting-scouts' in 1915.

The development of the fighting-scout or 'fighter' added a new dimension to the air war. As Lord Hugh Cecil observed, 'when the war began, the distinction between a fighting machine and a reconnaissance machine was scarcely recognized'[7] – by the end of 1915, it was. The Fokker E-type monoplane (or *Eindecker*) was an aeroplane specifically designed to hunt and shoot down the RFC's reconnaissance aeroplanes, and the disparity in fire-power and manoeuvrability between these respective machines, given their different functions, would prove fatal for many RFC pilots and observers in 1915, regardless of the individual skill of the pilot. The appearance of this machine was the catalyst for both pilots and designers to find tactical and technological solutions to the threat it posed to the RFC's reconnaissance machines. The solution was for the RFC to put its own fighting machines into the air to provide the reconnaissance machines with an escort. Subsequently, in early-to-mid 1916, more powerful fighting machines were given an offensive role, hunting the German fighters, by flying above and beyond the reconnaissance machines on routine fighting patrols. This tactical change brought into being the iconic figure of the fighter pilot (see Chapter 2), immortalised in modern memory by the classic 1938 film *The Dawn Patrol* starring Errol Flynn, David Niven and Basil Rathbone, and the more recent 1976 film *Aces High*.

More fighter squadrons and reconnaissance squadrons were made possible by the flow of volunteers into the RFC. The speed of the RFC's expansion was also due to the brevity of the pilot-training programme in England. The changing content and context of flight training both prior to and after the opening of Harlaxton aerodrome is discussed in Chapter 3. Meanwhile, the formation of more Reserve squadrons or Training squadrons in England also saw an increased demand for instructors (see Chapter 4). Instructors at Harlaxton, as elsewhere, were either seconded from operational squadrons or were some of the more talented trainee pilots who were held back once they had attained their 'wings'. These novice pilot-instructors were being pitched into the job alongside novice pilots. This exacerbated the already considerable risks inherent in flying machines made of wood, canvas and wire. Shockingly, over half the 14,166 pilots who lost their lives in the war did so in training.[8] Pilots were therefore, leaving England having already seen comrades killed or seriously wounded (see Chapter 5 and Appendix I). As a consequence of their experience in training they would, presumably, have become acclimatised to the precariousness of their future existence in an operational squadron, so why not, as it says in 1 Corinthians 15:32: 'Eat and drink for tomorrow we die'? There would certainly be little opportunity for dwelling on a death or injury given the very deliberate insistence of Sir Hugh Trenchard that there never be an empty chair at the breakfast table in the Officers' Mess.

In an effort to mitigate the losses being sustained in training, Harlaxton aerodrome was placed on the west-facing ridge above the Manor. This produced the additional lift needed to help novice pilots on take-off. This also meant that at Harlaxton Manor the war brought the modern technology of flight into the heart of an English countryside that was still home to the social elite of both Britain and the Empire. Significantly, the RFC was still only four years old. So, in addition to developing new tactical and strategic doctrines in response to the exigencies of the war, the Corps was still developing its own identity. Was the social identity of the pupil pilots who arrived in rural England for training influenced by a social context which allowed them to fly over the rooftops of the aristocracy and gentry? In 1917, a new training curriculum was also adopted by the RFC that allowed for more aerobatic flying in dual-control machines. Did this new curriculum, and these new machines, bring these trainee pilots, who would never have ridden a horse, closer to the fox-hunting and ex-cavalry officer originals whose reckless enthusiasm for stunting had had to be reigned in before 1914?

The latter belonged to a social elite recognisable across the Empire. Did an identification with their reckless enthusiasm in the air combine to produce a new sense of shared elitism and equality among a fledgling imperial officer elite? If so, this would echo the recommendation made after the war, by the South African soldier-politician Jan Smuts, for constitutional equality between Britain and the Dominions.[9] Coincidentally, in August 1917, Smuts had recommended establishing a new air service independent of both the War Office (overseeing the RFC) and the Admiralty (overseeing the Royal Naval Air Service).[10] This recommendation was accepted by the War Cabinet and resulted in the installation of a new Air Ministry in January 1918 in the Hotel Cecil on the Strand, in place of the former Air Board, and the appointment of a new Chief of the Air Staff. The new Ministry and the new Chief of the Air Staff (CAS) were responsible for the new Royal Air Force which was established on 1 April 1918.[11] The first CAS, Sir Hugh Trenchard, was determined that the RAF remain orientated, as the RFC had been, toward supplying information to the infantry and the artillery. In practice, as Malcolm Cooper states, 'because it was by far the larger of the existing air arms, the RFC contributed the majority of the RAF's senior officers. These men had been trained to believe that the aircraft was the servant of the army, and showed little sign of rethinking their position as long as the war lasted.'[12] Nonetheless, the technology needed to achieve this made its individual exponents the masters of one of modernity's most potent icons – the aeroplane. Unsurprisingly, the pilots who flew these machines saw themselves as belonging to a new officer elite. In 1917, Lieutenant Stanley Rutledge, a pilot-instructor at Harlaxton who had transferred into the RFC from the Canadian Expeditionary Force (CEF), described his new Corps as 'the premier service in the army today'.[13]

This new officer elite, drawn from across the Empire, was of course now training above Harlaxton Manor and an English countryside divided into a patchwork of estates owned by the social elite of Britain and the Empire. At Harlaxton we can glimpse an imperial air service, made up of officers from across Britain and the Empire, who saw themselves as a technological elite. Here, they also had the opportunity to model themselves on the aristocratic fox-hunting, cavalry officer originals. This opportunity arose from the respect the social elite had for good horsemanship extending to a respect for flying and the flying officer. But we can only glimpse this because, after 1919, not only did this imperial air service disperse to the four winds, the memory of the war in Britain and the then Dominions also diverged. In 1918, Lloyd George spoke of the readiness with which 'tens of thousands of young men, left comfortable and luxurious homes to face privation, torture and death, and the stateliest homes of England to-day are often the most desolate at this hour'.[14] In Britain, the grief experienced by the aristocracy has contributed to a story of loss, dislocation and disillusionment. Canadians, Australians and New Zealanders by contrast, 'typically reject the more bitter representations of the war'[15] that Britons have found so compelling, given that the war strengthened their sense of national identity. Similarly, in *Parti Patter*, a journal edited by a Canadian pilot to commemorate the coming together at Harlaxton in 1919 of pilots from across the Empire, a fellow Canadian declared:

> In raising our glass to the Memories of the Great Adventure, we have much to ponder in silent toast for those who have gone before – those pals of ours who ... passed on into Eternity ... we all know it was not gall to them, but rather that they realised in their last crowded hours the grand truth of the Roman's motto – *pulchrum et bonum est pro patria mori*.[16]

INTRODUCTION

The contrast with the poem *Dulce Et Decorum Est* by Wilfred Owen, published in 1920, is palpable:

> My friend, you would not tell with such high zest
> To children ardent for some desperate glory,
> The old Lie: *Dulce et decorum est*
> *Pro patria mori.*[17]

At Harlaxton, in 1919, we are looking at flying officers who, unlike the disillusioned temporary officers and gentlemen in the infantry, had much more positive associations with the war. This was after all a war in which they successfully transformed their social and self-identity by uniting the traditional identity of the officer and the gentleman with modernity and the aeroplane; producing contemporary comparisons between the airman and the chivalric knight.[18] These were also officers whose technical proficiency in killing the enemy, when married to the reckless courage of the cavalryman, allowed them to succeed as an individual, 'where the soldier failed'.[19] Thus, in contrast to the Army on the Somme in 1916 and then at Passchendaele in 1917, or the Royal Navy at Jutland in 1916, the RFC and 'the air war appeared to be the one positive success story of 1914–1918'.[20] This was because, it was only in the air that a decisive victory had been won in France.[21] This achievement was one that belonged to pilots from across the Empire and this is what bound together the flying officers from Britain, Australia, Canada, New Zealand and South Africa who gathered at Harlaxton in the summer of 1919 (see Appendix II). At this time the RAF still included some Australian pilots, although by now, the majority belonged to the three squadrons of the Australian Flying Corps (AFC) in France; the kernel of the future Royal Australian Air Force. These pilots had, however, trained in England (see Chapter 6).

Training in England was fraught with risks given the fragility of the machines pilots were flying. With fellow trainees being killed and maimed how were these fledgling pilot officers and gentlemen able to cope? According to Mark Bence-Jones and Hugh Montgomery-Massingberd, becoming a gentleman was achieved by the personal effort of the individual as 'behaving like a gentleman has always been more a matter of following the example of actual people',[22] but who to follow? To be an officer was to be a gentleman, and before the war the sons of Britain's social elite congregated in the socially exclusive Household Brigade (where officers in the Guards regiments as well as the cavalry were expected to ride) or one of the socially prestigious cavalry regiments. They were the officer elite. In 1914, Philip Sherwin Pearson Gregory, the heir to Harlaxton Manor and the surrounding estate, rejoined his regiment, the socially exclusive Coldstream Guards. He would return home after the Armistice, having won the Military Cross at Passchendaele in 1917, to resume his life as an English country gentleman. In the meantime, the inexorable demand during the war for ever more subalterns had brought into being a large number of officers with temporary wartime commissions, producing a pool of so-called temporary gentlemen.

Commissioned rank was 'traditionally the expression or confirmation of social status: the fact that one was an officer made it possible to assume one was also a gentleman',[23] albeit temporarily. These officers would have looked to follow the only example available to them, that of an Edwardian officer corps whose identity was, in turn, influenced by the officers drawn from a social elite; an officer elite that, tragically, saw military service as the best way to defend itself from the land reforms of the Edwardian Liberal party. These officers and gentlemen provided the quintessential role model – never displaying any of the weakness of character that 'the squirearchs expected [of] each other to show themselves gentlemen'.[24] Furthermore, whilst history holds that 'the

Figure 2. Harlaxton Manor.

trenches ... saw, quite literally, the death of the English gentleman and the end of an era ... it can be argued that gentlemanly values were after all vital for survival in the trenches'[25] and in the air. To quote the editor of *Parti Patter*, 2nd Lieutenant Howard Wallace:

> It would be difficult to estimate the greater of the friendships made by and those fostered by this land in all the intermingling of the flower of the Empire's manhood within the bounds of its shores. The four-odd years of a fellow-effort have granted all of its individuals ample opportunities for appreciating each other's character and style ... the Canadian has come to pass a new assay upon the real Old Countryman and to learn that within the portals of that 'woefully virtuous' reserve there stands the most finished gentleman in the world. This revision of personal opinion has been reciprocated on all sides ... and those who have been so placed as to have been received into the hospitable homes of Britain will realise all the more why the Empire has been re-welded into a comity of nations.[26]

This new imperial air service was made up of flying officers whose wings and commissions made them temporary gentlemen in a Corps whose identity was still taking shape. The early officers of the Corps would have been drawn from the Edwardian officer class, from landed families, with family ties to distinguished infantry, or more frequently, cavalry regiments. They brought the dash of the cavalry to the air. This was because they had the cash necessary to become pilots, as would-be pilots wishing to join the Corps had to first obtain a certificate or 'ticket' at their own expense from the civilian Royal Aero Club. Consequently, when Duncan Bell-Irving, a Canadian pilot, joined No. 7 Squadron in France in 1915, he found his fellow officers were:

> immaculately dressed ex-cavalry officers, with well-trained servants ... to ensure they remained polished ... Nearly all of them bore a proud family association with the British cavalry and they had put away regimental saddles and spurs reluctantly. Generations of tradition had to be set aside as obsolete. One vestige of the old ways remained, however. As in most [operational] RFC squadrons, several horses were kept for the recreational use of officers ... thundering around the fields of France on horse-back.[27]

Similarly, in the Bayeux-Armentières sector, 'a most distinguished field, beautifully mounted on their first chargers'[28] hunted hares with hounds behind the gun lines. These officers brought to the Edwardian Corps the *élan* of the cavalry, who were now sitting redundant on the ground, on the basis that a good 'seat' was considered a key prerequisite for being a good flyer, and by extension they also brought the character of the hunting-field, where it was:

> likely to be a sad day for the meadows, gates, and hedges. At all cost they must crash through and over. A ducking in the stream, a fall at a fence came as a penalty for the unskilful. At the end, for those few who could manage to reach it safely, there was the glorious who-whoop as the fox was broken up by the hounds. The glory of it consisted not in the death of the fox nor only in the exhilaration of a break-neck ride across country but in a sense of victory over one's fellows ... [having] shown [one]self better than many another ... reckless fellow who had been distanced. There was another joy in the hunt, too. Few pleasures have been discovered to rival the satisfaction derived from hurrying across country upon a powerful animal under the control of the rider, moving in sympathy with his commands, and accepting his dictation.[29]

In the early twentieth century, flying an aeroplane was a rival to the reckless exhilaration of riding to hounds by giving a pilot command of a machine moving in sympathy with his commands and accepting his dictation. This represented the attainment of a level of technical proficiency where, as Rutledge states, 'man and aeroplane become one ... [through the] excitement ... emphasised in aviation'.[30] This excitement was expressed in the new jargon of aerobatics described by Lord Cecil of 'climbing and falling, the "nose-diving" and "zooming-up" ... [and] dodging in and out of the clouds'.[31] In this mastery of flight we see the blending of mechanical prowess with the horsemanship associated with the 'life of a country gentleman'.[32] But were the temporary officers and gentlemen of this new Corps having to 'masquerade as a gentleman'?[33] Were they simply mimicking the lifestyle of an English country squire and the example of the original cadre of polished Edwardian cavalry officers? Or was there a genuine refashioning of individual social and self-identity by officers who, like Rutledge, saw themselves as a new elite? Surely, if it was simple mimicry, the continual expansion of the Corps, which inevitably saw the proportion of officers from the elite cavalry regiments decline in relation to flyers from non-aristocratic and non-landed families, would also have diluted the example of the originals, fuelling the growth of the technician airman as opposed to the gentleman pilot?

INTRODUCTION

Up to 1917, the Corps had recruited heavily from among the ready-made subaltern-pool of the public schools, where, as Sir Walter Raleigh wrote, the Corps obtained 'a body of youth fitted by temperament for the work of the air, and educated, as if by design, to take the risks with a light heart'.[34] The public schoolboy flying officer was also 'educated in a gentlemanly tradition'[35] and was thus 'equipped ... with enough stiff upper lip to pull through'.[36] This combination, unsurprisingly, had a great influence on the character of the new RFC; however, where could these young, inexperienced, officers look for their role model of how to behave like an officer and gentleman? Clearly, as 'gentleman' pilots they would have been highly susceptible to the dash of the elite Edwardian cavalry officers. In 1917 and 1918, as the Corps continued to expand, the pool of would-be pilots was extended still further with successful applicants arriving from overseas, alongside a smaller proportion of British air mechanics who serviced the aeroplanes, and gunner/observers who served alongside the artillery officers who had traditionally swapped the observer's cockpit for the pilot's seat. These pilots all belonged to a Corps where, as flying officers, they were all equals sharing in the risks of training and in the eventual mastery of flight.

In this technological meritocracy the 'bright plumage'[37] of the original cadre of Edwardian officers, who grew up in and around the world of the English country house, could have been obscured by a new twentieth-century machine-man. The men awaiting repatriation at Harlaxton in 1919 were now the heroic embodiment of modernity. They were airmen and:

> In the battles now won Man – Twentieth Century Man – discovered himself. No more need he of the desk or the work-bench bow to the Ancients. Ulysses and Paris and Hercules – all the ideals and glories of the Greek Gods, live in the hearts of the heroes of Today: and that Man, humble ordinary Man, is a hero in the measure of his Will, is the lesson his Effort in this War has unfolded in unexampled splendour ... [these] Men were struck, by the revelation of the possibilities of Self – the heights to which ... [they] could soar when borne by Simple Courage.[38]

Nonetheless, the vibrant colour of the original aristocratic cavalry officer and gentleman remained, because the individuals who succeeded them were trained amidst the social geography of the same country house estates that produced the dashing Edwardian flying officer originals. The landed aristocracy were also captivated by this modern aerial technocracy, given that the technical skills of flying an aeroplane and riding a horse were considered to be comparable. This comparison is enhanced when one considers the cavalry-inspired uniform of the flying officer with jodhpurs, riding boots and a Sam Browne belt. The coming together of these social and technological elites is best summed up by Lord Cecil in 1918:

> The Flying Corps is the greatest of the novelties of the war. And it appeals to people in several ways. Its military importance is great and increasing; it unites in a singular degree the interests of a sport with the deeper and stronger interest of war; the gallantry of its flying-officers touches sympathy and thrills the imagination; and the development of its mechanical and scientific apparatus inspires wonder and almost astounds belief.[39]

The risks inherent in exploring the 'possibilities of Self' and refashioning one's social and self-identity were of course very high, but any allusion to these could never be expressed by flying officers in an imperial air service who were marrying their skill in the air to the example of the elite cavalry officers of Edwardian England. To do so would immediately bring into question their temperament to be an officer and a gentleman, especially as they were also being regularly entertained by the social elite from which that example emanated. The disappointment of Lieutenant H.J.N. Rowe, an Australian flight instructor at Harlaxton refused a transfer to an operational squadron, was balanced by the consolation prize of 'flying to many of the stately homes of England for weekend parties conducted for "Officers and Gentlemen" by the nobility of the time'.[40] This was a continuation of an Edwardian tradition of social flying where aristocratic cavalry officers borrowed a machine to fulfil a social engagement or go to a country house party at the weekend.[41] The intermingling of a new, more meritocratic, officer elite with the old aristocracy during the war in these same country houses is evidenced by the hospitality offered by Sir Charles Welby Bt, the owner of the 25,000-acre Denton Manor estate across the valley from Harlaxton Manor. Sir Charles 'extended hospitality widely to the young [flying] officers in the neighbourhood'.[42] And, in consequence, a 'large number of young officers serving in the neighbourhood ... were inclined to see themselves as potential suitors'[43] for the hand of his youngest daughter, Joan Welby. Joan would eventually marry Charles Portal in 1918. Portal was the officer commanding the 24th Training Wing, which included RAF Spittlegate and RAF Harlaxton. This gave him certain advantages over his fellow officers in the neighbourhood, for example, on one occasion he landed his Avro 504 in the Park.

INTRODUCTION

Figure 3. Denton Manor.

Harlaxton Manor and Belvoir Castle were also open to officers and gentlemen whose style and skill reflected the elite fox-hunting officers of Edwardian England. After the Armistice, pilots at Harlaxton found that 'one of the most pleasant features of … Harlaxton Aerodrome has been their full use of the thousand acre estate of their neighbour, Mr T.S. Pearson Gregory, whose particular pleasure it has been to extend his hospitality to Major Butler and his little band, and to point out some of the rare beauties of his furniture, antiques and the various gardens'.[44] Similarly, Lady Diana Manners, the daughter of the Duke and Duchess of Rutland, who lived at Belvoir Castle, had 'hoped to entertain the boys before they left'.[45] When these 'Air Force Argonauts'[46] left, they departed for homes across the globe and the memory of what had been an imperial flight training programme at Harlaxton aerodrome dissipated. 'Harry' Cobby, the leading Australian air ace of World War One, who completed his advanced flight training at Harlaxton in 1917, lamented that having received their wings many pilots qualified for the 'heavenly variety only too soon … We felt something akin to friend Icarus, only our names would not be immortalised as his.'[47] Hopefully, this book will immortalise the names of the pilots who trained, and who died in training, at Harlaxton aerodrome. They were the reckless fellows who flew above Harlaxton Manor in 1917 and 1918, and who looked to the recklessness of the fox-hunting Edwardian cavalryman for a role model. Alongside them stand the officers and gentlemen of an imperial air service who assembled at Harlaxton Manor in 1919. These were officers who, like their predecessors at Harlaxton, trained as pilots in rural England, where their new social and self-identity as a new officer elite of the air was formed. This would have put them at their ease among the social elite of Britain and the Empire for 'five weeks of playing fields and lounging in the sun on lordly estates ... five weeks of healing from war's wound'.[48]

CHAPTER 1

Poor Bloody Observers and Aerial Reconnaissance

In 1917, in resisting calls to redeploy more squadrons from France to defend London against air raids by German Gotha bombers, in what was the first 'Blitz' against the metropolis, the Prime Minister, David Lloyd George, stressed to a secret session of the House of Commons the vital importance of aerial reconnaissance for the effective prosecution of the war in France. This meant keeping a sufficient number of fighting-scout machines in France to protect the reconnaissance and artillery machines whilst they did their job of observing the enemy, as they were:

> the eyes of the Army, which cannot advance without them ... By their means the Army discovers the enemy's trenches, guns and machine-gun emplacements. To photograph these requires air supremacy, and without that air supremacy it is sheer murder to allow troops to advance ... the slightest deficiency in the work of observation from the air, a single machine-gun emplacement overlooked, might in a few minutes mean the loss of thousands of gallant lives.[1]

The importance of aerial reconnaissance had been recognised five years earlier with the establishment of the RFC and a new Central Flying School (CFS) to give trainee pilots a course of instruction, that in addition to providing 'progressive instruction in the art of flying'[2] also included training in aerial observation and photography, training in flying cross-country and signalling by all methods. In 1915, the RFC identified: 'The most important role of aeroplanes in war is reconnaissance ... like that carried out by the cavalry.'[3] On the other hand, in the Edwardian RFC, aerobatic or 'stunt' flying had been 'generally discouraged'[4] in training in England, given the operational requirements of flying straight and level to take photographs or 'spot' for the artillery.

Figure 4. BE2e (A2847), Harlaxton, 1917. By 1917, the BE2c and BE2e equipped training squadrons in England.

Artillery was the dominant weapon of the war. By July 1915: 'The location of targets and the direction of artillery fire [was] ... one of the regular functions of aeroplanes'[5] thereby providing 'guidance to the gunners by reporting the fall of their shells against enemy targets'.[6] In performing this task, RFC pilots had to fly their reconnaissance machines accordingly. This requirement was reflected in the BE2 reconnaissance machine chosen by the War Office to be the RFC's reconnaissance workhorse. It was designed by the newly renamed Royal Aircraft Factory to be an 'inherently stable aeroplane'.[7] The designation 'BE' stood for Blériot Experimental machine. The 'BE' series adopted a so-called 'tractor' design where the pilot and observer sat facing toward the engine. This design was also applied to the 'RE' series of Reconnaissance Experimental machines. Alongside these designs the Royal Aircraft Factory developed a third, so-called 'pusher', machine where the pilot and observer sat in front of the engine. This series was designated 'FE' for Farman Experimental machines. All three types were stable flying platforms ideally suited to observation work, photographic reconnaissance and artillery-spotting, and so the instruction needed to fly them could be 'fairly rudimentary'.[8] Training pilots how to take off, fly straight, make a turn, and how to land in an inherently stable machine, at the expense of training a pilot to fly more aerobatically, ignored how 'actions like looping the loop trained pilots in the mastery of their machines'.[9] On the other hand, a rudimentary level of instruction allowed pilots to be trained quickly by instructors, sometimes only recently trained to fly themselves, and thereby facilitated the training of the extra pilots urgently needed by the RFC.

In 1912, it was envisioned that the RFC would have seven squadrons ready to go to France with the BEF; and as the likelihood of war increased the formation of these squadrons became 'imperatively urgent'.[10] This meant having a sufficient number of trained pilots to make these squadrons operationally viable. With each squadron due to have three 'flights' of four planes, the wartime strength of an RFC squadron could be calculated accordingly (see Table 1). In 1912, the Government's scheme also proposed flight sergeants and air mechanics (the rank assigned to all members of the Corps below the rank of sergeant) should be selected for flight training because whilst 'up to the present time the authorities have only attempted to train officers as flyers ... the minimum number of trained flyers should be two per aeroplane'.[11] In consequence, the new figure of the pilot NCO, or the non-commissioned officer flyer, appeared alongside that of the commanding officer, squadron commander, flight commander and flying officer, who at this stage, given the subordination of the RFC to the Army, were all accorded equivalent ranks in the Army of lieutenant colonel, major, captain and lieutenant.[12] The 1912 requirement to double-up on the number of available flyers for seven operational squadrons, with twelve aeroplanes per squadron, meant training 182 pilots comprising 91 flying officers (84 flying officers and seven commanding officers) and 91

Detail	Officers	Warrant officers and sergeants	Rank and file		Total
			Air mechanics	Others	
Headquarters (excluding attached)	7	2	12	—	21
Headquarters attached	—	—	—	3	3
Three flights	12	21	96	—	129
Total squadron (excluding attached)	19	23	108	—	150
Total squadron (including attached)	19	23	108	3	153

Table 1. The establishment of an aeroplane squadron, 1912.
Source: 'Royal Flying Corps: The Military Wing', *The Times*, 16 April 1912, p. 5.

NCOs. This figure was to be doubled again to ensure there was a 100 per cent reserve of trained pilots 'to meet casualties'.[13] Training a total of 364 pilots at the new CFS would, 'occupy some considerable time'[14] and this was time the RFC simply did not have. In the event, only four squadrons were ready when war was declared on 4 August 1914.

Despite having only four squadrons available, the RFC succeeded in 1914, in providing a punctual supply of information to the ground commanders, foiling the German attempt to envelop the BEF at Mons, and subsequent attempted envelopments during the retreat from Mons. In September 1914, Sir John French, the commander of the BEF, gave a particular mention to:

> the admirable work done by the Royal Flying Corps under Sir David Henderson [General Officer Commanding the RFC in the field, up to August 1915]. Their skill, energy and perseverance have been beyond all praise. They have furnished me with the most complete and accurate information which has been of incalculable value in the conduct of the operations. Fired at constantly both by friend and foe, and not hesitating to fly in every kind of weather, they have remained undaunted throughout ... [even] actually fighting in the air.[15]

It was friendly fire that resulted in both sides adopting clear markings on their aeroplanes, for the Germans this would be a black cross on a white square, whilst the British adopted a roundel made up of three concentric circles coloured red, white and blue. Flying evasively through the shell-bursts of German anti-aircraft batteries was becoming a part of the everyday experience of the RFC's growing number of reconnaissance pilots. This was because, as the divisional strength of the BEF increased in 1915, and as new corps and armies were formed, there was a comparable expansion in the overall number of operational squadrons. In 1912, a total of seven squadrons had been projected, by July 1915 there were already eleven operational squadrons in France, 'engaged on reconnaissance and its associated tasks'.[16] The new projected total was for 50 squadrons to keep all the BEF's new divisions, corps and armies fully informed of the enemy's dispositions to their front.[17]

With more squadrons appearing in the skies over France in 1915, it made operational sense to begin to group them into wings, under the command of a lieutenant colonel.[18] Over the winter of 1915–16 these wings were grouped together to form brigades commanded by a brigadier-general.[19] If these additional squadrons, wings and brigades, were to remain operational there also needed to be a reserve of pilots in training in England. However, having deployed the bulk of the RFC to France, 'once the need for replacements and reinforcements became clear'[20] there was, as Michael Armitage points out, 'no cadres at home on which to build'.[21] England had been denuded of aeroplanes, mechanics and pilots, leading to problems staffing a training system to produce replacements.[22] The pilots now in France 'were a remarkable group of pioneers ... [who] could ill be spared'[23] and so they were rotated back to England to work as instructors alongside the novice instructors in the newly formed No. 1 Reserve aeroplane squadron. This system of finding instructors allowed the number of Reserve squadrons in England to be expanded, equally, the speed of this expansion, and the need to quickly train more pilots, combined to encourage a rudimentary approach to instruction. This meant the training system in England was soon lagging behind the operational developments occurring in France, and which would, therefore, have to be learned in France by new pilots sent out from England.

Most significantly, RFC pilots in France in 1915 were confronted with the operational reality that: 'As in other forms of reconnaissance, information may sometimes have to be fought for, and reconnoitring aeroplanes must always be prepared to do so.'[24] In 1915, therefore, alongside the development of techniques for aerial photography, turning its aeroplanes into 'a platform for the camera',[25] the RFC began to develop a doctrine for establishing 'ascendancy in the air'.[26] This was in recognition of the fact that aircrews had been left to hurriedly improvise ways to defend their aircraft in a contested space; reconnaissance machines having been sent to France unarmed. With pre-war air theory confounded, and observers, mechanics/gunners and pilots now taking pot shots at one another, the RFC issued the following guidelines in 1915:

> Fire arms are selected for their suitability for types of aeroplanes. In many aeroplanes a machine gun can be used to great effect, a rifle or carbine is better adapted to others, and in some, such as single-seater scouts, automatic pistols are all that can be readily used ... Rifles and pistols should be loaded before starting and placed where they can be readily used.[27]

Clearly, adding a machine gun was the best of these options and in early 1915, the RFC began mounting a Lewis machine gun onto the forward nacelle of its 'pusher' machines.[28] This was the best solution available at this time because: 'The gun mounting must allow the largest possible area of traverse, elevation and depression. Large arcs are difficult to obtain in tractor aeroplanes ... [but] even in those of a propeller type it is necessary to move the gun bodily in order to enable the gunner to see over the sights.'[29]

Responding to these developments, the Germans pioneered the first modern 'fighter' aeroplane, the Fokker monoplane. Being a 'tractor' design it was faster and more manoeuvrable than the RFC's 'pusher' designs. It was also armed with a Spandau machine gun which, in a revolutionary innovation, had an interrupter mechanism that synchronised the machine gun with the rotation of the propellers allowing the pilot to fire through the propeller arc and point the aeroplane at the target. Even more alarmingly for the pilots and observers of the RFC's reconnaissance machines, were the tactics developed by Max Immelmann and Oswald Boelcke to maximise the attacking possibilities of this new fighting machine. Diving past an RFC machine from above, German pilots would then effect an 'Immelmann turn', pulling out of the dive and into a loop and then performing a half roll at the top of the loop to right the aeroplane ready for another attack. These aerobatic tactics allowed German pilots to mount repeated attacks with what was in effect a flying machine gun. Unsurprisingly, this 'fighter' was very adept at shooting down RFC reconnaissance aeroplanes and its main victim was the two-seat BE2c. Given its 'tractor' design precluded the mounting of a forward machine gun, the result was the 'Fokker scourge' of the winter and spring of 1915–16 as the Germans sought to disrupt the RFC's artillery and reconnaissance work.[30]

The BE2c was everything it was designed to be. It was easy to fly and ultra stable, but 'against the nimble, front-gunned Fokker monoplane fighters the BE2c was virtually helpless; it was far too stable to outmanoeuvre the enemy, too slow to run away from him and ... had no hope at all of out-climbing him'.[31] So the very stability that made the BE2c an excellent reconnaissance and artillery-spotting machine, hence its adoption by the RFC, was its Achilles' heel and earned it the grim appellation of 'Fokker-fodder'. In another bitter irony, the observer/gunner sat in front of the pilot in the BE2c, so even after a Lewis machine gun was mounted to the observer's cockpit to try to fend off the Fokker E-type, the gun could only be fired forwards, with a limited traverse, through a cut-out in the upper wing. The observer could swing the machine gun round to fire on an aeroplane on the tail of the BE2c, but only by firing over the head of the pilot. Firing the machine gun to either side of the aeroplane was also hampered by the wooden struts supporting the wings which would be macerated. These defensive deficiencies were rectified in the RE8 which superseded the BE2c in 1917. In this machine the pilot sat in the front cockpit with a forward-firing Vickers machine gun, mounted under the port-side engine panels and synchronised with the propeller by the Constantinesco interrupter gearing-system. The observer, now sitting in the cockpit behind the pilot, was given a swivel-mounted Lewis machine gun. The RE8 also had a more powerful engine and so was faster than the BE2c and had a better rate of climb.³²

The adoption of this new workhorse did not change the functions for which it would be used: the deeply unglamorous work of photographic reconnaissance and artillery-spotting, when compared to the glamour of the new fighting-scouts. But their fighting patrols were only occurring to allow the former to carry out their observation work which was essential to the prosecution of the land war. As a consequence, the pilots of the reconnaissance machines, and especially the observers and the air-gunners, remained the unsung heroes of the RFC:

> Observers, as their name implies, fly with the pilot, but their work consists of a great deal more than observing only. The observer is a trained wireless operator; he is an expert at photography under difficulties; he is a crack shot; and understands thoroughly the intricacies of machine guns; he is a man of iron nerve and unblenching courage – in fact, he is a compendium of all the special branches of the Army, and second only to the pilot in expert knowledge. The majority of observers eventually train as pilots and they are, naturally, with their double-training, amongst the best men in the Corps.³³

This is why, when the new training aerodrome at Harlaxton was opened in late 1916, in addition to the training of pilots, the station also trained observers in photography, hence the existence of the Harlaxton Photographic Section in 1918. The training of observers in photography at Harlaxton was facilitated by the decision to build a machine-gun training range in Harlaxton Park, with opposing trenches divided by a 'No Man's Land' complete with shell craters. Who gave the order for this training facility to be built is unclear, or when in 1915/16 it was built, but it would seem reasonable to suppose that it was a satellite of the Machine Gun Corps Training Centre at nearby Belton Park. Whatever its origins, clearly this facility would also have had great advantages for observers in the Photographic Section, training to use a camera from the cockpit of a BE2c or an RE8. In 1917, pilots and observers were required to take photographs 'from a height of from 1,500 to 5,000 feet, six out of eighteen points given by

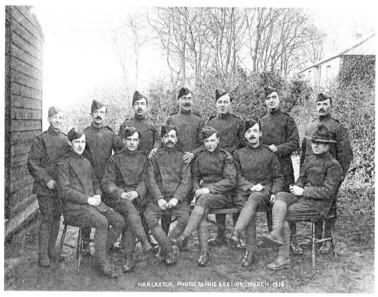

Figure 5. Harlaxton Photographic Section. The sergeant (front row, third from right) wears the crossed Vickers machine gun insignia of the Machine Gun Corps. There is also an American airman seated on the front row, first right (see Chapter 5).

Figure 6. Trenches, Harlaxton Park.

map-reference'.³⁴ These photographic images were then processed and studied in the office of the Photography Officer by trainee observers and pilots.

Aerial photography was, as Lord Cecil described it, one of the triumphs of the RFC for 'ingenuity, technical skill, knowledge and efficiency [thus these crews] ... deserve much more recognition and praise than they have yet received'.³⁵ This lack of recognition was because the crews of the RFC's reconnaissance and artillery machines were not fighting the air war of popular memory, of dogfights high in the clouds, they were fighting in the artillery-man's war and consequently, took 'enormous risks and seldom [got] ... any of the glory'.³⁶ This was especially true in artillery-spotting, when a single machine, working with an individual battery had:

> to circle above a German battery observing for half an hour or more ... tossing about in air, tortured by exploding shells and black shrapnel puffballs ... [but] in the air service this work is never done. Everywhere along the line the big guns wait daily for the wireless touch of aeroplanes to set them booming at targets selected from a previous day's observation.³⁷

Alongside the experimental mounting of machine guns and cameras in 1915, therefore, the RFC had also been exploring how best to send signals between the air and the ground. Having first experimented with coloured lights and lamps, this rudimentary system was quickly superseded by wireless telegraphy, with a wireless receiver placed in an artillery battery and a wireless transmitter in an artillery machine.

Having established this communications link the observer was able to direct the artillery fire onto the target using Morse code. The observer and the battery commander were both issued with the most recent photograph of the target, they could then both overlay this photograph with a celluloid sheet marked with eight concentric circles lettered Y, Z, A, B, C, D, E, F. These circles, extending out from 10 to 500 yards, were intersected by twelve points of the compass. This meant the position of the shell-bursts could be plotted by the observer and a letter and number transmitted to the battery commander who could then see where the shells were falling in relation to the target and adjust his battery's fire accordingly with 'deadly precision'.³⁸ By 1917, the training system in England had also come into alignment with the operational changes occurring in France. Pupils at Harlaxton were required to make 'at least one successful shoot on a picture target on the ground and one successful shoot from the air, with a puff target, observations being sent down by wireless'.[39] As a result of this training in England the 'deadly and effective method of directing artillery fire on hostile batteries by means of wireless telegraphy played a part in winning the war'.[40] Indeed, by 1917, 90 per cent of British counter-battery observation was achieved by this method.[41]

In 1917, the British developed the Counter-Battery Staff Office (CBSO) whose sole purpose was to 'destroy the enemy's [artillery] equipment and personnel, reduce the morale and capabilities of hostile batteries and, at the moment of assault, so thoroughly silence the German artillery that it would no longer be a factor in the battle'.[42] To achieve this objective, the CBSO needed the RFC. The Royal Field Artillery did have ground observers, and in an interesting intertwining of stories, Arthur Measures who was born in Harlaxton, joined the Royal Regiment of Artillery in 1914 and served throughout the war in the RFA. He was awarded the Distinguished Conduct Medal (DCM) in 1917, following his actions on the Somme in 1916:

> For conspicuous gallantry during an attack. [Service No. 98891, Acting] Bombardier Measures ['A' Battery, 52nd Brigade, Royal Field Artillery], in company with the Forward Observation Officer, operated the telephone under very heavy shell and rifle fire, being the whole time exposed on the top of the dump, where it was necessary to remain for observation purposes.[43]

But only the pilots and observers in the Corps' reconnaissance machines could observe the German batteries and 'render our artillery fire effective'.[44]

Up to early 1916, the development of artillery cooperation between the RFC and the RFA relied on the former continuing to fly cumbersome reconnaissance machines in a sky still dominated by the Fokker E-type. The latter's vulnerability was compounded by the equipment it had to carry. The RFC's *Technical Notes* for 1916 stipulated: 'Never attempt stunts on an aeroplane fitted with wireless.'[45] Given this limitation and given the risk of interception, reconnaissance and observation work could only be accomplished by providing these machines with an escort. In 1915, the RFC stipulated that: 'Aeroplanes constructed and equipped with the primary object of fighting in the air will usually be employed to protect those with little offensive power, such as wireless machines.'[46] These fighting machines were also designed to fulfil the RFC's new priority that:

> Hostile aircraft should, as a rule, be attacked wherever met ... to gain or retain a moral and material ascendancy in the air ... [because, the] artillery of a force which is best served by its aircraft will be enabled to gain the ascendancy ... when ... there is little movement on either side. The attainment of this superiority of our artillery will be greatly facilitated if our aircraft have established over those of the enemy an ascendancy so marked that he is unable to use his aeroplanes for the observation of the fire of his guns.⁴⁷

However, the RFC's currently available fighting machines were simply outclassed by the Fokker E-type. Rather than the RFC clearing the Germans from the skies, and leaving it free for the reconnaissance machines to go about their work unhindered, on 14 January 1916, the following order was issued to the RFC squadrons in France:

> Until the RFC are in possession of a machine as good as or better than the German Fokker, it seems that a change in the tactics employed becomes necessary ... In the meantime it must be laid down as a hard and fast rule that a machine proceeding on reconnaissance must be escorted by at least three other fighting machines. These machines must fly in close formation ... From recent experience it seems that the Germans are now employing their aeroplanes in groups of three or four, and these numbers are frequently encountered by our aeroplanes. Flying in close formation must be practised by all pilots.⁴⁸

This was relatively straightforward to accomplish given that in January 1916, an RFC squadron still contained a mix of aeroplane types. These early fighting machines included the Vickers FB5 'Gun Bus' and the BE12 (a converted BE2c), whose job was to fulfil the temporary expedient of simply getting more machine guns in the air. But the days of having a mixed squadron with different aeroplane types of varying capabilities and speeds were numbered. This mix had been 'of little consequence ... when neither formation flying nor co-ordinated air tactics had yet been developed'.⁴⁹ As the 'principles and tactics of air fighting began to be formulated as experience was gained'⁵⁰ the obvious next step, in the pursuit of aerial ascendancy, was to form specialist fighting squadrons to allow these tactics to be honed, once faster, more powerful fighting machines were available. This tactical development would again highlight how far the training programme in England was lagging behind what was happening in France. As a result, flying in formation and air-fighting began to appear in the training programme in England in 1916 and 1917, as would gunnery, with observers and gunners (as well as pilots, see Chapter 2) learning to fire a machine gun in England when previously they had been recruited straight from the trenches and trained on the job in France.[51]

Over time the observer became 'little more than a glorified look-out and gunner'[52] as it was found that pilots in fighter-reconnaissance machines were better able to 'watch for the fall of shot when working with the artillery or for taking photographs'.[53] This reduced role was, though, one that still required considerable skill, as Lord Cecil recognised: 'The working of a machine-gun in an aeroplane ... of firing effectively out of an aeroplane moving unsteadily at a great pace, and hitting another aeroplane also moving unsteadily at a great pace, have had to be studied and mastered.'[54] In 1917 and 1918, the training of observer/gunners would, presumably, have also included the live-firing of a Lewis machine gun from the air at ground targets, following instruction from the Gunnery Instruction staff, given that pilots were also learning how to strafe ground targets using the Vickers machine gun mounted to the front of an RE8. Tragically, in 1917, the sergeant armourer at Harlaxton was killed in a flying accident when the pilot of an RE8 crashed practising this manoeuvre. As Alexander Griffiths, an Australian wireless operator, explains:

Figure 7. Machine Gun Lecture Room, Harlaxton.

POOR BLOODY OBSERVERS AND AERIAL RECONNAISSANCE

I think it was – Harlaxton from memory. That was a training squadron for pilots on reconnaissance work. It was necessary for the pilots [and observers] to learn the Morse Code for [artillery co-operation work] … and gunnery instruction, that's handling a machine-gun.

Did you have much to do with the pilots in those days?

Not a great deal, only just this once when I'm speaking on. I had a wireless hut on the aerodrome and the sergeant armourer who was in charge of machine-guns had a hut next door. We were great friends but now on these observation aeroplanes it was necessary to either have two men in the plane when they were up or the pilot and a sandbag for balance. Now, very often they used to … either the sergeant armourer or I used to go up just for a ride instead of the sandbag. Well, this day I was going up with the pilot.

Can you remember the type of aircraft?

Yes, RE8 I was seated in the aeroplane ready to go up when the sergeant armourer came out and he said, 'Look, I think I better go up, they've got some ammunition that's playing up. I don't want the gun to stick. I'll go up.' So I got out and he got in. Well all right, the pilot went up, circled the aerodrome and then, in training they used to fire the machine-gun on targets on the ground. He went round and fired the gun, up again, all right, went round again, round to fire the second time and just as he pulled out of the dive his right wing broke off. He just did two turns into the ground and the plane caught fire and they were both killed.

What were your thoughts immediately after that happened, Alec?

Well, it's hard to think. The propeller was a four-bladed wooden propeller and when the plane hit the ground the propeller splintered. I got one of those small splinters and I kept it in my kitbag right until I came home.[55]

There was a key distinction between an observer/gunner and a mechanic doubling-up as an air-gunner/observer. An observer was often an infantry or gunnery officer who had transferred from a line regiment, who also acted as a gunner to get in his three months 'over the line' to automatically qualify for flight training. An air-gunner was anything from a private to a sergeant who had volunteered from the ranks of a line regiment, or, as was more often the case, an air mechanic doubling-up as an air-gunner and observer but their 'prospects of advancement were poor',[56] and they 'stood little chance of getting any further'.[57] By examining the recruitment programme in Canada, in the first half of the war, we can see the significant social obstacles that existed in the Corps. In Canada, British recruiting officers had been concerned about the perceived social suitability of applicants, often considering them to be better suited to serve as flight sergeants rather than commissioned officers, because 'most are of the class who would have difficulty securing admission to the RFC no matter how good mechanics they may be'.[58] The preference was to recruit 'only well-bred young gentlemen'[59] from good families. In the latter years of the war, as the need for pilots increased, the question of social suitability had to become a secondary consideration, although many of the officers commanding in operational squadrons were still reluctant to lose a skilled mechanic. Put simply, a pilot was more easily replaced than a mechanic.

As the war progressed therefore, it was no longer the social hurdle it once was for a working-class mechanic from Britain or the Empire to make the jump from the ranks into the Officers' Mess. In 1918, William Leedham, having joined the RFC in February as an air mechanic (3rd class) was selected for pilot training and sent to No. 40 Training Depot Station, Harlaxton, where he was transformed into a flying officer. By 1918, a Corps desperate for ever more pilots could not afford to ignore applications from suitable candidates in the mechanics' workshops or

Figure 8. Royal Flying Corps pilots at Mess, Harlaxton, 1917.

from among the ranks of the gunner/observers who had accumulated considerable experience in France. In 1917 my great uncle, Albert Stanton Curtis, was an air-gunner and observer flying in a BE2e, an Armstrong Whitworth and an RE8, 'directing our guns onto enemy targets using Morse-code, the old dot-dash'.[60] He too now had the chance to become a flying officer, when in March 1917 he was asked if he would like to train as a pilot. 'I jumped at the chance, I passed flying, but you had to pass a paper at 85%, I just failed by 2%',[61] whereupon he was offered the chance to pass as a 1st class gunner/observer, eventually attaining the rank of sergeant gunner/observer, rather than a pilot NCO.

By 1917, the pilot NCO was an increasingly rare anomaly. In 1912, half of the RFC's trained pilots were going to be NCOs. This scheme was soon shelved and by 1913 the RFC had introduced a two-tier training system for its pilot officers and pilot NCOs. As a result, the training of pilot NCOs failed to keep pace with the training of pilot officers, due in part to the opinion 'that not many men of the skilled mechanic class would be ready or willing to risk their lives as pilots'.[62] Subsequently, in 1916, the utility of keeping a two-tier training system was questioned by the Bailhache Committee, for whilst: 'In the early days of the war some 50 non-commissioned officers became pilots ... Every pilot must now be an officer. There are few exceptions.'[63] One of the exceptions was Albert Jackson. Walking through Harlaxton village in 1917, Stanley Rutledge recalled seeing a black ribbon running across the corner of a card that was proudly displayed in a cottage window. The card declared that Albert Jackson, a pilot NCO in the RFC was 'Serving King and Country'. Being acquainted with the family: 'The old man came out to see me. He had remembered my visit. "Albert has been shot down from 18,000 feet by Mueller, the crack German airman" was all that he said.'[64] Contrary to pre-war opinion, pilot NCOs were willing to risk their lives for their country. By 1917, however, circumstances and attitudes had changed ensuring that the RFC's policy of universal commissions encompassed candidates from the skilled mechanic classes on the basis that if a man is 'of the right type and good to be a fighting pilot in a fighting unit, he should be commissioned'.[65]

Significantly, in 1917, when the War Office returned to the Government's 1912 scheme and proposed a major increase in the number of pilot NCOs, the Director of Air Organisation, Sir Sefton Brancker, voiced his opposition. He argued that the whole point of giving a commission to a pilot was that 'it raised his social status and brought him into the officers' Mess, with the result that his morale was higher'.[66] The social exclusivity of the Edwardian Corps was also being undermined by operational necessity because, as Raleigh points out, 'the surest and readiest way to obtain the services of skilled flyers was to offer them commissions'.[67] In essence, if a pilot was an officer and a gentleman and expected to possess 'the same personal qualities as those traditionally associated with a commission'[68] he did not need to be born a gentleman to be able to display these qualities. George Jones (the future Australian Air Marshal and Knight) arrived at Harlaxton in 1917 as an air mechanic (2nd class) with No. 68 (Australian) Squadron. Jones had initially gone overseas as a private in the 9th Australian Light Horse, but on returning to Egypt from Gallipoli he transferred into the Australian Flying Corps as a mechanic, having been a motor mechanic before the war. After arriving at Harlaxton he decided that he would apply for pilot training like many of his fellow mechanics:

> I thought about this a great deal, and finally lodged my application on the very day that applications closed. When our commanding officer [Major Oswald Watt, see Chapter 6] asked me why I had not applied earlier, I admitted that I had felt that it would be necessary to have a recommendation from someone at least of the rank of Colonel in order to be considered [as in the days of the Edwardian Corps]. 'Do you know what I would do with such recommendations?' he asked. 'I would put them in the waste paper basket.' I was selected and sent with the first party to … Oxford, to attend a short course in aerodynamics, engines, wireless, and various other subjects essential for an air force officer. It was the beginning of a totally new way of life – playing tennis, punting on the river, and learning to live like a gentleman.[69]

The newly commissioned officers or cadets who arrived at Harlaxton had the additional opportunity of socialising with the English aristocracy and gentry, from among whom the cavalry officer originals had sprung. They would then be posted to France to fulfil the Corps' primary function of supplying the infantry with photographic reconnaissance or artillery targeting information, or fighting-off the enemy machines trying to stop this information from being gathered.

In 1915, observers had also been given their own distinguishing badge – an 'O' with a half-wing – but the chances of becoming a flying officer via the observer's cockpit, whether one was an officer/observer or a gunner/observer, was one fraught with risk. The lives of the 'Poor Bloody Observers' were in the hands of the pilots.[70] By contrast, a pilot newly arrived from England had, in the former, an individual who had built up considerable experience in France by routinely flying over the

Figure 9. Billiard Room, Officers' Mess, Harlaxton.

line with different pilots. The bond that could develop between regular pairings of pilots and gunner/observers is revealed in a small but telling incident that occurred before my great uncle, Albert Curtis, went on a dawn patrol to photograph enemy targets for the artillery without an escort. The absence of an escort reflected the new operational reality that a machine like the RE8 or FK8 was often fast enough and capable of flying at a high enough altitude to 'carry out such reconnaissance by itself'.[71] This was in marked contrast to the old BE2s in which a crew could be 'engaged in a running fight in which the enemy can outpace you, out-climb you and out-run you'.[72] Despite the addition of extra speed and altitude, Flying Officer Biddle still took my great uncle 'into the Officers' Mess and give me a double whiskey before we went up'.[73] Sadly, Albert's best friend Gunner/Observer Fred Jones was killed, when his pilot, on his first mission, 'lost flying speed too soon and came down like a stone to crash right on the landing strip ... The CO said he was sent out too soon.'[74] This tragedy serves to illustrate the potentially fatal imbalance in the relationship between the pilot and the gunner/observer. Nonetheless, the newly qualified pilots being sent out from England, to join the squadrons now specialising in observation work in France, were immensely lucky to have experienced observers/gunners able to get them up to speed. But what of the pilots joining the RFC's new 'fighting-scout' squadrons that first appeared in France in February 1916?[75]

CHAPTER 2
Reckless Fellows and Aerial Superiority

The 4 RFC squadrons which went to France in 1914, flew a mixture of BE2c, Blériot, Henri Farman, Avro and BE8 machines. Operationally, 'a single type of machine for a single squadron ... [was] a thing to be desired; [as] the squadron ... [was] easier for the pilots and mechanics to handle'.[1] In 1916, the RFC dispensed with multi-purpose or general squadrons: 'gone were the days of a unit having a mixture of machines'[2] and in their place there appeared dedicated squadrons of BE2c, Nieuport, DH2 and FE8, Sopwith 1½-Strutter and the multi-purpose FE2b and FE2d machines. This, in turn, allowed for the RFC's doctrine and tactics 'to be evolved more quickly and efficiently'.[3] Dedicated fighter or reconnaissance squadrons could also be grouped together to form whole wings specialising in these respective tasks. By 1918, these wings were being 'symmetrically paired'[4] together to give a brigade, working alongside an army, a balanced mix of aeroplane types.[5] The wing with squadrons now specialising in 'long reconnaissance and offensive patrols, bombing the enemy, attacking him in the air and in effect, protecting the machines which did the observation work above the lines'[6] worked in tandem with the HQ of an army; hence, the respective designations of Army wing and Army, fighting-scout or fighter squadrons. In the other wing of the brigade, specialising in photographic observation and artillery cooperation, squadrons worked locally with the respective Corps HQs within an army, hence the respective designations of Corps wing and Corps or artillery squadrons.[7] Their war was thus 'local in character ... [because their] knowledge of the particular piece of country over which they did their work [was] ... very important'.[8]

By contrast, the RFC's fighting squadrons were committed to an offensive strategy of combat patrols to establish what Lloyd George termed aerial supremacy over the German air service. One has to be cautious with this term, aerial supremacy suggests a complete mastery of the air but the Imperial German Air Force was still a formidable foe in 1918. What the RFC and, after April 1918, the RAF did succeed in establishing was aerial superiority over its opponent. This resulted from a superiority in aeroplane numbers and a qualitative equivalency to the German machines. With regard to numbers, the production of aeroplanes had increased exponentially following the decision in the winter of 1916–17 to transfer aeroplane production to the Ministry of Munitions, as this 'reduced the chaos, and friction, over the supply of aircraft and engines'.[9] As the new Air Board explained, 'the old system of divided responsibility between the naval and military air arms had prevented proper organisation of the national resources in this field'.[10] Subsequently, in 1918, the new Air Ministry ended the 'competition, friction and waste'[11] that had bedevilled an air service subordinated to both the Army and the Royal Navy.

It was not simply a matter of quantity, there was also the issue of quality. By early 1917, a qualitative gap had temporarily opened up that left the RFC at an obvious operational disadvantage given its fighting machines were now 'inferior in ... performance, to those of the enemy ... [and] given the marked increase in the number and efficiency of German aeroplanes ... [the RFC] cannot expect to gain supremacy in the air in April'.[12] The expectation of air supremacy would remain precisely that. The combination of a quantitative advantage and eventual qualitative comparability did enable the RFC/RAF to attain and retain aerial superiority over the Germans in 1918. In regards to quantity and quality, by early 1918, the RFC had a total of 54 squadrons in France comprising 27 Corps or artillery squadrons equipped with the RE8 (16 squadrons, and replacing the BE2 series), the FK8 (5 squadrons) and the DH4 (6 squadrons) for reconnaissance, artillery-spotting and bombing work. Meanwhile, the 27 Army, fighting, or fighter-reconnaissance squadrons were equipped with the Royal Aircraft Factory designed SE5a (10 squadrons), the Sopwith Camel (10 squadrons), the Sopwith Dolphin (2 squadrons) and the Bristol F2A and F2B Fighter (5 squadrons).[13]

Nonetheless, even before these machines came into service in large enough numbers to irrevocably tilt the air war in the RAF's favour in 1918, the RFC had a sufficient quantity of pilots and machines, if not necessarily the quality of machine or sufficiency of experienced pilots, to challenge the Germans for aerial superiority. This air battle had swung back and forth ever since the introduction of the Fokker E-type in 1915, as both sides sought to produce more and better fighting machines and to train more and more pilots capable of flying them. The key, therefore, to the RFC regaining aerial superiority in 1916 was the arrival of a new generation of fighting-scout machines, grouped into specialist fighting squadrons, which were capable of engaging the Fokker. These fighting machines were the new Royal Aircraft Factory multi-purpose FE2b (a twin-seater) and the single-seat DH2 Scout developed in the De Havilland factory.

Both were 'pusher' designs like the Vickers FB5 'Gun Bus', which meant a Lewis machine gun could be mounted forward of the engine with an uninterrupted field of fire obviating the need for a synchronised interrupter gear. The DH2, being a single-seat aeroplane, had a single Lewis machine gun on a pivot-mounting on the port side of the cockpit. It was also lighter and faster than the Fokker, and thus 'possibly did more than any other Allied aeroplane to overcome the Fokker threat'.[14] The success of the DH2 in quelling the Fokker threat was achieved in collaboration with its fellow 'Fokker-beater' the FE2b which mounted a forward-firing Lewis machine gun and a second Lewis machine gun on a mounting on the top wing allowing a gun to be fired upwards and towards the rear. In addition, the RFC also deployed the Nieuport 11, a fast, single-seat 'tractor', with a single Lewis machine gun mounted over the top wing. This trio of aeroplanes tilted the balance of air-superiority back in favour of the RFC by mid 1916.

These 'pusher' and 'tractor' aeroplanes were complemented in 1916 by the Sopwith 1½-Strutter fighter-reconnaissance machine, the RFC's first 'tractor' aircraft armed with a machine gun that was synchronised to fire through the propeller arc instead of an over-wing machine gun firing outside the arc of the propeller.[15] More importantly, these squadrons of new, faster, more powerful fighting machines were no longer tied to the coat-tails of the slower BE2c machines of the Corps squadrons. Instead, they could now be pushed forward on offensive, fighting patrols to screen the reconnaissance machines from attack.[16] This was not 'an inevitable push towards aggressive combat, but came from the [same] need to implement a system to protect observation, which was the primary purpose of the Royal Flying Corps throughout the war'.[17] More significantly, Maryam Philpott argues that in sending these fighters on patrol, in formation (see Chapter 4), the RFC was now using technology in a 'system' and that this was to be 'the RFC's most significant tactic'.[18] Indeed, the system that developed between the reconnaissance machines spotting for the artillery, now screened by fighting machines capable of flying aggressive patrols far ahead and high above them, would be 'a winning strategy for the RFC'.[19]

This was a system that developed in the field and was learnt there rather than in England, as the training system in 1916 continued to lag behind the operational changes occurring in France. This was 'a time when the pilot got the best part of his training in the war itself'.[20] On the other hand, so long as the majority of the RFC's new fighting machines were a match for the existing German fighters, the balance of aerial superiority was tilted in favour of the RFC and its observation machines. Consequently, over the Somme in 1916, the latter 'were able to carry out reconnaissance, artillery observation and photography with minimum interruption, while the German planes were so hard-pressed to defend their place in the air that they could seldom guide their own guns or collect useful information'.[21] This strategy of 'relentless and incessant offensive'[22] was, of course, the result of tactical and technological changes which, when combined, led to large numbers of technically superior British fighters being flown in compact formations on aggressive or fighting patrols behind the German line.[23] Meanwhile, 'a linear screen of patrols confined the Germans behind their own front'.[24] These were the patrols that produced the dogfights out of which arose the myth of a war being fought in the air with 'residual chivalry when compared to the mechanical killing of the ground war'.[25] In practice, in 1917 and 1918, the air war became a relentless routine of fighting patrols and thus, mechanical killing.

Pursuing a constant offensive strategy of patrols was a costly business and by the end of the war the RFC had suffered four times as many casualties as the Germans.[26] Tragically, the system for training replacement pilots in England, prior to mid 1917, only served to exacerbate these losses by sending out to France 'cursorily trained novices whose life expectancy by the autumn [of 1916] was barely a month'.[27] These were the odds the pilots and observers of the RFC willingly accepted to ensure the Corps fulfilled its primary function of supplying information to the artillery and the infantry on the Somme. Sir Hubert Gough, commanding the BEF's 5th Army, reported that the work done by the RFC over the Somme:

> was invaluable – especially in the ... 'blanketing' [of] the enemy's observation of his artillery fire, while they assisted, guided and directed ours most helpfully. No one of the complicated miscellany of services which comprise a modern army so commanded the respect and admiration of the infantry as did our air service.[28]

On the ground, among the artillerymen was Arthur Measures of the RFA, and among the infantry was Stanley Rutledge, then in the 28th Infantry Battalion of the CEF. He has left a vivid description of the battle being fought by the ordinary infantryman, which is why the RFC stayed in the air, enabling the artillery to cooperate with the infantry with its:

> batteries concentrating on the position to be attacked ... [during the bombardment] in the trenches the boys exchange a word or two, and then it is 'over and at them', and the best of luck ... [with] German machine-guns ... rattling away ... Men stumble up and on ... Bayonets, yes, how the foe hate the long slender steel. We engage and chances are the familiar 'Mercy, kamerad,' will drown all other noises ... [then] when it is all over a great weariness seizes one. The tension relaxes ... The men gather in small groups, telling of this or that adventure ... A regular rabble, dirty, clothing torn, no caps, they form the remnant of the battalion that went out 'spick and span' ... [thoughts of] the glorious adventure [are replaced by] silent grief ... The little company is formed up – the roll is called. My God, how many are gone? They move off. The news goes around that the battalion had achieved its objective – an official way of saying that 'The boys did well'. And then it is back for a few days. Reinforcements are sent. New officers 'take over'. In a few days again it is 'Over boys, and at them, and best of luck'. Thus we carry on.[29]

Toward the end of 1916, the balance of aerial superiority over the Somme was tilted back in favour of the German air service with the introduction of a new generation of fighters that outclassed the Sopwith 1½-Strutter and the FE2d and took a heavy toll of the RFC stable of DH2, FE8, BE12 and the BE2 machines.[30] The new lead German fighter was the Albatros DI/II and III. The Albatros was the first fighter to be armed with twin machine guns firing through the arc of the propeller, setting a new standard for fighters. Added tactical punch was given to these new fighters by grouping them together into hunting-squadrons or *Jagdstaffeln* of which the Germans had 33 by the end of 1916. This concentration of technologically superior machines produced a sharp rise in RFC losses, with battles having to be fought 'on a large scale ... in order to get information and to allow artillery machines to carry on their work'.[31]

By the end of 1916, the RFC had a total of 38 operational squadrons, of whom half were Corps or artillery-spotting squadrons, the other half being Army or fighting squadrons, with 18 aeroplanes per squadron, facing the *Jagdstaffeln* or *Jastas* with 14 aeroplanes per squadron.[32] In this ongoing technological battle for aerial superiority a greater quantity of higher quality machines was going to be needed by the RFC; as a corollary pilots would have to be trained to fly these more powerful machines. In regard to quantity, in December 1916, the Army Council gave its approval for the expansion of the RFC to a projected total of 106 operational squadrons. In 1914, the RFC had deployed 4 operational squadrons to France, by early 1918, it would have 54.[33] In addition, qualitatively, the Sopwith 'Pup' and the DH5 (with which No. 68 [Australian] Squadron would be equipped during training at Harlaxton and during the early stages of its deployment in France) were valuable additions to the RFC's stable of fighting machines in France in late 1916 and early 1917 respectively.[34] The 'Pup' was described by Arthur Gould Lee as 'really the most thrilling aeroplane. You feel you're riding the Pegasus of your dreams.'[35] The 'Pup' could also turn inside the Albatros, but the latter remained faster, better armed and had a faster rate of climb.[36] Both the 'Pup' and the DH5 were superseded by the end of 1917, by the arrival of the Sopwith F1 Camel (which also replaced the Sopwith 1½-Strutter), the SE5a and the Bristol Fighter, all three of which became available in quantity from mid 1917 onwards. Having closed the qualitative gap with the German Albatros DIII and DV, the RFC now had the 'material to make its numbers, inexperienced as many of its pilots were, tell against the German veterans'[37] in the battles of late 1917 and 1918.

Back in April 1917, over Arras, the RFC faced the prospect of maintaining a system of cooperation between its reconnaissance machines and its fighting machines, when many of the latters' machines were simply outclassed.[38] The German air service now had 37 *Jastas* and the Albatros fighter, and so despite being 'inferior in overall numbers … they had the edge in performance'.[39] Knowing they would be obviating this qualitative imbalance with quantity, the pilots of the RFC continued to fly offensive patrols. The offensive patrol or 'OP' included the distant offensive patrol or 'DOP' flown into German territory, 'looking for trouble'.[40] These patrols were complemented by the line offensive patrol or 'LOP', where pilots would fly along the line looking to jump on any German scouts 'trying to attack our BE's and other two-seaters doing art[illery] obs[ervation] below'.[41] This had to be accomplished at a time when the Germans were in possession of a 'considerable number of fighting aeroplanes that were faster, handier and could attain a greater height than any British machines with the exception of the Nieuport [17], FE and Sopwith [Pup]'.[42] Engaging the *Jagdstaffeln* in machines that were either outclassed, or only approaching comparable levels of performance, was the ultimate test of the 'possibilities of the Self' to be 'unflappable in every situation'[43] or at least to 'pretend to be unperturbed'[44] in the company of one's fellow officers. Especially, as the air battle over Arras was soon consuming the reserves of qualified pilots, which necessitated replacements being rushed out from England without adequate training. These noviatiates could be granted no gradual introduction to air combat, but were sent straight into action, usually on obsolescent craft, against experienced German pilots mounted on much superior planes, and were thus, with tragic frequency, shot down on their first patrols.[45]

The need for more and more replacement pilots to sustain the strategy of aerial attrition over Arras would mean a pitiless winnowing of many of the early graduates of Harlaxton, as the aerodrome had opened in late 1916. This was because, the life expectancy of pilots in 'Bloody April' 1917 was just 17 days.[46] As Richards states, the RFC 'with numerical but not technical superiority, made an all-out effort to drive the enemy away from the battle area and secure freedom of action for the artillery-observation aircraft. The cost was grievous ... the result in many cases of insufficient training.'[47]

On the other hand, the supply of information needed by the infantry and the artillery was not curtailed and, having endured the qualitative imbalances of the spring, by the autumn, during the great battles of Passchendaele and Cambrai, the RFC attained a qualitative equivalency to the Albatros fighter and regained aerial superiority. In addition, the growing sufficiency of aeroplanes, whose performance and armament made them a match for the best German fighters, was now, at last, being complemented by a sufficiency of pilots whose training had prepared them to fly these machines. But where were all the extra pilots coming from? Having survived the Somme, Stanley Rutledge and his brother Wilfred decided they would carry on their war by transferring to the RFC and get away from the infantry and the days 'when the shells were overhead, when the mud was knee high, and when the flares went up into a dirty sky'.[48] Their decision was not just about getting out of the mud, because the RFC also offered individuals a 'heroic alternative to the squalid and anonymous war in the trenches'.[49] Having received a field commission, like his brother Wilfred, 2nd Lieutenant Stanley A. Rutledge wrote home, 'I am keen to be a pilot, and feel I can fit the bill.'[50] On 2 May 1917, he wrote: 'I am making application for pilot in RFC, I saw the RFC people at the Hotel Cecil this morning.'[51] Unlike his brother who opted to become a pilot by becoming an observer, Stanley hoped to miss this intermediate stage, and did so, eventually arriving at Harlaxton aerodrome for flight training in September 1917.

In 1917, the flight training programme at aerodromes like Harlaxton now included instruction in aerial fighting (see Chapter 4); nonetheless,

Figure 10. 2nd Lieutenant Stanley Arthur Rutledge, RFC.

the overall life expectancy of an RFC pilot was both precarious and pitiless flying at high speed in a flimsy, highly flammable machine of metal, varnished wood and lacquered canvass, filled with oil, petrol and ammunition, without a parachute, against a skilled opponent. On average, an RFC pilot or observer in a two-seater reconnaissance aeroplane could expect to survive four months' war service. By comparison, pilots flying a two-seater day bomber or a fighter-reconnaissance aeroplane had an estimated average war service of three and a half months. The pilot of a single-seat fighter could, on average, expect to last only two and a half months.⁵² These sobering statistics emphasise the risks inherent in joining the Flying Corps, but also suggest that the men who gathered at Harlaxton in 1917 and 1918 were attracted to the risks of being a war-pilot. As Lord Cecil put it:

> the danger of fire, the danger of falling, the struggling home with a broken machine [against the westerly winds that had carried them over the German line and which, ironically, had earlier helped them take off from the westerly facing ridges of the training aerodromes in Lincolnshire] the triumph of seeing the enemy crash to the ground – such doings as these make up a story at which the heart beats.⁵³

The last 18 months of the war, from the summer of 1917 onwards, during the period that Harlaxton was in operation as a training aerodrome was therefore 'the era of the great aces'⁵⁴ flying the single-seat SE5a and the Sopwith Camel. These pilots were now flying machines with which they could show themselves, to quote Kirby, 'better than many another reckless fellow who had been distanced'. Of course, 'no war was ever won just by the actions of a few gifted and aggressive pilots [but] … would the other pilots have achieved as much if they had not been inspired by the spectacular success of the great flyers?'⁵⁵ It was these gifted flyers who provided the heroic example to be followed by the rest of the RFC and its Australian offspring, the AFC. In so doing, they added further embellishments to the reputation of an air service and its new officer elite, who were recognised as such in both Britain and across the Empire.

When a large contingent of Australian airmen and mechanics of the AFC returned home aboard a mail steamer, the *West Australian* described these 'Heroes of the Air' coming home with 'honours thick upon them'.⁵⁶ Among them were three alumni of the training programme at Harlaxton, namely Major Oswald Watt (see Chapter 6), Major Roy Phillipps and Captain 'Harry' Cobby, the latter two being reunited on the journey home after 'doing their initial flights together in Harlaxton'.⁵⁷ Phillipps was returning home with the Military Cross and bar and the Distinguished Flying Cross (DFC). He also had 14 'kills' to his credit in a SE5a. Cobby had 29 'kills' to his credit in a Sopwith Camel. Cobby was also returning home with the Distinguished Service Order (DSO) and the DFC with two bars. In 1919, these were Australian heroes belonging to the new AFC squadrons established in 1916. This explains the markedly fewer Australians among the flyers awaiting repatriation at Harlaxton in 1919, especially when compared to the number of

Canadians (see Appendix II). However, Watt, Cobby, Phillipps and the rest of No. 68 (Australian) Squadron all trained in England.

By contrast, the Canadians established their own pilot training programme with 20 Reserve squadrons, rather than a comparable Flying Corps. This helped to ameliorate the pilot supply problem[58] but, it also meant transfers into the RFC from the CEF like Stanley Rutledge, would increasingly become the exception to the rule. Indeed, by the end of the war, in addition to constituting nearly one-quarter of the pilot-strength of the RFC, 'two-thirds of all Canadians in the British Air Services had enlisted and been trained in Canada'.[59] Nonetheless, despite the Australians forming the AFC and the Canadians forming their own training programme, both were still part of an imperial air service in which the majority of their fellow flyers, including the majority of the Australians, had completed their training in England. Similarly, even if two-thirds of Canadian pilots trained in Canada, this still meant that one in three Canadians had trained in England. Stanley Rutledge and 2nd Lieutenant Alick Charlesworth both trained at Harlaxton, the latter having transferred into the RFC in 1917 from the 88th Battalion, Victoria Fusiliers (CEF).[60]

The number of Canadian pilots serving with the RFC by 1918, together with the development of the AFC was all 'a far cry from the early days of the war when the British had been reluctant to enlist colonial pilots'.[61] Furthermore, given the demands of the infantry for young subalterns from the public schools, the attrition of trained

Figure 11. Royal Flying Corps pilots from Canada, Harlaxton, 1917. Left to right: Lieuts Christian Burgener, Wardlaw, Lang, Weatherall, Yonge and Gilmore.

pilots, the need to rest pilots, and the need to find more pilots for more squadrons, the RFC 'could no longer take a superior attitude to recruits from the colonies'.[62] As a result, where once questions of social suitability or social exclusivity had ensured a 'scant welcome'[63] to pilots from overseas or from the ranks, the RFC was now actively looking for capable and aggressive individuals who, as Rutledge put it, 'fit the bill' regardless of their background. The Canadians were looked upon by the RFC as 'wonderful chaps, breath of the wide open spaces, great pilots, likely to destroy a mess or anything in five minutes at a guest night'.[64] The Australians were considered even more rambunctious; however, in Britain, only 'a few men from the lower classes ... the sons of army non-commissioned officers ... [compared to] many from the Dominions ... filled the ranks of the RFC during the last two years of the war'.[65] This suggests that candidates from the Dominions perhaps had the edge over their British working-class air-gunner/observer/mechanic counterparts applying for flight training and a commission, given their classless accent.

Allowing for the anomaly of the pilot NCO, flying was still the preserve of the flying officer, and thus the individual with the requisite gentlemanly qualities associated with a commission. These qualities had been embodied by the original Edwardian cavalry officers, but as the Corps became more cosmopolitan, how was the identity of the original cadre of flying officers transmitted to their successors? The theory that a pilot needed to be a good horseman and have a 'good "seat", a natural equilibrium, and a sensitive pair of hands'[66] remained unquestioned throughout the war. This, of course, made the troopers of the Australian Light Horse ideal pilot candidates when the new Australian squadrons were formed in 1916 (see Chapter 6). But what if one did not ride? For all the comparisons between riding a horse and flying, a mechanic, gunner, observer, or young subaltern, was learning to fly an aeroplane not ride a horse, and they were very different, especially when flying in clouds where an inexperienced pilot could easily become disorientated. The subsequent symbiosis of technology and individual skill that occurred in training would transform them into skilled pilots. Their pupillage also included the transformation of their self-identity within a social context imbued with the memory of the reckless courage of the fox-hunting country gentlemen and ex-cavalrymen who had joined the Edwardian Corps. Is it purely coincidental that the more technically proficient RAF pilots of 1918, who trained in the English countryside, exhibited the same reckless dash as the aristocratic RFC originals of 1912?

In 1919, prior to returning home, pilots from across the Empire came under the command of Major James Butler, officer commanding the Harlaxton Repatriation Camp. Butler was a lifelong soldier who had started his military career in the ranks. He was born in Manchester and served in the South African War (1899–1902) with the Royal Irish Fusiliers (No. 6982). Staying in the Army he attained the rank of company sergeant major (CSM) and joined the BEF as a warrant officer. In early 1915, he was awarded his MC, giving him the distinction of appearing in the inaugural list 'one month after he was promoted to one of the first commissions won in the field'.[67] In 1916, having fought on the Somme in the infantry, he transferred into the RFC in August, and ended the year back in France flying over the line with No. 53 Squadron. Eventually, in 1918, having survived 'Bloody April' and the battle of Cambrai in 1917, he was made a flight commander in No. 16 Squadron, Home Establishment.[68]

Rising through the ranks, Butler had transformed himself into an 'English gentleman and soldier'.[69] As a Major, serving with the RAF, he now commanded men who 'fit the bill' as pilots due to their individuality, self-reliance and knowing 'how to play the game'.[70] The last is a trait associated with the public schoolboy who was 'particularly, drawn to the British fighter arm, where he seems to have set the tone'[71] at least initially.[72] Playing the game was, in practice, a luxury that pilots could ill afford to indulge; indeed, Morrow suggests that 'in the brutal war of 1917 chivalry and sportsmanship were gone'.[73] By 1917, the RFC was also becoming a rich social mix, as *The Lancet* commented: 'Flying is not now confined to the public school boy, the cavalry officer, or the athlete. We take many of our pilots at present from the lower middle classes and the artisan class.'[74] Joining them were the Australians, New Zealanders, South Africans and Canadians, 'in large numbers'.[75] This was because, as Stanley Rutledge explained, 'flying calls for initiative and other qualities which the chaps from overseas seem to possess in a high degree'.[76] Butler was particularly impressed with them:

> having been brought into touch a good deal both in the field and at home with the boys from Overseas … the more I see of them the greater is my admiration for them. My experience in the War was that whenever the boys got a task to do, they never failed to carry it through; the more difficult it was considered the more they liked it.[77]

The RFC training schools in England were rapidly becoming social melting pots supplying the RFC and then the RAF operational

Figure 12. 'Waiting for a bus': RFC pilots under training, Harlaxton, 1917. Second from left: Lieutenant Land; sixth from left: Lieutenant C. Burgener.

squadrons with an 'infinite individuality and variety ... [and] cosmopolitanism'.[78] What brought all these individuals together was their 'pluck, determination and the will to see a thing through'.[79] The RFC went further and encouraged pilots to see themselves as uniting the chivalric and the heroic, the twin, 'qualities of ancient and of the most modern warfare'.[80] This comment appears in the 1917–18 RFC manual *Work and Training*, a manual from which Lord Cecil was quoting from when he wrote:

> The officers of the Flying Corps ... in their lonely self-reliance and dependence on their own individual prowess ... remind us of the knights of old; and certainly since the days of the knights there has been no such opportunity in war for the display of the personal qualities of the individual ... [but] in their association with ... science and mechanics they belong to the very latest hours of our own day ... for we see our knights-errant of the air go forth in an aeroplane furnished with wireless telegraphy and a photographic apparatus; and we stand looking on with open mouth ... admiring at once the gallantry and the ingenuity of the enterprise.[81]

Lloyd George described the pilots in similar terms: 'they are the cavalry of the clouds ... They are the knighthood of this war ... let us think [then] of the chivalry of the air'.[82] In the opinion of Arthur Gould Lee this 'false image of ... intrepid, daredevil, hell-bent, fearless aviators

– left pilots "cynically amused"'.[83] On the other hand, as Morrow states, Lee was not entirely immune to the heroic imagery himself, describing his fellow pilots as a 'winged aristocracy of warriors'.[84] Cecil Lewis, in his memoir *Sagittarius Rising* (1936), wrote that the RFC attracted the adventurous:

> devil-may-care young bloods of England [and the Empire], the fast-livers, the furious drivers. This invested the Corps with a certain style ... We had the sense of being the last word in warfare, the advance guard of the wars to come and felt, I suppose, that we could afford to be a little extravagant.[85]

Was this all illusion or, as Morrow suggests, 'bunk'? Or, do we need to draw a distinction between the chivalric and the heroic? The new technology of the machine gun, when combined with the aeroplane, had, 'made chivalry possible in the air, just as it destroyed it on the ground'[86] but, chivalry was 'exaggerated, for air combat was a serious, deadly and ruthless business that some confused with the tourney's [sic] of the Middle Ages'.[87] Whilst *this* was the heroic illusion[88] of the air war, the actions taken by the pilots themselves remained heroic, which is why they came to see themselves as a new winged aristocracy, 'with a sense of mastery over space, over nature, over life itself'.[89]

Was this sense of belonging to a new aristocracy of the air transmitted to pilots from the ranks and from across the Empire during their training? A training environment which opened the doors of manor houses emblazoned with coats of arms to these pupil pilots, and which allowed them to fly over the battlements of Belvoir Castle, would have done little to dispel the idea that they were the modern equivalents of the knights of old, and by extension the Corps' cavalry officer originals whose obituaries could read as follows: 'a keen sportsman, a good shot, and a good rider to hounds'.[90] As Patrick Bishop states, 'the air force was to act ... as a machine of social transformation, elevating likely young men from the lower classes and making them officers'.[91] Flying over Belvoir Castle in 1918, Leslie McNab, an instructor at Harlaxton, went 'all round it hoping to see ... Lady Diana Manners whom many say [is] the most beautiful woman in England. Someone on the turrets [was] drying their hair ... but no doubt a serving maid.'[92] He was now part of a training programme that had come into alignment with the requirements of the air war in France. Prior to the opening of Harlaxton aerodrome at the end of 1916, as Raleigh observed, 'the various activities which had developed at the front, such as artillery observation, fighting and bombing, had no counterpart ... in the training establishments'.[93] This would change in 1917. Previously 'the great practical School of Research for pilots was the war',[94] the great practical school would now be England rather than France.

Figure 13. Belvoir Castle.

CHAPTER 3
Young Icarus and Flight Training

During its operational existence Harlaxton aerodrome was a bustle of different squadrons and aeroplanes. The first squadron to arrive at Harlaxton aerodrome on 13 November 1916 was No. 44 Reserve Squadron (see Appendix I). On 23 December 1916, it was designated as a Higher Reserve Squadron equipped with BE2, RE7, DH4 and Avro 504 machines.[1] On 17 March 1917, No. 44 HRS was joined at Harlaxton by No. 54 HRS which was equipped with Avro 504, DH6 and Bristol Scout machines.[2] Subsequently, on 22 September 1917, No. 26 Training Squadron arrived at Harlaxton. Initially, designated No. 26 Elementary Reserve Squadron, in May 1917 all Higher and Elementary Reserve squadrons were re-designated as Higher or Elementary Training squadrons to more accurately reflect their function. No. 26 Squadron was therefore, equipped with Maurice Farman 'Shorthorns' and 'Longhorns'.[3] These Reserve/Training squadrons and their various machines were all components in a burgeoning training programme. In 1912, the Central Flying School (CFS) had been set up to produce pilots for 7 squadrons. By the end of 1914 the work of the CFS had been complemented by three new Reserve squadrons. By the end of 1915 this had increased to 18.[4] In 1916, the RFC had 33 Reserve squadrons and 22 Training stations. By early 1917, this had increased to 42 Reserve squadrons.[5] In December 1916, the Army Council approved the expansion of the RFC to 95 Reserve squadrons and 106 operational squadrons.[6] In 1917, this was raised still further to 117 operational squadrons and 109 Training squadrons or schools.[7]

In July 1916, responsibility for coordinating the work of the increasing number of Reserve squadrons was given to the RFC's Training Brigade (which was raised to the status of a Division in 1917) and which, in January 1917, was divided into three geographical Group commands in Northern, Eastern and Southern England.[8] This

Figure 14. Aerial view of Harlaxton Manor and aerodrome.

was because, accommodating the expansion of the training programme in England to 95, and then to 97, Reserve squadrons could only be achieved through a geographical expansion of the training infrastructure, to ease the overcrowding and congestion that was developing in the air in the south of England. In late 1916, it was decided to build new aerodromes in Lincolnshire at Spittlegate, Waddington, South Carlton and Harlaxton.[9] The county is famous for a geological feature called the Lincolnshire Cliff. This ridge runs the length of the county and provided an invaluable source of additional lift to trainee pilots taking off into the prevailing south-westerly wind. This advantage was complemented by Lincolnshire's, 'open countryside [and] ... lack of industrial haze'.[10] This combination of factors is what brought the county to the attention of the aerodrome planners. The result was a series of aerodromes running along the Cliff and thus, through the heart of England's premier agricultural county.

In 1917, Harlaxton aerodrome, situated at the southernmost tip of this chain, together with the new aerodrome on Spittlegate Hill overlooking Grantham, provided the training infrastructure for the training squadrons belonging to No. 24 Reserve/Training Wing, which was part of the Northern Group Command (Northern Training Brigade) headquartered at York.[11] Arriving there in July 1918, to join

Figure 15. Hangar construction, Harlaxton.

Figure 16. Harlaxton, interior of hangar, 13 April 1917.

No. 20 Training Squadron, Leslie McNab found the aerodrome 'prettily situated with many pleasant clumps of trees and growing crops and a mess of big proportions. Nearby is the Manor of Harlaxton – a great rambling building too ornate with one old man who lives there in all this solitude.'[12] Work on the aerodrome had begun in October 1916, when workmen arrived from the Ministry of Munitions to clear hedges and trees from the fields and to construct the new roads needed to facilitate access to the aerodrome and the delivery of the prefabricated wooden huts and corrugated-iron buildings that were all assembled on the aerodrome; which was also supplied with mains water and electricity which even Harlaxton Manor lacked up to the 1930s.[13] The most spectacular of these buildings were the six huge hangars, measuring 170 feet × 80 feet × 20 feet which housed the all-important aeroplanes. These conformed to the 1917 standard pattern General Service Shed with 13 bays and 'Belfast' timber roof trusses giving them their characteristic bowstring roofs.[14] These rose up out of the arable fields requisitioned for the aerodrome, following the harvest in 1916, hence the stubbles we can see in Figure 15. Despite the competing needs to produce more food and to produce more pilots, the Defence of the Realm (Acquisitioning of Land) Act in 1916, gave aerodrome planners the statutory right to requisition the 386 acres needed for Harlaxton aerodrome.[15]

But what kind of training were the fighter and reconnaissance pilots[16] receiving in the reserve/training squadrons stationed at Harlaxton? Before the war, prospective flying officers were expected to arrive at the new CFS for their further instruction in the art of flying having already mastered the rudiments of flying around an aerodrome and, more importantly, the art of landing an aeroplane. This was probably the most dangerous aspect of flying, as an inexperienced pilot could descend at too steep an angle and crash into the ground before flattening out; or he could descend at an insufficiently steep angle and stall the engine and crash; or he could 'pancake' and crash in a heap by flattening out too early; or he could simply misjudge the landing and crash into a hedge or a tree.[17] Teaching pilots how to take off, fly straight, make a turn and land, was the job of the pioneering civilian aviators of Edwardian England who gave flying lessons to make ends meet. These flying lessons were geared to preparing would-be pilots to 'take their ticket' and obtain their Aviators Certificate from the Royal Aero Club.[18]

In 'taking one's ticket', a fledgling pilot was required to ascend twice and fly five figures-of-eight around two posts over 500 yards apart and then land within 50 yards of a point specified before taking off. In addition, he was expected to climb to a specified height, switch off the engine and glide to the ground.[19] The successful completion of these tests resulted in an Aviators Certificate issued by the Royal Aero Club. This was the all-important passport into the RFC for those Edwardian officers able to afford the £75 fee. As *The Times* explained in 1912, officers transferring into the Corps from the Army would need to obtain the Royal Aero Club certificate privately before joining the CFS. The link between the Royal Aero Club and the RFC persisted after 1914 with successfully 'taking one's ticket' continuing to be 'recognised as the register of qualified pilots throughout the war',[20] and thus, initially, it continued to act as another way to perpetuate the social exclusivity of the Corps. In Canada, in 1915, as in Britain, it was, 'expensive to take the training required to get one of these certificates, a fact which tended to restrict entry to young men from "good families"'.[21] Of course, as we have seen in the preceding chapters, these social considerations had to give way to the need to produce more pilots to keep an ever-growing number of squadrons in the air. In this context, the Corps' pilot-training programme, of necessity, had to become more and more accepting of recruits with the necessary individual characteristics to be pilots regardless of their upbringing. Put simply, more squadrons equalled more pilots and ever more replacements. And so the former social hurdle of 'taking one's ticket' was absorbed into a training programme operated exclusively by the RFC, with pupils being tested for their RAC brevet by their RFC instructors. If successful a form was filled in and 'sent to the Royal Aero Club, together with a cheque – to become a certified aviator – but not yet a Flying Officer of the RFC'.[22]

By the end of 1915 it had become obvious that a more specialised system of pilot training was required, to give pupils preparatory technical training before they went to one of the Reserve squadrons or the CFS, 'which could then concentrate on their flying training'.[23] This ground course was taught at a new School of Instruction (established in December 1915) at the University of Reading's Wantage Hall. Subsequently, this became the RFC's No. 1 School of Instruction (or School of Military Aeronautics) following the opening of a second school at Christ Church College, Oxford in April 1916.[24] There were around 1,000 'Gentleman Cadets' from Britain and, 'all over the Empire'[25] enrolled at Oxford at any one time. Officers transferring into the Corps from the Army were allowed to keep their distinctive regimental uniforms whilst their fellow cadets wore the distinctive RFC wrap-over tunic, 'with breeches and puttees and a white "flash" in their

Figure 17. Group photograph of flight cadets of No. 40 Training Depot Station, Harlaxton.

service caps'.[26] All cadets sat written examinations after studying the workings of aero engines, instruments, airframes, rigging, meteorology, map-reading, cross-country navigation, signalling using wireless and Morse code, aerial observation, photography, artillery and infantry cooperation, fitting fuses to bombs and the workings of the Lewis and Vickers machine gun.[27] The successful graduates were then given a passing-out parade, prior to which they also had to choose a tailor. This was because if the inspecting officer spotted a loose or untidy uniform, the offender would be asked for the name of his tailor which was then bellowed out by the sergeant major, whereupon a tailor, 'complete with a tape measure … [would] rush across to the … officer to take details of the necessary alterations and get them done at the workroom, immediately after "fall out"'.[28]

Cadets passed out of the Schools of Aeronautics with their commissions as a 2nd lieutenant, unless they were already officers.[29] They were now officers and gentlemen in a Corps that modelled itself on the elite cavalry regiments of the British Army and a smart uniform was the visual signifier of this elite status. Hence, their RFC tunic was modelled on the tunic of the elite lancer regiments. Subsequently, on becoming a flying officer, having gained their RFC brevet or wings, they could also put on their classic Sam Browne belts. Before they did so they had, of course, to learn how to fly and this meant having now mastered 'the technical part of the game [going] … to a flying squadron for the actual work as a pilot'.[30] This meant going on to an Elementary Reserve/Training squadron to learn the rudiments of flying sat alongside an instructor, before they went solo, took their 'tickets', and moved onto a Higher Reserve/Training squadron. The decision to change from Reserve squadrons being 'all-through' schools, to some being responsible for elementary flying and others taking charge of higher training, reflected the growing realisation that simply 'taking one's ticket' did not qualify a pupil to be a service pilot.[31] On the other hand, up to mid 1917, what kind of instruction was given in these higher training squadrons given the Corps' earlier disapproval of stunt flying?

This disapproval is evidenced in the training guidelines given to instructors working at the CFS in 1914. Instruction should 'only take place in calm weather, as the pupil would become confused if a sudden gust or *remous* [swirl] necessitated an abnormal use of the controls'.[32] Indeed, 'a sharp turn is seldom necessary, but the pupil should be shown what it is like, in case he ever finds himself in such a position that it is necessary'.[33] In 1915, the training given at the CFS and other training stations 'was still very elementary in character'.[34] The great irony is that prior to 1914, those pupils taking flying lessons privately to obtain their Royal Aero Club Aviation Certificate, were being taught by the pioneers of Edwardian aviation. These pilots earned their living by giving rudimentary flying lessons and by putting on air shows and aeroplane races. According to Eric Furlong, who trained at Harlaxton in 1917, these pre-war exhibitions 'made for very spectacular flying'.[35] The steep banks, climbs and dives used by these pioneer flyers were not, however, taught to RFC pilots prior to mid 1917. Their flight training was in consequence 'poor preparation for operational realities'.[36] This would, according the Michael Paris, change after mid 1917 but, prior to this, a training programme rooted in pre-1914 theory produced pilots who, with their 'tickets', *appeared* competent 'after only a few hours' instruction and could be rushed off to the Front'.[37] The problem with this system was that the pilots, 'thus trained had to be retrained [in operational squadrons] to cope with the complex manoeuvres being developed in France'[38] where, in 1915, experience was showing that an abnormal use of the controls and sharp turns were absolutely necessary to avoid the shell-bursts of German anti-aircraft batteries or to evade the machine gun of the Fokker E-types.

The system of training prior to mid 1917 actually exacerbated the problem of keeping a rising number of squadrons supplied with new and replacement pilots. In 1916, the average life expectancy of a pilot in France was just three weeks, following a course of instruction 'wholly directed to producing air-worthiness in the pupil'.[39] Experienced observers in the Corps squadrons in France could give a new pilot additional instruction on working a camera, a machine gun, liaising with a battery and flying through anti-aircraft fire, given the protection they received from the roving patrols of the RFC's fighting-scouts.[40] Unfortunately, so long as the main part of the pupils' business in England was learning to fly safely, those pilots sent to the fighting squadrons arrived 'innocent of all … fighting manoeuvres'.[41] A period of particularly high attrition only served to highlight the inherent flaws in a training programme that was filling the cockpits of the machines on patrol above rural France with 'vulnerably inexperienced aircrew'[42] or 'inadequately trained beginners',[43] resulting in a deadly spiral whereby more pilots had to be sent out even earlier. The roots of the tragedy of April 1917 in the air over Arras, were in England, as training was curtailed and pilots were rushed out to France with an average of only 17½ hours' flying time.[44] As a consequence, the most adept pupils often had the least training, and when matched against more experienced German pilots they became, as Peter Hart describes it, 'willing Albatros fodder'.[45]

Alongside the curtailment of the training programme in early 1917, there is still the question of what was actually being taught. By 1916, it was recognised that while the 1914 training model gave a pupil

Figure 18. Aerial view of Harlaxton aerodrome.

sufficient instruction for 'taking a ticket' on a Maurice Farman, and for then flying a BE2c, BE2d or BE2e that was so stable that it virtually flew itself, this was an elementary level of flying. Hence, the distinction between an elementary training squadron and higher training squadron and the realisation that more could be done in training at the higher level. Especially, as the appearance of more powerful machines, coupled to the development of more complex aerial fighting, combined with a high attrition rate 'was giving cause for concern'.[46] Consequently, in March 1916, a new curriculum was introduced by the Director of the Training Brigade, Sir John Salmond, who returned to England from France in early 1916 to command and reorganise a training system that needed to overcome pilot 'shortages and inexperience'.[47] Before getting their coveted wings pupils were now required to climb to 6,000 feet (raised to 8,000 in 1917) before switching off their engine, gliding down to earth and landing within a circular mark 50 yards in diameter.[48] In addition, a pilots' pupillage now included making two landings in the dark assisted by flares. This is why the officer commanding No. 24 Training Wing, which comprised Harlaxton and Spittlegate aerodromes, was forced to write the following memo to Training Brigade Headquarters:

Ref. yr Secret TB/809 dated 3. 1. 17.

I was up at Harlaxton yesterday and am of the opinion that the Aerodrome is not fit to be classed as a Night Landing Aerodrome until the tree stumps on the aerodrome have been removed. Urgent application has been made to the contractors to do this.[49]

Pupils also needed to successfully complete a 60-mile cross-country flight during which they had to land at two other aerodromes. More importantly, this new curriculum provided a new benchmark for the number of solo hours a pupil, with an RAC brevet, had to complete before they graduated from their flight training and received their RFC brevet, or wings, and were sent to France.[50] From August 1914 to December 1916, pupils had, on average, a total of 15 solo hours' flying time when they arrived in France.[51] In 1916, 15 hours' solo flying time became the new *minimum* requirement.[52] This was subsequently raised to a new minimum total of 20 solo hours in December 1916, before a pilot received his wings, before falling back to an average of 17 in the spring of 1917.[53] According to Arthur Gould Lee, in May 1917, 'most pilots average 15–20 hours' flying when they arrive here, with maybe

[only] 10–12 solo, 5 on the type they're expected to fight on. With that amount of piloting, they can't even fly, let alone fight.'[54]

By late 1917, 'a sum total of twenty hours' solo [including time in elementary machines] was necessary before a pilot could graduate as a pilot ... and was given permission to wear his "wings"'.[55] In addition, in December 1916, a series of special tests were added covering elementary tests in gunnery (stripping, assembling and firing Vickers and Lewis machine guns on a ground range), artillery observation and photography, bomb-dropping (see Chapter 7) and also, '"trick" flying was [at last] encouraged'.[56] In 1917, pilots also had to complete tests in flying in formation and elementary fighting practice using a camera gun.[57] This was accompanied by further increases in the time spent in the air in training to between, '25–30 hours actual flying in the air'[58] before a pilot-pupil was passed 'fit to graduate as a Flying Officer'[59] and receive his wings.

After mid 1917, before going to France, newly qualified pilots were also sent on a specialist fighting course, finally bringing together the theory and practice of military aviation. As Ray Sturtivant states, further specialist training was 'becoming increasingly necessary if the RFC was to cope with the improved machines and tactics of their German opponents'.[60] Newly graduated pilots were now expected to complete at least five hours' flying time on a service machine, or a close equivalent, as 2nd Lieutenant T.H. Hampshire, training with No. 54 Squadron in 1917 states, 'I shall always remember Harlaxton, as it was there I completed my five precious hours on the little Bristol Scout, prior to being posted overseas.'[61] By mid 1918, pupils were spending a minimum of 35 hours in the air completing the RFC's new curriculum.[62] These changes in both the length and rigour of the training programme in England were, of course, occasioned by the appearance of the RFC's more powerful fighting-scout machines and fighter-reconnaissance machines, which new pilots had to be able to handle. Conversely, it was the appearance of these new machines that turned the tide against the *Jastas* and allowed pupils to double their flying times.

This transition from a quasi-civilian pilot-training programme, to an advanced fighter training programme, can be observed at Harlaxton through the experiences of Eric Furlong, who trained at the aerodrome in 1917, after transferring into the RFC from the Royal Inniskilling Fusiliers. Furlong became an infantry officer in 1915, straight out of public school, having been in the school's Officer Training Corps (OTC). Whilst still at school he had taken private flying lessons at Hendon aerodrome. Learning to fly on a single-seat Caudron machine was, unsurprisingly, not without incident. When making a turn his instructor had told him to simply 'kick-on rudder' rather than bank. This dropped the nose of the aeroplane which then, as he variously described it, skidded, flopped, slewed or fell around the corner. In retrospect, he blamed this suicidal piece of instruction on the current 'lack of knowledge of aerodynamics',[63] but he could at least now make a circuit of the aerodrome and he duly took his 'ticket' in 1915.[64] He then applied to join the RFC and was promptly turned down by the interviewing officer because he was 'too heavy for our aircraft',[65] necessitating his sojourn in the infantry. Not to be deterred he re-applied, and was eventually accepted, and arrived at Harlaxton aerodrome in mid 1917 for his service training in learning to fly – again.

At Harlaxton he began his elementary flight training on the two-seat Maurice Farman MF7, before progressing to the Martynsyde Scout and the DH4 used by the higher training squadrons. The Farman, or 'Longhorn', a nickname derived from its long, curved outriggers, was, in Furlong's opinion, 'quite a delightful machine to fly'.[66] Going up for his first flight in the Farman his instructor immediately spotted that he had flown before and told him 'alright well you fly it [but] ... he didn't like the way I went round corners because I'd learnt to turn flat corners

Figure 19. 'A bad landing', in a Maurice Farman Shorthorn, Harlaxton.

whereas the air force, and in fact, I suppose, most other training by then had advanced to proper banked corners so I learnt how to bank the machine'.[67] On this first flight:

> as soon as he realized I was doing flat turns he wrenched the controls out of my hand and threw it into a bank 'this is what I want, do it like this' ... we got to the next corner he wrenched it out my hands *again* and showed me how to go round and on the last corner he didn't give it back to me and I just sat there and watched and we were gliding in and we went straight in, slap into the ground, wallop, and smashed the machines to smithers and he said 'what did you do that for' and I said 'well I didn't touch it' and he said 'neither did I', he thought I'd got it and I hadn't ... that was my first ... exciting landing in ... a Maurice Farman Longhorn.[68]

Furlong, had in fact, decided not to reveal he had his 'ticket' in the belief he would find out more from his instructor, but for the true beginner taking over from the instructor must have been a daunting experience, especially before all instructional machines were fitted with dual controls.[69] Dual control enabled a pupil to put his hands on the controls and his feet on the rudder bar and feel how the instructor made an aeroplane climb, turn and descend. The pupil could then attempt these manoeuvres with the instructor able to make any adjustments. In the unmodified machines, where the instructor and the pupil operated one set of controls the experience of learning to fly, in readiness for going solo and then 'taking one's ticket', was a far more dangerous business. Indeed, some of the pilots less suited or inclined to the business of instruction (see Chapter 4) would refer to their pupils as 'Huns' on the basis that they were equally as dangerous.[70]

Having secured his 'ticket' the pupil pilot now moved to one of the Higher Training squadrons to complete the new curriculum introduced in 1916 which now involved flying cross-country in a BE2d or BE2e. This was because their stability, which had made them so vulnerable to the Fokker E-type in corps or artillery squadrons, made them an ideal step up for pupils moving from flying a Maurice Farman in a circuit around an aerodrome to flying a more powerful machine in a circuit cross-country.[71] Navigating cross-country was one of the key flying skills for pilots in a Corps whose primary function was to reconnoitre over enemy territory. Flying cross-country in machines whose engines could stall resulted in pupils regularly having to make forced landings, which

YOUNG ICARUS AND FLIGHT TRAINING

Figure 20. Lieutenant W.J. Dalziel in a BE2e aircraft prior to his first solo flight, Harlaxton, 11 December 1917.

was another test in itself of the pilot's flying skill and ability to repair his aeroplane's engine. This experience was described by Stanley Rutledge:

> I had my first forced landing on Friday morning, which really means landing without aid of an engine. The majority of these landings, need I say, turn out badly. Sometimes the machine is broken and sometimes the pilot is battered. Luckily, I drew up ten feet from a hedge, and didn't do any damage. I had to wire, though, for an engine expert, and the machine had to be dismantled.[72]

Ironically, for Eric Furlong, having already made a forced landing in his DH4 after his engine cut out, it was his attempt to fly out of the field that led to him becoming somewhat battered and bruised. As he bumped his way across the ploughed field he quickly realised that he was not going to be able to clear the hedge that was looming up before him. He just managed to jump it, whereupon the engine promptly stalled:

> and I fell in a heap on the other side wrapped the wings right down the machine and I remember finishing up upside down with the wings all round me and looking through I could see petrol dropping on the hot engine ... and I thought the sooner I get out of this the better so I fought my way out tearing whatever I could and climbed out ... and that was the end of that.[73]

Given the primary function of the RFC was to provide aerial reconnaissance for the BEF, mastering cross-country flying was the final test before a pupil received his wings, as Stanley Rutledge explained:

> Yesterday [24th September 1917] I went for my cross-country flight test. This is really the final test one does on the BE machines, because after twenty hours' flying one passes on to a scout machine, with more speed and more tricks. Windover, another Canadian, and I went off together and landed at South Carleton and Waddington [aerodromes], and then circled above Nottingham, covering in all about one hundred miles. We had no exciting escapades, engine troubles or any moments of awful suspense. I am now flying Martinsydes, and in a few days' time will be on my final machine, a very powerful bi-plane of great speed and climbing ability.[74]

Having successfully completed his cross-country test on 24 September 1917, and having now flown several different types of machine and amassed the requisite number of solo hours flying time, his qualification as a pilot was confirmed by the wing commander: 'To be Flying Officer (pilot) – Lieutenant S.A. Rutledge.'[75] This was followed by the arrival of a graduation certificate.[76] Having obtained his wings Rutledge continued to train at Harlaxton because, by this stage of the war, pilots were required to master a more powerful service machine on a specialist fighting course before being sent to France, as he wrote on 21 October:

> Yesterday I completed my last test to make me a service pilot and ready for overseas. Of course I graduated as a pilot on September 25th, but one has to undergo subsequent training before he is counted ready for combat. Brown and I have been going along neck and neck in our tuition work, and we both finished together. He is a Canadian from the Maritime Provinces, and was out in France for some months as an observer.[77]

Similarly, Brian Garrett, who attended Harlaxton in 1918 was subject to a requirement that service pilots, 'will not wear wings until they are qualified for service overseas'.[78]

The shift, in 1917, toward sending pilots to France who had already experienced an operational style of flying in training in England, is evidenced by the progression of pilots through a succession of ever more powerful machines, culminating in flying a service machine. This is why the handling qualities of the aeroplanes they flew in training

YOUNG ICARUS AND FLIGHT TRAINING

at Harlaxton features so heavily in the recollection of both Stanley Rutledge and Eric Furlong. The latter, for instance, summed up the qualities of the Martinsyde Scout, given it:

> wasn't a scout in the true sense of the word, it was simply a single seater and a bit faster than some of the others, but it wasn't a very nice machine to fly … [because] it was heavy, I don't think I'd liked to have been a scout [in this machine] … because it didn't throw about very easily and I think you would have been a sitting duck for any of the more modern machines, anyway, it was used as a training machine and it was cheap and cheerful, I suppose, if you broke it.[79]

As a machine the Martinsyde was in marked contrast to the DH4 flown both in operational squadrons in France and in the training programme in England, where it received a glowing report from Furlong as:

> a lovely machine, that was a first class machine, it was fast, the fastest machine in the air at that time, and in fact you were told, and you soon realised, that your safest way of escape was to turn and run because you were faster than the other chap and could fly higher most of the time … [but, it] wasn't an aerobatic machine, it wasn't strong enough, it was too light really, you could do a few aerobatics but it wasn't a good thing to do nothing like some of the others, so it really relied on its climb and its speed, that's what it was famous for.[80]

The 'others' would be the DH5, a genuine scout-fighter, but this was only flown at Harlaxton by No. 68 (Australian) squadron as it was working up as a fighter squadron; also the Sopwith Pup and the Sopwith 1½-Strutter which were flown at Harlaxton (see Appendix I). Similarly, the DH4, with its speed and rate of climb, was a machine whose performance was comparable to a fighter.

With pilots now flying ever more powerful machines in training, up to and including service machines such as the DH4 and the RE8, the earlier prohibitions on stunt flying were abandoned. As Lord Cecil observed in 1918, 'at the beginning of the war much that is now part of the ordinary training of a pilot would have been forbidden as impossible to achieve and dangerous to attempt. Aeroplanes to-day can climb … five times as quickly as they could three years ago. They can defy the wind …'[81] The DH4 was to be the final machine Rutledge was to fly in training at Harlaxton, and like Furlong he considered it to be 'a wonderful aeroplane; well engined; in fact, there is an enormous reserve of power, and has a speed at high altitudes that will compare with any of the machines now in use'.[82] And with this speed and power it could do a few aerobatics as he described in a letter home dated 7 October 1917:

> I do not know any sensation to equal that of stunting. Suppose one goes up for a loop. The nose of the aeroplane is thrust down until a speed of a hundred miles is registered. Then one pulls the 'joy-stick' (control lever) back, and the plane begins to climb. Then, applying pressure gradually one points the nose heavenwards, and the plane stalls and flops over. It is when one is upside down (at the height of the loop) that one gets a sinking feeling like unto nothing I know, and one wonders if the thing will go over or stay upside down for ever ... But the spin is the greatest spectacular stunt. One comes hurtling down, inside out and outside in, as it were. The uninitiated would swear that the aeroplane was out of control and falling to earth. But generally, all comes right. The pilot puts on a little rudder and waggles the 'joy stick', and the 'bus', obedient to his touch, straightens out and floats away. Thus do we carry on in the Flying Corps.[83]

Deliberately spinning a machine is perhaps the clearest indication of the change that had occurred in regard to the progressive instruction of pilots after mid 1917. This was a routine manoeuvre in France, but it had not been a routine manoeuvre practised in training in England, where 'if a pilot lost control it was usually due to chance rather than skill if he recovered again'.[84] This was because there was, as Lee states, 'no instruction technique, no standard method. Nobody could explain in simple, practical terms how a plane was piloted.'[85] After mid 1917, this all changed thanks to one man – Robert Smith Barry:

> The great Smith Barry – the man who taught the air forces of the world how to fly.[86]
> Marshal of the Air Force,
> Lord Trenchard.

CHAPTER 4

Gosport and the Flight Instructor

In late 1917, pupils and instructors at Harlaxton were rolling, looping, spinning and slide-slipping powerful machines. This was in marked contrast to early 1917, when 'trick' flying had only just begun to be encouraged. As stunting literally took off after mid 1917, the skies above the Manor echoed to the roar of engines as pilots closed the gap on the more experienced *Jasta* pilots whom they would soon encounter in France. This transformation in the theory and practice of flight instruction was due to the vision of Robert Smith Barry, a scion of the fox-hunting Anglo-Irish Ascendancy, who assumed command of No. 1 Reserve Squadron, stationed at Gosport, in December 1916, just as No. 44 Squadron was arriving at Harlaxton. One of his protégés at Gosport has provided an excellent illustration of the reactionary attitudes that were then endemic to the training programme. Borrowing a 'Shorthorn':

> I found that it could be jazzed about in the air with considerable grace and ease, and after about fifteen minutes of various evolutions I landed and found the CO waiting for me. He was in a furious mood and being one stripe my senior severely reprimanded me for setting a bad example to his pupils. I was flabbergasted that such antiquated feelings could still exist … it taught me a lesson that the work being done at Gosport had only just begun, and that it was going to be some time before we flew everywhere with the complete confidence that a steeplechaser rides his horse.[1]

In 1917, the 'Gosport' method would quickly and completely overturn these antiquated ideas inherited from the Edwardian Flying Corps. The supposed benefit of the earlier system had been its simplicity, which allowed for the mass-production of pilots by newly appointed instructors. These benefits were, as Michael Paris points out, illusory[2] as they obscured the true capabilities of pilots thus trained, who quickly became casualties encouraging the mass-production of more replacements. By contrast, pupils training after mid 1917 were exposed to the loops, dives and spins now commonplace in France. These manoeuvres were practised in dual-control machines. This provided a controlled air environment in which the instructor could test the pupils' aptitude for flying – 'it is here that the beginner's weak points are quickly found'[3] – and the pupil could master these same manoeuvres before going solo. Arthur Gould Lee, recalling his training in 1916, in the days before spinning aeroplanes became commonplace, wrote: 'nobody tried a spin, for this would have been a suicidal act. Nobody knew how to get out of one, and anyway, this was too reliable a way of being killed accidentally.'[4] By comparison, when training at RAF Wittering, Philip Brereton Townsend's instructor 'when on dual RE8 deliberately spun the aircraft, and then allowed me to do the same ... this gave me great confidence'.[5] Stanley Rutledge's and Eric Furlong's time in training at Harlaxton in 1917 coincided with this transition between two very different approaches to instruction. The key to this new method of training was raising the standard of the instructors in the training squadrons. So how had instructors been chosen and allocated to the training squadrons?

Having only been established in 1912, by 1914 the CFS had simply not had the time needed to build a large enough reserve of trained pilots to cope with the 'wastage'[6] of pilots experienced in 1914 and 1915. Training enough pilots to compensate for this wastage was compounded by the need to train more pilots to ensure the size of the RFC in France remained commensurate with the size of Britain's Expeditionary Force. In these circumstances, the priority was to produce pilots quickly and so quantity superseded quality. By 1916, the drawbacks of this focus on quantity over quality was becoming 'more pronounced as aeroplanes became more powerful and the roles of fighting-scouts and fighter reconnaissance emerged'.[7] An approach to training which encouraged the production of pilots with the minimum of fuss, also allowed the RFC to find the extra pilot-instructors needed 'in-house', by recalling operational pilots from France to serve as instructors in one of the new Reserve squadrons now being formed in England. These Reserve squadrons added extra capacity to the training programme in England given that, on its own, the CFS was simply not going to be able to produce enough pilots.[8]

The policy of rotating experienced pilots between operational squadrons and the Reserve/Training squadrons was a feature of the training programme in England throughout the war, especially as more Reserve/Training squadrons were formed. In so doing, the RFC succeeded in creating a reserve of pilots in training in the UK. This allowed for new pilots to be continuously sent out to France, although sometimes too soon, to keep the Corps and fighting squadrons at full strength. This, in turn, made possible a system of daily photographic reconnaissance work and artillery observation by the Corps squadrons, with fighting squadrons defending them in their work by flying daily fighting patrols. With its emphasis on quantity, the training system in England was successfully producing a ready supply of replacements for those pilots who were killed, or were wounded and needed to recuperate in England, or those pilots who were simply in need of a rest. Indeed, 'the single largest cause of wastage … was the requirement to rest aircrew before their efficiency was impaired'.[9] Ironically, another cause of wastage was 'the need to feed experienced instructors into the flying training system'.[10] The expanding training system in England was thus seen by the RFC as an opportunity to 'kill two birds with one stone', as experienced pilots could be rotated through the training system as instructors having 'done their bit at the front and … been sent home for a rest'.[11]

Was it really a rest when pilots who had done their bit in France found the only rest they could expect, given the shortage of pilots, was to go to a Reserve squadron as a flying instructor?[12] Even as accomplished a pilot as 'Harry' Cobby found the strain of instruction 'much worse than flying in France'.[13] Pilots who were resting, or preparing to go back overseas also had, in Smith Barry's opinion, 'other interests paramount'.[14] For example, James Fitz Morris, following his recovery from a serious accident in August 1916, returned to duty as an instructor at Harlaxton aerodrome. Given the date, he would have been attached to No. 44 Reserve Squadron under the command of Major Jenkins. He subsequently returned to duty in France in July 1917 where, by the end of August, he had become an 'ace' having scored five victories. Thereafter, he went on to win the MC with bar, the Belgian *Croix de Guerre* and was recommended for the DSO. Eventually, as a decorated fighter ace with a total of 14 victories, he was sent to the United States with the British Aviation Mission where he was killed flying a Sopwith Camel during an air exhibition at Cincinnati.[15] Being in need of rest, probably explains Cobby's observation that having initially:

> felt that I could never achieve the jaunty outlook on life that seemed so characteristically part of the make-up of the pilot who had been overseas.

I little knew that quite a large proposition of his perkiness was due to the fact that whilst in England the enemy was not throwing lead and heavy shells at him.[16]

The biggest problem in the training programme was thus the haphazard approach of finding instructors and the consequent variation in the quality of training a pupil was receiving. This was especially true if a qualified service pilot was assigned to a training squadron because they were:

> useless for anything else [and whose] ... results were not watched or compared. They received no praise or blame. They worked without guidance or system, and they looked on the whole business as drudgery. To them pupils were 'odious Huns', and their indifference was contagious.[17]

As Cobby again observed:

> We did not then realise that quite a large number of the instructors with whom we had come into contact, had seen very little fighting for quite a number of reasons. The Air Force had developed so quickly and was still expanding at a fast rate. Almost any pilots who had returned from overseas, irrespective of the cause, whether from incompetence, disability or for a rest from the War, were put on to instructing, and a large number of the more advanced pupils themselves were given similar duties. Consequently, the general knowledge of air tactics and War fighting among instructors was rather low.[18]

This was especially true of the best of the new graduates who were held back to be instructors. It was 'not at all unusual for a pilot to be teaching his juniors to fly the day after he himself had qualified for his wings'.[19] This was the case for both Stanley Rutledge and Eric Furlong who began giving formal training as service instructors in a system where, according to Furlong:

> it was more or less left to the instructor to devise his own method of instructing, I don't think there were any books on the subject, and each instructor appeared to, and it certainly happened when I was instructing, you got up your own ideas as to how to train, and you told the fellow what happened, on the ground, you then took him up in the air and showed him what happened, demonstrated the controls, how they worked, and then you let him have a go, and if necessary correct him

while he was doing it otherwise telling him afterwards what he'd done wrong, this was the system.[20]

In September 1916, just as the hangars were about to go up at Harlaxton, the CFS had published its *Hints for Young Instructors on How to Instruct in Flying*. It defined the business of formal instruction in the following terms: 'It is universally acknowledged that the best type of pilot is the man with a well-disciplined mind, and, therefore, *any method* of instruction or training which assists in the cultivation of this fundamental power of control may be regarded as fulfilling a purpose of paramount importance'.[21] Precise guidelines for training had in fact been avoided for fear it would stifle initiative on the part of the instructor. As Sir Sefton Brancker explained, an instructor was 'a man whose business it is to break young horses'.[22] During 1916 and 1917, under the tutelage of Sir John Salmond, 'trick' flying had been introduced into a training system which had also increased from 47 to 78 Reserve/Training squadrons.[23] This meant that, by 1917, there was a growing pool of pilots, and thus former pupils, with experience of flying patrols in fast, powerful service machines in France, being seconded to the training squadrons in England. Would these experienced pilots have been indifferent to the lacklustre approach to training adopted by some of their fellow instructors? Arthur Gould Lee, reviewing the instructors he had encountered, sorted them accordingly:

> Some were beginners too, and just didn't know how. Some were not even confident pilots, unable to do a vertical turn, and shying off aerobatics. Many were reluctant to entrust their lives to ... pupils, and never surrendered full control. Some were nervy after active service, and some, it was rumoured, were throw outs from squadrons in France ... But mostly the fault was that they simply didn't know how to teach.[24]

The existence of a pool of progressive opinion among instructors looking for guidance on what to teach and how to teach it, would certainly help explain the speed with which the training system in England switched over to the new method of instruction pioneered by Smith Barry at Gosport. With 'trick' flying or stunting having been added into the curriculum by Sir John Salmond, pupils at Gosport were now encouraged by Smith Barry's team of instructors to go further and undertake even:

> more adventurous forms of flying, to enable them to cope with all manner of difficult manoeuvres. They were taught how to cope with

tricky wind conditions, especially during take-off and landing, and to recover control from various unaccustomed circumstances induced deliberately by their instructors ... Graduates of the school emerged confident of their own abilities, undertaking by instinct much of the manoeuvring necessary for survival, and consequently devote a much greater proportion of their attention to their opponents.[25]

The benefits of 'enabling pilots to master new manoeuvres and to understand the strengths and limitations of their aircraft'[26] were so self-evident, that the 'Gosport' method was adopted after mid 1917 as the RFC's new standard model for pilot instruction. The keys to the success of this new approach were with the instructors working in the training system and as Arthur Gould Lee suggests:

> It was obvious to us all that instructors should have been taught their job. There were competent instructors at the civil flying schools at Hendon and Brooklands, who were engaged mostly in teaching novice *pilots* [like Eric Furlong] to get the RAC brevet, but these should long ago have been assembled into a school to give crash courses to RFC novice *instructors*.[27]

By 1918, all instructors, no matter how experienced, were detached from their squadrons and given a two-week School of Special Flying course, where they were graded 'A' as suitable for teaching other instructors, 'B' as suitable for all types of flying instruction, 'C' as licensed to instruct pilots but requiring supervision and additional training, or 'D' as unsuitable to be an instructor.[28] The last category eliminated those instructors who 'consider it their duty to carry out their work with a minimum of risk to themselves and the minimum of risk to their pupils and their machines'.[29] In November 1917, Smith Barry had recommended the establishment of an instructors' school so that the 'instructors themselves could convert Instructional Squadrons to the improved system'[30] of teaching. This was because:

> A school where pilots drawn from the front-line squadrons [and the training squadrons could] ... become instructors would [ensure that] ... their flying [was] brought to a very high pitch, and ... they would acquire an *esprit de corps* that would improve the whole atmosphere surrounding pilot-training.[31]

Training was being taken out of the hands of pilots who considered instruction 'a terrible job [and] ... were afraid to give pupils full control of an aircraft for fear they would crash'[32] or those who had no interest at all in instructing.[33] Meanwhile, pilots seconded to the work as part of their recuperation would now be given instruction on how to teach, as 'courage and simple skill in flying were not enough to make a flying instructor and neither were battle fatigue and the need for a rest. Instructors had to be taught, and that became the task of the CFS.'[34] The work of the CFS was complemented by the opening of flying instructors' schools in each of the new RAF Area commands, based at Ayr, Redcar, Shoreham, Lilbourne and Gosport, which became the No. 1 School of Special Flying in May 1918.[35]

In October 1917, Smith Barry's 'Notes on Teaching Flying for the Instructor's Courses at No. 1 Training Squadron Gosport, May 1917' were reissued by the War Office as a pamphlet titled *General Methods of Teaching Scout Pilots*. This was because the War Office had decided that 'everyone in the UK and overseas in the Dominions and Colonies should adopt Gosport's methods at once'.[36] Stunting was now 'positively encouraged ... through practical demonstrations with experienced instructors'[37] in Britain, Canada and also Egypt where the RFC's Middle Eastern Brigade (established in 1916) was headquartered. A very useful offshoot of the Brigade was No. 20 Reserve Wing which, unlike its counterparts in England, could carry on with a programme on instruction during the winter without being interrupted by the weather. This made it an invaluable source of trained pilots.[38] For example, Leslie McNab (No. 3/432) had originally gone overseas with the Medical Corps of the New Zealand Expeditionary Force (NZEF). After serving at Gallipoli he was in Egypt, in 1917, when he was recommended for a field commission by his colonel. His commission coincided with his successful application to join the RFC in Egypt and he began his flight training on a DH6 at Amrid aerodrome. This was followed by flying on an Avro at Aboukir aerodrome. He graduated at Amria aerodrome on a BE2c, having accumulated 22½ solo flying hours. He then returned to Aboukir for training on the RE8 and received his wings on 4 May 1918. Subsequently, in July he arrived in England and reported to RAF Headquarters at the Hotel Cecil in London. He was then informed he was being posted to Harlaxton to fly RE8s, despite his 'protest, having been told previously I am for Bristol fighters, but this is useless, being informed that if a man ... [can] successfully fly RE8s he cannot get off them. This is a sad outlook for me, on these cranky machines'.[39]

On arrival at Harlaxton he was informed he would have to have additional training on the assumption that the training programme in Egypt was inferior to that in England and that he was not yet entitled

Figure 21. Sopwith two-seater crash, Harlaxton.

to wear his wings. This assumption was quickly dispelled as his re-tests were 'but a repetition of Egypt'.[40] He could now get on with the business of learning the various operational-styles of flying namely, flying in formation, dogfighting and strafing targets on the ground. As we saw in Chapter 1, when an RE8 crashed when circling Harlaxton aerodrome, live-firing was a feature of the range built in the Park, and aerial gunnery was a skill pilots as well as observers and gunners had to master following their ground gunnery course in the aerodrome's lecture hall. Once in the air, McNab's instructor fired 'on a target on the ground, cutting off the engine and diving very steeply like a hawk from 800 to 100 feet shooting out bullets in a stream. All very exciting and never forgetting to pull the bus out straight near the ground.'[41] In completing his course in strafing, and flying solo, he was very lucky not to become another name on the aerodromes' Roll of Honour (see Appendix I):

> I am … at the aerodrome [late] in the evening … when Lieutenant Jimmy James, a Canadian [instructor] … say[s], 'Hop up and finish the rest of your rounds it looks all right for a while up top'. This at 25 to 9 at night in the twilight, and I am soon shooting [targets on the ground] and to my annoyance I get a No. 4 stoppage. I try to remedy this … and the next thing I am all in fog … to add to my misfortune I realise that night is coming on. Its neck or nothing now, and I cut off my engine and glide

downwards seeing nothing ... suddenly dim shapes of trees and hedges whizz past at a terrific speed ... I touch ground ... [with] a hedge dead straight in front of me. On with the engine and I hop it like a steeple chaser, keeping her nose in the air to make a pancake landing ... Praise be! I am on an even keel ... [and] quickly scramble from the wreckage fumbling for a cigarette to soothe me ... At the aerodrome I find many flares lighted for me ... [then] To Lieutenant James' hut to report ... [and he] welcome[s] me with much warmth. This proves how lucky I am in being alive – most instructors hiding their feelings very successfully under similar circumstances and enquiring after the fate of their machines. In the mess ... they inform me that all are on the aerodrome firing Very lights in the air and they ... thank me for the opportunity of having the best fireworks display for years.[42]

The fact that instructors felt it necessary to hide their feelings was all part of the same unflappable imperturbability, and stiff upper lip, highlighted by Berberich, which helped officers cope with the cacophony of crashes in the fields surrounding the aerodrome. By contrast, with death and serious injury their constant companions, the junior officers and gentlemen cadets were, unsurprisingly, prone to bouts of horseplay. McNab records an incident where a pupil at Harlaxton, who was not allowed to go solo pinched a machine and landed miles away, 'sending a cheeky card "Who said I couldn't fly?"'[43]

Before going overseas, a pupil also needed to learn how to fire a machine gun at an opponent when flying. This was achieved through mock aerial combats. As a result, the skills of dogfighting, developed and executed on a daily basis by scout pilots in France, were learnt in England. In late 1917, Stanley Rutledge, having received his wings, was enrolled on a specialist air-fighting course at nearby Spittlegate aerodrome, which he described in a letter home:

> Well, this has been quite a week. Have been ... on what is termed a fighting course. The purpose of such instruction is to prepare pilots for the conditions which have to be met when overseas. A pilot's efficiency must necessarily depend on his ability to manoeuvre his aeroplane in such a way as to ward off the opposing plane, and place his opponent in a hazardous position. Thus he must know how to stunt. If one flies straight a Hun can simply sit on his tail, as the expression goes, and pump lead into one's machine. But supposing the pilot has mastered his plane, then ... his opponent is thwarted. That is what our programme consisted of. We stunt – one goes aloft and throws the machine about,

Figure 22. Practice aerial scrap at 10,000ft in an Armstrong Whitworth FK8.

careless of equilibrium and negligent of the laws of gravity. Thus does man and aeroplane become one. Thus does a pilot get a great measure of confidence in his ability to meet any contingency in the air.[44]

Subsequently, in 1918, Leslie McNab took the same air-fighting course by flying a machine mounting a camera gun:

> This is just as a machine gun in appearance and [has] the same controls, so that in fighting the trigger is pressed on the joystick, and the gun instead of firing … take[s] photographs, which is much safer. Afterwards they develop the negatives and make allowance for the forward speed of the aeroplane as in duck shooting, and allot points if we get the mock enemy in the proper circles on the photographs. This I think [is] very ingenious, and clever, and of great value in training as very few instructors I think would allow themselves to be shot at with bullets for the training of pupils, in spite of their comments on the ground on the accuracy of our shooting.[45]

Given the social context in which the RFC/RAF was training its pilots in England, in 1917 and 1918, another option open to trainee pilots wishing to improve the accuracy of their shooting was to go clay pigeon shooting.[46] During the war the Edwardian obsession with the rearing, preservation and shooting of pheasants and partridges for shooting had to be curtailed due to the lack of gamekeepers. This would have been

Figure 23. Clay pigeon shooting, Harlaxton.

particularly vexing for one of the leading shots and recognised experts in the rearing of game in Edwardian England, namely Thomas Sherwin Pearson Gregory. In another change, the right to shoot on the estate, a privilege formerly only enjoyed by the squire, or by tenant farmers with the permission of the squire, was extended to the neighbouring gentlemen of the air, although the unpredictability of the 'sport' was somewhat lessened by the smooth flight of a clay pigeon.

Back up the hill, on the aerodrome, the use of DH4 service machines was complemented by the use of RE8 machines, but whereas the former was considered by instructors like Furlong and Rutledge to be an excellent machine, the RE8 had a reputation as a much more 'cranky' machine.[47] What is beyond doubt is that it was a considerably heavier and more powerful machine, with its 150 hp engine, than the machines used by pupils in their initial flight training, which at Harlaxton included the 70 hp Henry Farman 'Rumpety' and the Maurice Farman 'Shorthorn' and the 70 to 90 hp BE2 series.[48] Even these machines could not be taken lightly by the inexperienced pilot. On 11 November 1917, 2nd Lieutenant Duncan Alexander Robertson was killed when flying a 'Shorthorn' (see Appendix I). However, the RE8 remained a machine with a reputation for being especially unpredictable which is why it made sense to keep hold of an experienced RE8 instructor such as Lieutenant Rowe. This would also explain why Leslie McNab, given

Figure 24. Officers and air mechanics in front of an RE8, Harlaxton.

his experience on RE8s, was recommended for work as an instructor. But this was 1918, not 1917, and holding back talented graduates to be instructors was now subject to a much more stringent programme of training. In 1917, within a month of graduating Stanley Rutledge had begun working as an instructor. In a letter home dated 28 October 1917, he wrote: 'Since returning from leave my time has been employed flying, and I have done some instruction work – training new men … While here I have done very well indeed, and my superior officer has entrusted me with several dual trips, e.g., instruction of embryo pilots.'[49] By contrast, before McNab and 'Pratt an engineer from Harlaxton'[50] were allowed to begin work as instructors they were sent to Lilbourne, 'an offspring of Gosport, a famous training school. The pilots are super-airmen who instruct instructors.'[51]

The speed with which the training system in England adapted to this new approach has to be considered one of the great successes of the RFC/RAF. One might also speculate that the move from being in the doldrums of the air war, in a reserve or training squadron, to being centre stage in the training of potential fighter pilots must have engendered a bit more swagger in the Officers' Mess and when instructors visited the local aristocracy and gentry. Instructors could also test pupils much more closely, and if, according to Smith Barry, 'the pupil considers this dangerous let him find some other employment as whatever risks I ask him to run here, he will have to run a hundred times as much when he gets to France'.[52] Conversely, McNab and his fellow instructors were now taught to show 'great consideration to our pupils [at Harlaxton who] ... expect us to allow them to make mistakes in the air, and we ... calmly correct them by the telephone and [do] not touch the controls'.[53] Ironically, he found the officer teaching him to be an instructor 'very weak in the true sense of teaching, in that he shouts too frequently to me "My God! How is it you haven't killed yourself before this?" Which is not encouraging.'[54]

Offering encouragement to novice pilots was now the order of the day. T.H. Hampshire found the adjutant of No. 54 Squadron, Captain B.S. Lyon Williams, to be 'a most human and companionable officer ... [he was] tall and academic looking ... He had rather a bookish and schoolmaster way with him in my youthful eyes at the age of nineteen years!'[55] McNab, meanwhile, passed his instructors course and returned to Harlaxton on 4 September 1918 where he began to take his pupils:

> through all the different machines ... and not as in Egypt, a different instructor each time ... instruct[ing] from the back seat, giving the pupil the seat he is to go solo in – which is only fair. Pupils also ... get many more hours dual before going solo, and are check-tested by the OC flight. This takes a big responsibility from the instructors.[56]

Working with the same instructor was another innovation of Smith Barry's. In early 1918 all higher training squadrons in England were converted to 'all-through' squadrons where an instructor would instruct a pupil from the time they joined the squadron until they gained their flying brevets and were posted to their 'finishing schools', such as the Aerial Fighting School at Ayr in Scotland.[57]

Two new aeroplanes had also been added to the roster of machines that were used for instruction at Harlaxton, namely the DH6, which was then replaced by the Avro 504. This too was another innovation of Smith Barry who had recommended that the training squadrons adopt a single machine, the Avro 504, which would replace the multiplicity of different machines then in use throughout the training system for both elementary and intermediate instruction.[58] The twin-seat Avro was an ideal trainer as it was 'a fully aerobatic machine'.[59] Many of the instructors at the aerodrome had never flown it before and, according to McNab, this resulted in 'forced landings in all directions. I congratulate myself on having trained on them

Figure 25. Harlaxton crash – Avro 504.

[at Lilbourne] but instead have four forced landings in five trips.'[60] The transition to the Avro 504, however, proceeded apace, and:

> with the sun rising behind a wood nearby and a pleasant tang in the air of the English Autumn … We fly low over the huts where those not flying are asleep – until we come. Joystick to the left, press on the rudder bar with your feet, and the left wing tip goes down, and we swing round on a glorious bank … Right rudder – joy-stick to the right, we flatten out, and you speak down the phone. The pupil takes over. He makes a mistake – you correct him, showing him his faults and how he should do the different movements … Half an hour's instruction, you cut the engine off and drop the nose to a gliding angle.[61]

Pupils would then progress to flying cross-country, and 'knowing the capacity of our pupils for trouble, we listen with horror to any tale of a forced landing'.[62] When one occurred, and if the machine was still intact, it was the rule for the pupil's instructor to fly it out of whichever field it was in. Thus it was, that McNab cleared another hedge, 'then in front of me two trees … but a narrow gap, and I cannot clear them flying straight. This is the best bit of flying ever I did as I tip one wing in the air and just enough to clear the tree (the other being in the gap) urging her over like a tired steeple chaser'.[63]

The pupils' programme of instruction meanwhile, progressed onto strafing, mock air-combats and flying in formation, all of which brought the training programme in England, finally, into full alignment with the operational realties in France. Back in 1914: 'The main part of the pupils' business was to learn to fly with safety, and when he could do this he was passed out to the squadrons. Such a training would have been terribly inadequate a year or two later, when no one could hope to fly long without fighting.'[64] The fact the training programme now mirrored this operational reality was commented upon by James McCudden when he was brought back from France in 1917 to instruct pupils in the 'aerial acrobatics which are only one part of the qualifications of the successful air fighter'.[65] In England, he 'often explained how much better off they were in their training than were the pilots who had gone out to fight in the air a year previously, for at this time the pilots were receiving very good training indeed, and [had] … a good chance of downing an opponent'.[66] By contrast:

> At the time I went to France to fly a fighter aeroplane I had not even flown the type which I was to fly over the lines the next morning, let alone not having received any fighting instruction … [given the speed] aerial fighting take[s] place [in a scout], as distinct from that of the artillery, bombing and reconnaissance aeroplanes.[67]

If fighting in the air in France now meant learning how to fight in the skies above rural England, it also meant having to learn how to fly in formation. This was, after all, the key 'tactical revolution'[68] that made possible a system of line offensive patrols and distant offensive patrols high above and beyond the reconnaissance machines. These offensive patrols into German airspace represented the tactical extension of the formation flying adopted by the RFC in response to the 'Fokker scourge'. Pilots in France, in 1915 and early 1916, in mixed squadrons flying either a BE2c or its Vickers 'Gun Bus' escort, had been required to develop techniques for 'keeping station'.[69] This technique was then adopted by the dedicated fighter squadrons, especially those equipped with single-seat fighters. The RFC's 1916 *Notes on Aeroplane Fighting in Single Seat Scouts* state that as 'a general principle a single-seater should never cruise alone, and an attack by an isolated single-seater should be the exception'.[70] This was because a single-seat fighter was vulnerable to an attack from the rear when flying alone, but this risk was reduced when pilots flew together in mutually supporting pairs.[71]

In 1916, the size of the RFC's operational squadrons was also increased from 12 to 18 machines, and from three flights of 4 machines to three flights of 6 machines. As a result of this change, patrols of two, four, five or six machines, with two or more pairs working together, became the accepted practice.[72] In a dedicated fighter squadron, flying machines with the same levels of performance, pilots could become more confident in 'keeping station'. Initially 'wingmen' tended to concentrate on holding their position rather than keeping on the look-out for the enemy but, 'with experience, the formation would be opened out on approaching enemy lines so that the wingmen could relax more and look around them'.[73] A patrol of five machines would cruise in the classic stepped 'V' formation, with machines flying above and astern of each other, flanking out to the left and right of the flight leader. The two rearward machines watched the tails of the rest of the formation and if they spotted the enemy astern would fire a red flare forward and above of the formation using a Verey pistol, 'rocking their wings and pointing rearward.'[74] Up ahead, the flight leader was identified by coloured streamers fixed to each of his rear struts; the deputy flight leader was identified by a streamer fixed to his rudder. The former would lead the formation into an attack by rocking his wings to signal German machines below and then diving 'with the formation following, firing as they go'.[75]

Formation flying enabled the RFC to keep its single-seat fighters on patrol continuously to contest control of the air with the German air service; indeed, 'the sole duty of offensive patrols is to drive down and destroy hostile aeroplanes'[76] and thereby protect the reconnaissance machines. In order to do so, offensive patrols had:

> to fly in formation in order to obtain the advantage of mutual support ... [in 1918 it was recognised that] single-seater scouts or even two-seaters, if superior in speed and climb to the great majority of the enemy machines, may be able to patrol very successfully alone or in pairs, taking advantage of their power of manoeuvre and acting largely by surprise, but in the case of machines which do not enjoy any marked superiority, formation flying is essential.[77]

The size of this formation could vary markedly. No. 68 (Australian) Squadron had trained at Harlaxton as a single-seat fighter squadron on the DH5. Subsequently, in France, the squadrons' DH5s were replaced by the SE5a, a fighter that was a match for the best German fighters, whereupon it was 'agreed to patrol in pairs, rather than full flights to entice the German pilots'[78] into aerial combat. Being able to 'keep station' was the key to flying in any formation. Indeed, as Lord Cecil noted in 1918:

> The loneliness of a flying officer ... is not quite what it used to be. He still usually has only one companion or flies alone. But nowadays flying in formation is a common practice; and the flying officer often fights as one of a flight or of a squadron rather than, as in earlier days, totally alone.[79]

On the other hand, this was still an era where there was no radio communication between aeroplanes and as Cobby explains:

> Although formation flying and fighting demanded a very close cohesion among the members of the flight, in the early days one felt very much alone and at the mercy of chance. Lack of means of communication with one's fellows was, I think, the principal cause of this. You could not communicate with the other chaps about what was going on. Every possible eventuality had to be studied before leaving the ground ... then your memory and a thorough understanding of the characteristics of your leader and your comrades had to be relied upon.[80]

Cobby, having trained with No. 68 (Australian) Squadron at Harlaxton, would fly with No. 71 (Australian) Squadron in France, alongside George Jones. Unlike No. 68 (Australian) Squadron, which flew the SE5a, No. 71 (Australian) Squadron flew Sopwith Camels. Given the higher operational ceiling of the former, the latter was 'much more likely to be surprised',[81] hence the importance of flying in formation when on patrol. The operational necessity of being able to 'keep station' in a Camel or in a SE5a explains the inclusion of formation and cloud flying in the training curriculum. Learning to keep station was highly dangerous. One of the worst accidents at Harlaxton occurred on 8 May 1918, when the RE8 being flown by 2nd Lieutenant Myer Levine (aged 18) of No. 53 Training Squadron and the RE8 being flown by Lieutenant Arthur Thorne (aged 23) together with 2nd Lieutenant Howard Watson (aged 18), both of No. 64 Training Squadron, collided when practising formation flying. As Lord Cecil again observed, whilst 'flying is [being] better and better understood and more and more safely conducted with improved machines and greater knowledge of aviation ... the dangers of training have rather increased than diminished'.[82]

Nonetheless, as Michael Paris points out, there can be little doubt that, after January 1918, the RFC pilots graduating from training aerodromes like Harlaxton 'were more thoroughly trained'[83] making these new pilot officers in their new fighting-scouts formidable opponents for the pilots of the German air service who, in consequence, eventually lost the strategic battle for aerial superiority in 1918. This was a victory won by the pilots who came back to Harlaxton, to reflect upon what they had achieved, before returning home to Australia, Canada, New Zealand or South Africa. Before they did so, they returned 'home' to England, to the country where they had learned to fly and where, as recently as the autumn, Leslie McNab was training pupils in whom 'I see myself again and recall my first few wonderful solos, with all the world at my feet, sublimely unconscious of my danger through my ignorance, and of the prayers of my instructors for the safety of their machines'.[84]

CHAPTER 5

Airmen and their American Mechanics

The losses sustained in the training programme in England produced a catalogue of accidents with machines written off and injuries and fatalities to their aircrews (see Appendix I). Approximately 8,000 of the 14,166 RFC/RAF pilots killed in the First World War died in England in training.[1] During his training in 1916/1917 Arthur Gould Lee:

> saw fatal crashes every few days, and usually through mysterious spins into the ground when taking off ... The instructors put these crashes down to sheer clumsy piloting, and so there it was, hanging over us – if you did a flat spin [cartwheeling horizontally] it was just too bad, practically an act of God. There seemed to be a funeral every week, and as the pupils still alive had to follow and act as pall-bearers, it was rather depressing, but it became something of a routine journey to the cemetery ... especially as the band always played the same funeral march, and so after two or three burials one got used to it. Afterwards I learned that the same sort of thing was happening at most RFC stations, and for the same reason – poor instruction. Not without reason did we feel that for RFC learners, the war, considered in terms of casualties, began in England.[2]

For the inexperienced pupil working with the experienced instructor schooled in the new training approach pioneered by Smith Barry, learning to fly still remained a dangerous business. This was because machines with wings made of wood and canvas could experience catastrophic structural failures, especially after stunts became an everyday part of training. In September 1917, Air Mechanic (2nd class) Walter Brown, of No. 44 training squadron, was killed when the port wings of his DH4 machine collapsed during a spin (see Appendix I).

Crashes around Harlaxton aerodrome occurred almost continuously. RFC statistics indicate that, whilst the techniques for training pilots

Figure 26. 'DH6 makes an attempt for the hangar', Harlaxton.

Figure 27. 'Captain Saint and pupil killed, August 1918', Harlaxton.

were improving rapidly, on average, every pilot completely wrecked two aeroplanes and destroyed six undercarriages.[3] In 1917, RFC pupils were still wrecking 3.11 per cent of their aeroplanes, although this was a significant reduction on the 10 per cent of aeroplanes wrecked in the pre-Smith Barry era.[4] As previously noted, Furlong, Rutledge and McNab had all crashed, or had to make a forced landing when flying cross-country. Given the evident propensity for aeroplanes to misbehave and for pilots to miscalculate, the law of averages dictated that whilst pilots like Furlong and McNab walked away from many of these forced landings and crashes with only scratches, other pilots would be seriously injured or killed. The Roll of Honour for Harlaxton Aerodrome compiled for this book, and which appears in Appendix I, is a testament to these fatal crashes and among these names we find Stanley Rutledge (aged 26). Having become an instructor at Harlaxton he wrote home on 28 October 1917:

> I have, strange to say, been referred to as quite daring, and overly-confident. But that does not seem to me to be a true statement of the case. I have looped and spun the DeH/4, not an unusual feat, but one which the ordinary chap does not do for some time. But by nature I am not of an adventurous disposition, and yet there is that within me which makes me want to be reasonably proficient. I always calculate and 'think over' the business in hand. I may take chances, but I am always looking ahead, and in little emergencies it is possible for my mind to work well. Rather egotistical this, I know.[5]

On 16 November Rutledge's father received the following alarming telegram from Lieutenant A.H. Beech of No. 44 Training Squadron: 'Regret to say Lieutenant S.A. Rutledge met with a serious accident this morning.'[6] The next day another telegram from the squadron confirmed what the earlier telegram portended: 'Regret to report death of your son … as result of aeroplane accident 16th instant, killed instantaneously.'[7] His pupil, 2nd Lieutenant J.W. Rhodes, was, thankfully for him, only injured as the DH4 they were flying in hit a tree on approaching the aerodrome to land (see Appendix I). A letter was then received from the OC of the squadron, which presumably was still Major Jenkins, in which he expressed his condolences:

> The Royal Flying Corps have lost the services of a really good officer and a very gallant pilot, who would have made a name for himself had he been spared to proceed overseas. I was personally very sorry indeed, to lose your son, as were all the officers, NCO's and all who knew him.

Major _____
No. 44 Training Squadron
Harlaxton, Grantham, England.
Nov. 21st 1917

The key line in this letter is his OC's assessment of Rutledge that had he been spared, he would have gone on to make a name for himself in France and escape the anonymity of the trenches. Attaining this immortality was fraught with risks, as Cobby recognised, with many being killed before they had the chance to make a name for themselves, but the chance to do so was compelling for individuals who, as was mentioned in the introduction, were struck by 'the possibilities of Self – [and] the heights to which ... [they] could soar when borne by Simple Courage'.[8] This symbiosis of individual courage, bordering on the reckless, and the technical proficiency that engendered this confidence (and perhaps overconfidence), was at the heart of the systematic refashioning of self-identity that occurred in training. This was also a training programme where pupils were under constant scrutiny; as a poem included in *Parti Patter* explains:

A Base Fabrication
Ruefully Robeyish
I pose as a Pilot. I know I'm hot stuff,
And I hate fellows swanking around
Giving advice that is far from polite
Picking holes where there's none to be found
I admit that I swerve just a shade on take offs.
I admit that I land a bit high,
But to say I've got the wind up, can't manage the bus,
It's a lie. It's a lie.
These choicest of merchants who blow on the 'drome
While I'm waiting my turn near the wing
Remark as they gaze at me over the side
'I'll fly first, you might smash it Old Thing.'
I confess that I've smashed up a V strut or two
A wing tip, once rev'd her too high
But for them to suggest that I'm likely to crash –
It's a lie.
I know all about these Star Stunters, you know,
Who come around dictating to you,
Then go up and do all their Immelmann turns,
Round a cloud, where they're well out of view.
Admitted my fuselage got a shade bent
My prop blade flew up pretty high,
But for them to infer that my flying is dud
Well, I mean, the idea is simply absurd.
The Hairy Coconut.[9]

Given that the training programme in England now encouraged stunting, both experienced and novice pilots alike had the opportunity to display their skill and courage to their fellows. In 1917 a truly exceptional 'star stunter' arrived with No. 68 (Australian) Squadron (see Chapter 6). The skill of this particular pilot was observed by a journalist visiting the aerodrome in late 1917:

> Here in the late hours of a sunny autumn day, I found Major Watt, and we watched a group of keen young Australians go through their evening 'stunts'. A Sopwith 'Pup' commenced to grunt vigorously as a mechanic in brown overalls gave a twist to its long broad propeller, which as the engine responded whizzed round at furious speed, the air-draft throwing up a cloud of dust and dirt ...
>
> A typical long-jawed young Anzac, wearing the ribbon of the Military Cross under the white wings of his tunic, detached himself from the group of officers, pulling on his leather coat and cap as he walked, jumped into the pilot's seat, glared keenly at the various controls, and raised his hand by way of signal to the mechanics to let go. For 50 yards or so the 'bus' ... ran over the rough ground, steadying up as it rose into the air. Then the pilot pulled his 'joystick' ... and at an amazing angle the little scout shot upwards ...
>
> Then commenced the wonderful aerial game that reminded me irresistibly of the aquatic revels of the sun-tanned lads of Sydney and Melbourne. Jumping off from the little wisp of cloud, the airman took a long graceful dive at an angle of about 45 degrees – a thousand foot dive, from which he 'zoomed' up with exquisite grace, coming out at the 2000ft, level on his back and swimming along thus with powerful strokes to his fleecy springboard.
>
> A few seconds breather, and then he appeared to just let the aeroplane go, and it turned over with its head pointing straight to earth. Down, down – the wings revolving in terrifying fashion, and indicating apparently a complete lack of control. But it was only part of the everyday game – the spinning-nose-dive. Until quite recently the spinning dive was the most dreaded of happenings, for it meant the end of both man and machine. Now the secret of how to get out of it is known to all, though the beginner, naturally, does not sample its exhilarating sensations.
>
> Back to high level again, the air swimmer turned on a whole box of tricks, cutting through the air on his side, travelling on his back for a mile at a stretch, looping backwards and forwards, and otherwise exhibiting the same mastery of the air as Cecil Healy and Frank Beaurepaire ...

As the airman glided down unerringly to the field again, Major Watt remarked 'That's Captain Stanley Keith Muir, of Melbourne, one of the finest flyers I have seen. With any luck he is certain to make a big name. He has already done good work in the Egyptian campaign, where he won his Military Cross' ... Major Watt has seen the flying man of every country, but he is absolutely certain none are superior to the Australians.[10]

This description of the reckless daring of the First World War flying officer retains its immediacy because 'despite the changing nature of heroism in the twentieth century, the pilot has retained an aura of glamour and manliness'.[11] The supposed 'chivalric heroism'[12] of individual aerial combats reinforced the idea of the pilot 'as the supreme figure of manliness'.[13] Individual pilots went on patrol in formation, and once the enemy was sighted they dived together, staying in formation, 'swooping down on them out of the sky, [in] the nearest thing to a cavalry charge'.[14] But the dive was designed to break-up the enemy formation, whereupon a series of individual combats commenced, and now it was the skill of the individual pilot that counted rather than tactics – the same skills being exhibited by Muir. As Philpott states: 'Pilot-led innovation facilitated daily flight over the German lines ... in a continual battle for technical and aerial superiority ... [that] effectively established systems for combat that were not wholly reliant on technology. Instead it was a combination of skilled flying and pilot's adaptability ...'[15] that counted. Displaying one's skill and adaptability in France allowed pilots to make a 'name' for themselves, but the jostling for a reputation clearly began in England. This was accompanied by an acceptance of the risks involved, as Lieutenant A.H. Beech explained in the letter of condolence he wrote concerning the death of his friend, Stanley Rutledge:

> I, too, belong to the 28th Canadians, and was with both Stan and Wilfred in France. I was in the Scout Section, and Stan and I used to sleep together there; and I must say I have never met a finer boy in my life, and thought as much of him as a brother; and he was generally liked immensely throughout the squadron, and by all who knew him. In regard to Stanley's work here, it was of the highest order, and he was a very brilliant pilot, and the unfortunate accident was and is liable to happen to any of us.

Lieut. A.H. Beech, 44th TS
Harlaxton, Grantham, England
18th November 1917

The death of Stanley Rutledge prompted the Canadian poet A.C. Stewart to write the following elegy to him:

> **In Memoriam, Lieut. S.A. Rutledge**
> Courier of the azure steeps,
> With Orion holding chase
> Flashing through the diamond deeps
> With the jocund Morn a-race;
> Wearied – curving from the skies -
> Calm, with folded pinion, lies.[16]

Stanley Rutledge is now buried in Harlaxton parish churchyard alongside his fellow Canadian 2nd Lieutenant Alick Charlesworth (aged 24) who had been killed earlier the same year on 30 May, having banked too steeply in a DH4 and had then spun in.[17] A similar fate was suffered by 2nd Lieutenant Jack Randell Falck (aged 19) of No. 54 Training Squadron whose Sopwith 'Pup' spun in on 7 December 1917. These were all tragic accidents, but what gives the death of Stanley Rutledge added poignancy is that he died in a field in Lincolnshire having survived the battlefield of the Somme. Sadly, this was a fate shared by another veteran of the Somme, and a fellow Canadian pilot, Lieutenant Gordon S.M. Gauld (aged 24).

Having graduated with a BA in Philosophy from University College, University of Toronto, Gauld attested to go overseas with the CEF on 9 February 1915. Subsequently, in England, he transferred into the Imperial Army receiving a commission in the RFA. He arrived in France in April 1916, serving with the 149th Brigade RFA on the Somme where he was awarded his MC for his actions on 5 and 6 July when:

> As Forward Observation Officer at the Briquetterie, he kept up, under heavy [shell] fire, visual communication with [Group] Headquarters after the [telephone] wires had been broken. This officer's name had already been submitted for great gallantry in putting out a fire in a gun pit after the gun had been destroyed by a premature explosion, and the ammunition set on fire, though he had been wounded and knocked out by the explosion.[18]

In the spring of 1917 he was seconded to the RFC and spent four months as an Artillery Observer with No. 8 Squadron, and having completed the requisite amount of time over the line as an observer and wanting to be a pilot he was sent for pilot training in England.

Whether this was at Harlaxton is unclear, but it is quite likely given that on completion of his training course he was taken on as an instructor with No. 20 Training Squadron. Both he and his pupil, 2nd Lieutenant Alexander Drysdale (aged 18), were killed on 25 March 1918 (see Appendix I) when flying an RE8: 'the machine crashed, from an unknown cause, killing both instantly'.[19]

Another Canadian instructor, Lieutenant William Kay Anderson (aged 25) of No. 20 Training Squadron, and formerly of the 156th Battalion of the CEF, was killed on 7 January 1918 when the DH6 he was flying, and the DH6 being flown by 2nd Lieutenant Arthur Charles Perryman (aged 29), collided in mid-air. Among those who, like Gauld, had also transferred from the RFA, and who met their end at Harlaxton, were the aforementioned Lieutenant Arthur Burrell Thorne (see Chapter 4) an instructor with No. 64 Training Squadron killed in May 1918 and 2nd Lieutenant Gerald Arthur Bloomfield (aged 23), a pupil pilot training with No. 53 Training Squadron killed in February 1918. Both were killed when flying in an RE8. The causes of fatal accidents, in addition to hitting a tree on approach, spinning-in when banking, colliding in mid-air, or having a wing collapse, also included the accident suffered by 2nd Lieutenant Cecil Reginald Bascombe (aged 19) of No. 44 Training Squadron, on 10 October 1917, whose DH4 stalled on take-off. Writing in 1918, a wing adjutant commented that when taking off an inexperienced:

> pilot may easily climb too quickly, or try to rise before the machine has gained sufficient speed, and thus 'stall' (come down tail first) or side-slip the aeroplane when he has not sufficient altitude in which to recover, but has ample in which to crash both the machine and himself.[20]

The loss of pupils and colleagues was therefore a constant occurrence in the training squadrons. As Leslie McNab noted on 3 August 1918: 'Two are killed here on RE8's in the last fortnight. It comes so unexpectedly – a short time before perhaps in the mess at lunch, laughing and talking, and a few minutes after snuffed out like a candle.'[21] The two pilots in question were most likely Flight Cadet Harold Buckley of No. 53 Training Squadron who was killed flying in an RE8 on 17 July and 2nd Lieutenant Arthur Moulton Cross (aged 23), with No. 20 Training Squadron, who was killed when training on an RE8 on 29 July 1918. A third pilot, killed in July, was 2nd Lieutenant John Arnold Sheperd, who was killed flying in an Avro 504 (see Appendix I). But in a Corps where the pilot had to ready himself in training to 'face the

Figure 28. 'Flight Cadet Iddon, killed, RE8, Harlaxton'.

combined terrors of aviation and war, depending on his own dexterity and presence of mind'[22] feelings of terror, like grief, had to be hidden and so when a serious injury or fatality occurred in a training squadron:

> We refrained from discussion of the subject as far as possible and then only to decide how such an accident could be avoided in future. Nevertheless, an unmistakable atmosphere pervaded the mess for which it was difficult to account at the time, and which, moreover, it was not easy to define.[23]

This, again, conforms to the imperturbable, stiff upper lip school of coping with grief and loss, highlighted by McNab and Berberich, but then to dwell on these risks ran contrary to the sense of adventure and, 'dismissal of the risk',[24] needed to carry on with the daily activity of training in England or going on patrol in France. Despite the risks inherent in flying, a favourite sport among the reckless fellows at Harlaxton was hedge-hopping, or 'flying low over the paddocks and zooming at the hedge like a race horse'.[25]

Accidents could occur on the ground as well as in the air. On 13 March 1917, Lieutenant Leonard Murray (aged 20) of No. 44 Reserve Squadron was accidentally killed when he was struck by the propeller of a DH4. This tragedy highlights the fact that all the activity in the air should not distract us from all the noise and activity of the aerodrome.

Each machine had its own crew of two riggers and two fitters, who would either be an air mechanic, 1st or 2nd class:

> Riggers look after the fabric, wiring, woodwork and general exterior of the machine, whilst the fitters are responsible for the condition and running of the engine. Other men work on the aeroplane as occasion arises – carpenters, sail-makers, etc.; blacksmiths, tinsmiths, instrument repairers, and men of countless other trades are in attendance to see to the ailments of engine, instruments, or any other of the delicate parts of the anatomy of the aeroplane. There are also drivers of cars and lorries, riders of motorcycles, wireless telegraphists, storemen and clerks galore.[26]

There was a whole community living on the hill above the village of Harlaxton from 1916 to 1919, comprising a cosmopolitan officer corps, the technical support staff teaching gunnery, photography and wireless telegraphy and the supporting ground trades all living in the growing assemblage of wooden huts brought onto site on the back of trucks in 1916 and 1917. Water was piped onto the aerodrome and stored in large wrought-iron water tanks capable of holding 9,000 gallons;[27] there were also storage tanks for the oil and petrol delivered to the aerodrome by tanker. In addition, the new corrugated-iron workshops provided workspace for an Aircraft Repair Section (ARS) that included carpenters, sail-makers, fitters, welders, blacksmiths and a dope section

Figure 29. Harlaxton, 1917.

(dope being the lacquer applied to canvas to make it taut and waterproof) as well as the mechanics.[28] Repair work and the erection of additional buildings were carried out by the civilian workmen employed by the Ministry of Munitions who also lived on the site. In August 1918 a report for His Majesty's Office of Works included a reference to bedsteads and bedding being supplied for workmen at 'Harlaxton Aerodrome Lines … for the Ministry of Munitions'.[29]

Within this community the social climb from the mechanics' workshop to the Officers' Mess, though a higher climb than many, also became more of a possibility in the latter stages of the war. Although the loss of a skilled mechanic was still felt more keenly than the gain of another pilot from the mechanic pool. This was because it was the mechanics that kept the squadrons' aeroplanes airworthy, and this was as true for a training squadron in England as it was for an army or corps squadron in France.[30] This had been true from the very beginning of the Corps. The Edwardian RFC was built around its air mechanics who had transferred from the Royal Engineers, with many of its NCOs coming from the Brigade of Guards, thereby combining 'the smartness of the Guards with the efficiency of the sappers'.[31] Elitism was built into the marrow of the Corps given this combination of the technological skill of the Royal Engineers and the spit-and-polish of the Guards; which is perhaps why mechanics like James McCudden or William Leedham could see themselves making the transition from wearing overalls, and keeping an aeroplane in the air, to wearing wings on their tunics and actually flying it.

The regard in which skilled mechanics were held by the pilots is revealed in a very telling incident at Harlaxton in 1917 when Stanley Muir overheard an RFC trainee pilot being a bit short with a No. 68 (Australian) Squadron rigger. Muir promptly told the pilot: 'Don't make trouble here, that laddie can do ten times as much for you as you can do for him, and civility is free.'[32] The level of respect accorded mechanics is a further reflection of their importance to the air service. In the opinion of Sir Hugh Trenchard, the ground tradesmen, the mechanics, fitters, riggers and armourers were the backbone of the Corps.[33] But where were all the extra mechanics to be found to allow for the projected expansion in the overall number of RFC/RAF operational squadrons? Even allowing for the 3,000 other ranks being trained, per month, in 1918, additional mechanics would have to be found.[34] In September 1917 the following advertisement appeared in the *Grantham Journal*: 'Recruits, skilled or unskilled men of almost any occupation, are wanted at once for the various Branches of the Royal Flying Corps.'[35] The eventual solution to this manpower problem was a scheme devised by the Director-General of Military Aeronautics, Sir John Salmond, and involved the use of American maintenance personnel to 'fill slots in the RFC training stations [in England], thus releasing British troops for France'.[36] The details of this scheme were worked out at the Allied Conference in Paris, in December 1917:

> The result of three years' experience … proves conclusively that the number of Other Ranks personnel required to maintain each active service plane … is 47.5 men … The position as to the personnel for the … RFC programme of 240 Squadrons [by July 1919] is not, however, as satisfactory [as the supply of machines]. There is great need for men in Great Britain for all branches of the Services and the supply of technical personnel is practically exhausted. Consequently the mechanics required for these additional Squadrons can only be obtained by depleting Infantry Units of men who are not actually qualified and will require a large amount of training. This in the present state of man-power available is manifestly impossible.
>
> The position with regard to personnel in the United States … is, I understand, exactly the converse of the position in Great Britain, there being a plentiful supply of man-power even with technical qualifications but not sufficient facilities for training rapidly, and … time is the paramount factor.
>
> In view of the foregoing a reciprocal and mutually advantageous proposal is set out hereunder, namely, that to assist in the training of American personnel and to provide mechanics for training Squadrons so that already trained personnel may be released for British service Squadrons in the Field, 15,000 American mechanics should be temporarily drafted for training to British training Units in Great Britain.[37]

In addition, given the competition from British industry for skilled workers, the agreement between the United States and Great Britain for the 'Training and Supply of Personnel for the Air Forces of Both Countries'[38] also contained the following stipulation:

> In conclusion I am to emphasize the fact that British mechanics, released by the supply of American mechanics, will be employed in completing the establishment of other RFC units, thus releasing personnel for the armies in the Field. On no account will the British mechanics thus released be utilised to work in factories under civilian conditions with civilian pay.[39]

Figure 30. The 50th Aero Squadron, US Army Aviation Service, at Harlaxton, 1918.

The plan to temporarily draft American mechanics into existing RFC training units to release British mechanics was modified with the American aviation mechanics being 'sent in Squadrons with enough officers for discipline and supply ... directly to England',[40] thereby relieving the United States Army Air Service of the 'very serious difficulties [of] training these men in France'.[41] This model also ensured these 'School' squadrons retained their identity prior to becoming service squadrons. Being 'dispatched in formed bodies under their own officers ... [they were] self-contained in every sense for discipline ... [and having been] kept together as units ... their officers would ... have plenary powers to punish according to American Law'.[42] These School squadrons were distinguished from service squadrons, as their name suggests, by their respective functions:

> By a service squadron is meant a squadron such as the layman thinks of. It is equipped with planes and flying personnel, pilots (and observers, if equipped with bi-plane machines), enlisted personnel consisting almost entirely of mechanics, wireless men, machine gun experts, or armourers, as they are called, and chauffeurs. The service squadron is the one that actually does the fighting. The school squadrons are made up mostly of mechanics, and they attend to the work of the aviation fields where pilots are trained.[43]

During 1918, as a result of the decisions taken in Paris, Harlaxton was to become home to the 50th and 85th Aero Squadrons, as well as flights of the 9th, 165th and 636th Aero Squadrons.

The two American squadrons, the 50th and the 85th, which were stationed at Harlaxton and which each comprised 150 men, were raised at Kelly Field near San Antonio in Texas. The 50th was raised on 6 August 1917 and the 85th on 17 August 1917. Raising these new squadrons was a perfunctory business. The 165th Aero Squadron was raised on 26 November 1917, when 150 men were simply counted off from among a 'multitude of men, some clad in khaki, some in half khaki and half civvies and others in badly dilapidated civilian clothing [all standing] on the sands of Texas'.[44] Subsequently, they were shipped to England and arrived at Harlaxton. The impression their new surroundings had on them was summed up in a letter written home by Alfred C. Beardslee, a mechanic with the 50th Aero Squadron. Having enjoyed an evening at the Inn in the neighbouring village, the mechanics walked back to the aerodrome:

> I will never forget [that] … walk back to camp … The moon was bright and our spirits were light … and we made the miles short by singing.
>
> The part of that walk that I shall always remember was – just on the outskirts of the camp there is a fine, old English country house known as Harlaxton Manor. It is almost a castle. The grounds are beautiful and the road by which we returned was the main road to this house.
>
> The manor sits on a hillside and is surrounded by trees … There are two large gates on the main road – they are also large and heavy. And looking straight up the road through the moonlight – with the shadows of the trees on the road – one can see the castle – or manor – setting against the hillside – with the large towers – and the smaller spires and the minarets showing up against the clouds. It surely was pretty and I will never forget it.[45]

During the day they were responsible for running the mechanics' workshops at Harlaxton aerodrome and keeping the aeroplanes, instructors and pupils of the RFC training squadrons at Harlaxton in the air. Unsurprisingly, this made for a somewhat complex picture with the three different RFC training squadrons (Nos 20, 53 and 64) having their machines being kept airworthy by American mechanics from five different American school squadrons!

Despite this complexity, the two programmes of training both pilots and mechanics were successfully integrated resulting in a highly advantageous arrangement for both the British and the Americans. According to Daniel P. Morse, the future officer commanding the 50th Aero Squadron, the arrival of the squadron on 4 February 1918 at the British Aviation Field at Harlaxton relieved:

> a British squadron for duty at the front and taking over the duties of a school squadron, running the English aerodrome at that place [which] was very wise, for it gave the English additional service squadrons and allowed our men to gain the experience and exactitude on airplanes so absolutely necessary for a service squadron to possess.[46]

Subsequently, in August 1918, the 50th Aero Squadron would become an operational service squadron in France, when it received its own machines and pilots. Between 8 February and 3 July, in its guise as a school squadron at Harlaxton, under the command of Lieutenant H.A. Sharret, and after 20 March, by 2nd Lieutenant C.D. Burrell, it received 'very excellent training'[47] with the men being 'given instruction for the first three weeks by a few English mechanics and then took over the entire work'.[48] The 50th Aero Squadron began training, and taking responsibility for keeping RFC machines in the air, on 8 February, the day after 'A' Flight of the 638th Aero Squadron left Harlaxton. The work of the squadron consisted of keeping the aeroplanes in good condition by working on both their rigging and their motors, the major repair of RFC machines (no small task given the number of crashes), running the central workshop and taking charge of transportation.

Some school squadrons were divided into flights and dispersed to RFC airfields for training, as in the case of the 638th squadron: 'A' Flight worked on 'airplane construction, motors etc.'[49] at Harlaxton with 'B' Flight stationed at Spittlegate, until it too moved on 8 February. Similarly, after disembarking at Liverpool on 7 December, the 9th Squadron was divided into four flights for training at RFC Stations in Lincolnshire. 'A' Flight went to South Carlton to work on Sopwith Camels, 'B' Flight was sent to Scampton for duty on scout planes, 'C' Flight went into observation plane work at Spittlegate, and 'D' Flight was ordered to Harlaxton for motor instruction. The Squadron then reassembled on 8 February 1918, under the command of 1st Lieutenant J.A. Richards, and shortly afterwards it became the first American squadron to be assigned exclusively to duty with a British flight.[50] From 8 February, with the 50th beginning its training, Harlaxton was 'taken over by the Americans'.[51] This was underlined on 16 March when the 50th was joined at Harlaxton by the 85th. There were now

Figure 31. Eleven officers and sixteen other ranks sitting and standing outside a tented hangar at Harlaxton. Five US Army Aviation Service personnel at left of rear row.

two full school squadrons at the aerodrome servicing the machines of the various RFC training squadrons. The official history of the 85th records that: 'Two flights of the 53rd Training Squadron were operated solely by mechanics from this organisation.'[52] And during a stay of more than five months at Harlaxton, 'mechanics were constantly employed in the hangars, machine shops, transport, gunnery and photography sections'.[53]

In the 50th Aero Squadron mechanics were rotated through gunnery, wireless, photography and bombing instruction 'from time to time to get a more thorough knowledge of all branches, and a complete record [sadly now lost] kept at all times as to their best qualifications'.[54] This accounts for the American observer in the photograph of the Harlaxton Photographic Section. The deployment of the 50th and the 85th to France necessitated another round of postings and on 16 August a detachment of the 165th Aero Squadron was posted to Harlaxton, to work on the machines of the new No. 40 Training Depot Station. Another detachment of the 165th was posted to Spittlegate, the squadron 'organisation' having been divided on arrival in England. At both stations the work was again of a 'purely mechanical nature in repairing motors and carrying on the work necessary to keep the planes

Figure 32. BE2c with US mechanics.

in the air';[55] both detachments being under the command of Lieutenant Arthur Kelley.

What is most remarkable about all these changes of personnel at Harlaxton is the relative ease with which the two air services cooperated at the aerodrome, and were able to work together to ensure machines were correctly serviced and the training of pilots was not interrupted when the mechanics were themselves in training. This is not to say there were no teething troubles, one of which was highlighted by Leslie McNab:

> We ... have here many Yankee mechanics, who practise on us ... [true] the pilots in France ... have many more dangers than us ... but these Yanks ... help to even things a little, and help to earn us our jeopardy pay. The top of a carburettor coming off in mid-air and I am wet with petrol and sweat, thinking of the closeness of the exhaust pipes and the easy burning of this 'gas' as they call it.[56]

In general, during their stay at Harlaxton, the professionalism of the US mechanics ensured that two air services successfully combined to run two mutually dependent training programmes on the same aerodrome. The 85th Squadron developed an excellent working relationship with their hosts which 'both along technical and disciplinary lines, was of the highest order, and the British authorities cooperated heartily'.[57] This hearty cooperation also encompassed the social life of the aerodrome, although there were also some shocks in store for Americans training

Figure 33. 'Yanks and Limeys' (Harlaxton).

in England. Writing home in March 1918, Alfred Beardslee described a concert in the Canteeen:

> The English can'teens are like bar-room and YMCA combined. They sell beer at certain hours at the bar – the can'teen counter sells coffee, cakes, cigarettes, candy and many other things that a can'teen usually handles. And in another part of the building there is a reading and writing room – a billiard room and a recreation room – with a stage and piano. Last nite there was a concert … Among the numbers were some American ragtime songs by one of the boys in our squadron … The audience (all soldiers) simply went wild.
>
> It's a peculiar thing the way these people take to ragtime – they simply go nuts over it … Dick sang us 'Kentucky Jubilee', 'Are you from Dixie', 'Where the Swanee River's Flowing', 'Hong Kong' and 'When Yankee Doodle learns to parley vous Francais' are the special favourites. The raggier the songs – the more they like them. When Carlton (the 'Yank' who sings) sang 'Pretty Papa' I tho't they would stamp the floor thro so vociferous was the applause.
>
> I saw something there last nite that, I suppose, would have shocked you speechless – I saw a WAAC (Women's Army Auxiliary Corps) … sitting there amongst the men her knees crossed, puffing vigorously away at a cigarette.

The majority of the women smoke cigarettes ... I received a letter from Homer ... and he had been to 'tea' with some very respectable and well-to-do-people – and he said that after tea, cigarettes and wine were in order – he was the only one that didn't indulge. Even the daughter and the hostess smoked and drank some wine. Shocking? It all depends on your point of view ... but it is considered quite proper over here.[58]

But what of the American pilots? American volunteers, having trained in Canada, had already joined the RFC and the RNAS prior to the United States entering the war and some remained with the RAF until the close of hostilities, as a result 'a representative number from all parts of the United States'[59] would come to Harlaxton in 1919. Their compatriots in the new United States Air Service, learning to fly in France, 'by the French method with French instructors ... [had] a completely foreign experience'.[60] Whether they trained in France or in Canada, American pilots were still participating in the same transformative experience being shared by pilots from Britain, Canada, Australia, New Zealand and South Africa, after all: 'Who would not want to wear a uniform with a Sam Browne belt from the cavalry days and a pair of wings on the left breast?'[61] Similarly, a US pilot, flying with a French squadron, wrote: 'It's the most wonderful sport I have ever participated in.'[62] This was a sport that, even with better machines and better instructors, continued to exact a heavy toll in England as well as France.

Figure 34. 'Lt Mather. Killed Harlaxton, 1918, RE8'.

CHAPTER 6
An Australian Odyssey from Egypt to England

The two largest pools of Empire pilots were from Canada and Australia. Unlike Canada, Australia formed its own operational Flying Corps with four squadrons flying alongside the RAF in 1918. This accounts for the strong Canadian, New Zealand and South African presence in the pages of the magazine *Parti Patter* and the absence of a strong Australian voice. There were Australians in the RFC/RAF because initially the Australian Flying Corps (AFC), established in 1912, had no operational squadrons. This anomaly was ended in 1916 with the establishment of four new squadrons. The first squadron to be formed was No. 67 (Australian) Squadron, RFC (No. 1 Squadron AFC, from February 1918). This squadron served in Egypt with the Egyptian Expeditionary Force (EEF). Confusingly, a second squadron was raised in Australia in September 1916 just as another 'second' squadron was being raised in Egypt. The former would become No. 69 (Australian) Squadron (No. 3 Squadron AFC, from January 1918) whilst the latter would become No. 68 (Australian) Squadron (No. 2 Squadron AFC, from January 1918).[1]

No. 68 (Australian) Squadron was raised at Kantara camp in Alexandria in Egypt from tradesmen and mechanics drawn from the original No. 67 (Australian) Squadron and from the Australian Light Horse. The transfer of men between the 'cavalry of the ground to the so-called cavalry of the clouds'[2] should not come as any surprise given that the military authorities 'perceived a correlation between riding horses and flying aircraft'.[3] As a pilot with No. 67 (Australian) Squadron explained:

> Aeroplanes are like horses. Some are docile, reliable, well-mouthed, and comfortable to ride. Others, like polo ponies, are sharp and snappy on

the turns ... lastly the outlaw, which fights man's mastery up to the last; in its record there is sure to be at least one victory, involving maiming or death for the vanquished.[4]

Figure 35. 'De Havilland 5, crash', Harlaxton.

In January 1917, these ex-light cavalrymen, together with a nucleus of experienced officers (themselves ex-light horsemen), wearing the AFC's distinctive blue and red triangle on their shoulders from No. 67 (Australian) Squadron, set off for England, where they would be joined by the squadron's fledgling pilots for training at Harlaxton.[5] Of the approximately 410 pilots who flew with the AFC in the First World War, the majority learned to fly in England in 1917 and 1918, and so the 'bulk of the AFC's pilots were fortunate to train ... under [the] ... improved "Smith Barry" system.'[6] However, for the pioneer pilots and mechanics of No. 68 (Australian) AFC, stationed in Egypt, the first order of business was to get to England.

Sailing across the Mediterranean, journeying by train across France, sailing across the English Channel, they eventually arrived at Waterloo Station in London. The scene there is described by Verner Knuckey, who had enlisted as a private with the 8th Australian Light Horse in 1915, and after seeing combat at Gallipoli and in Egypt, volunteered to serve as an electrician with the squadron, later becoming a wireless operator:

> Can you picture for yourself about 180 Australians getting out ... each with his swag of blankets strung over a shoulder like the tramps at home in the bush, every man burnt brown ... from the ... desert, hair not been brushed for weeks, whiskers an inch long, clothes in rags, twelve different varieties of colours as we were made up out of our twelve Regiments of Light Horse, a few of us with lovely Emu Plumes waving in our hats ... [and for the English civilians] we were Australians and that was enough [and] ... if ever Australians took the heart of the good, homely and kind hearted English civilian it was the 68th on this winter night at Waterloo Station, the very picture of misery and wretchedness and yet all [soon] singing, laughing, talking and shaking hands at once. All our troubles were forgotten ... we were back amongst our own countrymen ... [with] a huge Buffet run by English women ... where huge mugs of steaming tea and coffee was served to us together with sandwiches, buns, cake ... [then] to Charing Cross [by Tube] to board our north bound [Edinburgh Express] train ... to Grantham.[7]

The officer in overall command of this 'motley crew of diggers and light horsemen'[8] and the man tasked with building a fighter squadron over the coming months at Harlaxton was the remarkable Major Walter 'Ossie' Watt.

A graduate of Cambridge University, with a captaincy in the New South Wales Reserve of Officers, he returned to England on attachment in 1911, presumably to see the 1911 Army manoeuvres in Cambridgeshire which, incidentally, involved the forerunner to the RFC, the Royal Engineer Air Battalion which was formed in 1911. What is certain is that while he was in England, in August 1911, he obtained his Royal Aero Club 'ticket', making him one of the first Australian servicemen to do so.[9] Three years later, he was working for the Blériot Company in Paris, having purchased his own Blériot XI, and being in France in 1914, he joined the French air service flying a Maurice Farman 'Shorthorn' named 'Advance Australia'. Despite the award of the *Légion d'Honneur* and the *Croix de Guerre* in 1915, his lack of French citizenship precluded the possibility of command. He therefore transferred to the AFC in 1916, becoming a flight commander with No. 67 (Australian) Squadron following its arrival in the Middle East.[10] He was also, quite clearly, the outstanding choice to raise, train and then ultimately lead No. 68 (Australian) squadron into battle in the skies above the fields of France.

Arriving at Grantham around midnight the squadron discovered there was no one to meet them and show them the way to the aerodrome. The 'Tommy' officer sent from the aerodrome to meet the squadron had inexplicably missed their train! As it was snowing, and the aerodrome was a three-to-four mile march, Major Watt arranged for the squadron to bed down in Grantham station and bought every man a hot pie and a coffee from the Soldier's Rest Home over the road. The following morning the squadron marched to Harlaxton aerodrome where, according to Knuckey, on arriving at the aerodrome, it was discovered that:

> The Aerodrome we were going to had another Squadron on it [No. 44 Reserve Squadron and] ... they were advised that we would arrive at midnight. The men prepared huts for us, put four new blankets on each man's place, lit fires in every hut and put a guard on to keep them burning till we arrived, prepared a hot supper for us all and waited up till 3 a.m. to attend to our wants.[11]

No. 68 (Australian) squadron would now, in their turn, have to wait for the arrival of their aeroplanes whilst the aerodrome itself was completed. As Knuckey wrote in his diary:

> The Aerodrome we had come to was only being built and had very few conveniences but a large gang of workmen were employed at improving it all the time until it became as near to perfect as human means could

make it, all through the winter we had an open shed to wash in or to stand in the snow and ice around the tap. Later on we had hot and cold shower baths.[12]

These were also Light Horsemen who had fought at Gallipoli and in the Sinai desert and so whilst they were:

> keen on their work and proud of the way they turned the machines out ... there was one thing they objected to and did most unwillingly and that was every morning we had to turn out at 6.30 a.m. and do an hour's drill in the snow ... Needless to say we did the drill in a very half-hearted manner and as the Tommy Squadron was so good at it we showed up all the more.[13]

As tempers began to fray on both sides, Major Watt intervened to ensure relations between his men and the 'Tommy' officers under the command of Lieutenant Colonel Burdett did not deteriorate any further:

Figure 36. Group portrait of officers and ground staff of No. 68 Squadron arriving at Harlaxton, 1917. Second from the left in the front row is Major Walter Oswald Watt, the squadron commander.

> As regards this drill of a morning I want to tell you that ever since the Royal Flying Corps came into existence in England it has been compulsory for the mechanics to do some hours drill every day [a legacy, presumably, of the original NCO's coming from the Guards] ... You boys have had a hard time on Gallipoli and Sinai, most of you have been through Hell, now I want you to have as good a time as possible during your stay in England but I want you to remember that I am a Major and anyone before me will find I'm no milkson ... The morning Parade will be at 7.00 am instead of 6.30, it will be half an hour ... Parade Dismiss![14]

Watt had also been assigned a temporary British adjutant, the future military historian Basil Liddell Hart, who had been recuperating in England after being gassed. Liddell Hart has left an account of his time with the squadron at Harlaxton:

> After a few weeks I received the offer of an Adjutancy in the Royal Flying Corps and jumped at it. I was sent to an Australian squadron of the RFC which had just been formed and required an English Adjutant until an Australian was available. I joined it at Harlaxton aerodrome near Grantham. The first parade I inspected was a shock to anyone accustomed to British regimental ideas with hardly any man dressed identically or with a uniform complete in all respects. But I found them quite willing to come reasonably into line with what seemed to them curious customs. More importantly, they had the fundamental discipline of doing every job well and never neglecting any detail of their work on the aircraft.
>
> The officers were brilliant pilots but rather a wild lot when off duty ... Some of them liked to go out rabbit-shooting 'by air' before dinner in couples – one of them handling the machine, while the other took pot shots at rabbits from the gunners seat in its nose while it was [flying] very low over the fields and hedges. With the 'pusher' biplane then in use such 'rough' shooting was possible although the bag was scarcely in proportion to the effort and expenditure of shot.[15]

Ironically, this would prove to be excellent practice for the work of strafing the enemy in the squadron's DH5s in late 1917. The DH5 was an ideal choice for close-support, ground-attack patrols because its back-staggered wings, 'afforded plenty of vision from the pilot's seat'.[16] Similarly, the rugged individualism of the Australians, sometimes bordering on insubordination, also made them ideal candidates for pilot training.

Figure 37. Major Watt OC 68th Squadron (AFC) and Major Jenkins, OC 44th Squadron RFC, Harlaxton, June 1917.

We have seen already how George Jones made the jump from the workshop to the cockpit, and a similar opportunity was open to Verner Knuckey:

> One day I was busy in our Wireless Office ... when an Officer came in asking for me ... he came over to me and shook hands. I was absolutely at sea as to who he was ... He would not tell me his name but commenced asking me did I remember certain funny things that happened to three of us (Eddie Baker, Tom Grant and myself) down at Warrnambool in Victoria until I burst out with 'Surely you are not Tom Grant'. It was he right enough ... He was surprised that I had not taken up flying but I said I was only waiting to form my own opinion of it.

Tom took it upon himself to introduce Verner to flying. Having been detailed to go up in an 'Avro' to find a machine that had crashed in the vicinity he asked Major Watt if he could take Verner up with him. With permission granted, Verner:

> did not wait to think but hopped straight into the front seat. I had plenty of time to think all the same for the engine would not work satisfactorily ... this waiting was rather trying on the nerves, I remember Capt. Muir was standing by ... and he kept telling me it would be all right ... But at last we were ready ... taxi-ing smoothly out into the middle of the Aerodrome the machine was turned to face the wind ... then the pilot opened her full out and we flew along the ground at a terrific pace for about one hundred yards and then gracefully rose up into space ... it was a beautifully clear afternoon, not a cloud ... then he would fall down, down hundreds of feet, rise up again and dive again ... we [then] got as high as an Avro will go and then we started out across country ... The fields took on the shape and appearance of a patch work quilt ... We were soon over Nottingham with all its smoke ... [then] east until the sea was well within sight ... [then] a few more circles over Grantham, Harlaxton and Denton, and then getting up as high as he could he turned off his engine and we glided ... down so beautifully and gradually that I did not know we were falling until I got to about two thousand feet, when once more the woods and farms began to fly past at eighty and ninety miles per hour. Tom gave me a beautiful landing and we taxied up to the hangers as if we were in a modern car on a good hard road.[17]

The excitement and the freedom of flying is self-evident here and explains why learning to fly (despite the inherent risks) appealed to these young men training in England, and who trained knowing that on graduation the *Jagdstaffeln* were waiting for them in France.

The Captain Muir referred to by Verner was, of course, Captain Stanley Muir. He was one of the most experienced and accomplished of the squadron's officers who at this time were all acting as senior flight instructors; the squadron acting as a temporary training squadron for Australian pilots, prior to the arrival of its DH5 fighting-scout machines and training up as a fighter squadron. Muir was a native of Melbourne and in keeping with the character of the squadron he would later join, he had initially enlisted in August 1914 as a private in the 4th Australian Light Horse. Subsequently, he was commissioned as a 2nd lieutenant in the 20th Battalion of the King's Royal Rifle Corps (KRRC) and from there he transferred into the Royal Flying Corps. After taking his 'ticket' in England on a Maurice Farman on 11 May 1916, he completed his RFC training and joined No. 67 (Australian) Squadron in Egypt in July 1916.[18] He quickly distinguished himself as a bold and aggressive pilot as we can see in his recommendation for the MC:

> For conspicuous dash and skill on 22nd September 1916, in the attack on Tel-el-Sharia bridge, he dropped his bombs from a low height and very accurately. In addition he afforded great assistance to the machine photographing Bir Saba during the same flight, by skilful fighting. He was mainly instrumental in shooting down a Fokker, which he followed down from 10,000 feet to 2,000 ft. Further, on the 1st January 1917, he single handed, pursued two enemy machines from El Arish to Bir Saba, one of which flew to the south, and the other he drove down over its own aerodrome, coming down to 3,000 feet to do so. During the chase he was under the enemy observer's fire for 10 minutes, but with great coolness held his fire until within 70 yards, and must have inflicted severe damage on the enemy machine. He then waited over Bir Saba under heavy AA fire for the other machine, which flew in shortly afterwards, diving so fast to earth that he was unable to attack it.[19]

No. 68 (Australian) Squadron was therefore blessed with one of the most talented pilots in the AFC. Knuckey described Muir as:

> our best Pilot and perhaps one of the cleverest and ablest pilots in England. Our men absolutely swore by 'little Muir', he was daring to the last degree but unlike our other very clever pilot Captain Guilfoyle, he never seemed to be foolhardy, he would do things in the air to show

Figure 38. Capt. Muir, MC, AFC, with squadron mascot, Brrr the monkey.

that he could do them but would not court disaster by continually doing them.[20]

Whilst Captain Muir was clearly the squadron's talisman, the squadron included a nucleus of other experienced pilots and thus temporary instructors who, like Muir, had transferred from No. 67 (Australian) Squadron in Egypt. One of these was Captain William Guilfoyle. Born in Edinburgh, Guilfoyle had been an agricultural student in Melbourne in 1914, when he too enlisted as a private in the Australian Light Horse before obtaining a commission in the Royal Field Artillery (RFA) in 1915 and then transferring into the RFC. After taking his 'ticket' in England on a Maurice Farman on 14 October 1915, he served with No. 19 Squadron before joining No. 67 (Australian) Squadron in Egypt in 1916. Again, like Muir, he was awarded an MC in 1917. His citation in the *London Gazette* reads: 'For conspicuous gallantry in action. He carried out a daring bombing raid and made a valuable reconnaissance under heavy fire during the same flight. He has at all times set a fine example.'[21] Guilfoyle continued to set an example as one of the senior pilots and instructors with No. 68 (Australian) Squadron as it trained at Harlaxton.

By 1918 the AFC had its own permanent training squadrons in England. Prior to this, in 1917, Australian cadets, having graduated from one of the Schools of Military Aeronautics, were 'usually posted to British training units alone, or with perhaps just a couple of other colonials'.[22] After their elementary training, conducted on the reliable Maurice Farman 'Shorthorn' or 'Longhorn', 'Harry' Cobby and his three friends were posted to No. 68 (Australian) Squadron for their higher training. They could also have gone to No. 69 or No. 71 (Australian) Squadrons which were also training in England. Training with fellow Australians was not necessarily as advantageous as it would at first appear. In his autobiography *High Adventure*, Cobby explained there was:

> a vast difference in the manner in which we were treated at Harlaxton, to that meted out to us at Royal Flying Corps Schools. We were Australians with Australians and no longer gentlemen visitors from the Antipodes and instruction and comment was direct and to the point. The senior instructors were Guilfoyle, Muir and Matthews.[23]

This directness was in marked contrast to the experience of Australian cadets at the Schools of Military Aeronautics where their training had involved learning to be a gentleman, as George Jones had discovered.

Guilfoyle, Matthews, Muir, and Captain John Bell, a friend of Muir who came with the squadron from Egypt along with his pet monkey, were all highly experienced combat pilots. Their focus on turning these 'rookies'[24] into service pilots in a 'no frills'[25] training programme, was sharpened by the realisation that they would most likely be serving alongside some of these 'rookies'. Guilfoyle, Matthews, Muir and Bell, like the pioneering RFC pilots of the original four squadrons that went to France in 1914 were, after all, the nucleus of one of the new Australian service squadrons due to go to France later in 1917. The pupils under their tutelage were thus, potentially, the flying officers they would be serving alongside in France. In England, their higher training pupillage with No. 68 (Australian) Squadron was accomplished with 'A' Flight, and its Avro 504a and 504j machines and 'B' Flight with its mix of Sopwith 'Pups' and Sopwith 1½-Strutters.[26] Significantly, among the pupils training with No. 68 (Australian) Squadron, during its time as a temporary teaching squadron, was 'Harry' Cobby, 'the archetypal fighter pilot: courageous, dashing and good humoured'.[27]

Cobby would go on to become Australia's leading ace serving with No. 71 (Australian) Squadron in France and, as we saw in Chapter 2, he and his fellow Australian pilots were welcomed home as the embodiment of the 'professional skill … often complemented by the laconic confidence Australians like to think is a national characteristic'.[28] These were, however, characteristics common to flying officers in general, and were acquired during training where it became customary to smoke a cigarette after a crash, as this 'creates a great impression and everyone accordingly wonders and marvels at the coolness of the daring aviator'.[29] Crashes were commonplace in the RFC training squadrons, and 'it would not be an exaggeration to say that few, if any, Australian pilots didn't crash, or at least make a forced landing, while training'.[30] Following a crash, or a forced landing, the 'get back on the horse' approach of the RFC was one ideally suited to the Australian Light Horseman training with the squadron. But it was also an approach applied by instructors to new recruits like 'Harry' Cobby, who arrived at Harlaxton after moving between various training aerodromes for about two months and was now ready to progress from '*ab initio* types to something more advanced'.[31]

Having qualified for advanced training by soloing on 'Shorthorns' and 'Rumpeties' he, together with Tommy Hewson and O.J. Jones, were told to report to No. 68 (Australian) Squadron where they were introduced to Major Watt, an officer who 'knew the habits and instincts of his fellow Australians'[32] and on being shown into his office 'Ossie' tore into the trio:

> As soon as we saluted, he demanded to know where we had been, and we told him truthfully 'on 48 hours leave from so and so' and proceeded to show our passes. However, this was not what he was talking about. He was referring to the fact that the war had been going on for a couple of years or so and he wanted to know why we had not plucked up courage before to do something to help win the war. He dressed us down like a trio of pick-pockets and laid it on thick and heavy. It was rather extraordinary to be jumped on like that … In any case we were still only kids, although we thought we had assumed men's estate and resented his attitude. Tommy Hewson found his voice first and said he was astounded at such an attitude of mind from an Australian, particularly when every English person we had met had expressed themselves to the effect that it was very decent of the Dominions to hop in so thoroughly. We all had something to say, but not much, as 'Ossie' just silenced us and instructed the Adjutant, Roy Phillipps, to march us out.[33]

It transpired from, 'some of the other chaps on the 'drome … that he was terribly keen on beating up the enemy and that he was absolutely intolerant of everyone not in the War'.[34] Cobby and his companions 'agreed with this, but felt that a little reasonableness would not have been out of place'.[35] Stung as they were by this dressing down, they had been given every incentive to prove to their new OC just how good they were and just how unreasonable he had been. Oddly, enough, despite his unreasonableness, 'everyone said he was a particularly fine man, and an excellent Commanding Officer, and as nothing could be done about it, we just had to put up with it'.[36] This makes one suspect that this 'kindest and most thoughtful [of] people'[37] allowed himself a brief smile as they were marched out.

Cobby and his companions were then put through their hoops on the Avro, 'something in our experience that was more like a proper aeroplane than anything we had touched … I had already gone solo on a 'Rumpety', but you didn't throw those around, you just remained sedate, crouched over the controls with your feet on the rudder treadles, as though playing a harmonium'.[38] The Avro was a very different machine as 'it would stand almost anything. So I went solo';[39] pupils having had 'one dual flight right away and [then] you went "solo"'.[40] This no-frills approach to training in the new Australian squadrons also encouraged stunting from the off, as Cobby states: 'we were all under a moral obligation to loop the loop on our first solo'.[41] All his friends stopped to see him do so[42] which again underlines the collective transformation of social and self-identity being experienced by pupils on the training 'drome. As Cobby explains:

> Somebody had started the habit some little time before and although nothing was ever said until after you had done it, even amongst the pupils it had to be gone through otherwise you lost caste. It did not matter how many times you looped the loop later on, it had to be done on the first solo … It is of course, about the simplest evolution to perform, but we were all timid of carrying it out at that period in our flying history … Three or four times around the aerodrome to comply with instructions … then the custom was to move to a position just away from the 'drome where you could be seen, and then loop … after about four runs up and down, I realised it had to be done, so down I put the nose until the speed showed about 160 miles per hour, then easing the stick back I zoomed up and then while keeping the stick back, the machine went right over and just as the ground came back into sight I throttled the engine. A few feet more and I had looped the loop. It was just too easy so I did another one, and then returned to the 'drome and managed a fairly decent landing. Nothing was said by anyone, they had all disappeared except my instructor. But I felt like a million dollars, and as I have no idea how a million dollars feel, the description is apt. I did feel pretty good though.[43]

Training in the new Smith Barry era also meant, in addition to loops, pupils learnt how to make vertical turns, rolls and spins when 'just a year before, British instructors had been telling their pupils to avoid spinning at all costs because it was too dangerous'.[44] In addition to these basic combat manoeuvres they, like their RFC counterparts on the aerodrome, were learning to fly cross-country. In so doing, Cobby was lucky not to join the long list of fatalities that occurred in training at Harlaxton:

> I had force landed in a field alongside the aerodrome owing to the high tension ignition wires in the engine coming adrift, and had made it OK. The area was very small, about three hundred yards across at the longest run, and was surrounded by a built up stone wall about four feet high. Matthews asked if I could manage to get out all right after they had fixed up the engine and I was confident that I could, so getting into the far

corner I started off. Alas for the egotism of youth – I did not get right out, only the front end managed to. Just as I got off the ground the engine spluttered and I hit the wall with my undercarriage and broke the machine in two, with the tail inside the field and the nose sticking in the ground outside. A piece of broken longeron, which is one of the fore and aft members of the fuselage, stuck into my thigh ... and I had to stay in hospital for nearly three weeks. When I came out Hewson had gone to France ... I never saw Tommy again as he was shot down within a few days of going overseas. It was a sad business. After some eight or nine months of being together in the closest of friendships, it was a shock to realise he was gone. It also brought to mind that there *was* a serious side of the war.[45]

And 'here we were about to give battle in the air to the enemy as fighting pilots'[46] when, apart from the AFC's nucleus of instructors, there was a shortage of experience among his fellow pilots. This would not have been felt so keenly if 'we had been attached to well-established units where we could have been mothered for a while, until we found our "air" feet or wings'.[47]

On the other hand, whilst few pilots were naturally heroic, 'most of them would be able to do the Horatius act per medium of their "bus" and Vickers', if they came up against fearful odds'[48] for like Horatius, as Macauley observed, 'how can a man die better than facing fearful odds'.[49] There would certainly be no lack of aggression on the part of the Australians when they got to France.[50] Additionally, during their eight months of training in England, Australian pilots and observers had become familiar:

> with every possible type of aeroplane which they might have to use in France. The time had arrived when pilots and observers were really taught the new science, and were not, as in the earlier days, sent abroad to pick it up as best they could over the battle lines. Besides the technique of the aeroplane, they were called upon to learn intimately the construction of machine guns and Lewis guns, shooting from the air, navigation by compass, observation of country and the tricks of distinguishing ground objects ... the practice of photography from the air, and the artillery-officer's work of battery-ranging and 'spotting' for fire effect ... [and] the latest tactics in the science of air fighting.[51]

Pilots' training now concluded with a two-week course at the School of Aerial Gunnery in Scotland, which also involved shooting at clay pigeons to improve pilot reflexes,[52] and a week at the School of Aerial Fighting where pupils were given the confidence to 'do the most reckless things'.[53] These reckless fellows were now flying officers. They were at finishing school having completed their higher instruction. They had completed five hours on a service machine – either a fighting-scout or a reconnaissance machine, depending on whether the pilot was earmarked for an Army or Corps squadron. They had completed all their tests – flying cross-country, landing from 8,000 feet with the engine switched off, and a night landing – and had graduated as pilots. This entitled them to sew their AFC wings onto their tunic and 'wear a Sam Browne belt and, most importantly for the majority, draw a pay rise to finance their new, gentlemanly lifestyle'.[54] As Stanley Rutledge had found, 'messing is higher in the RFC [than in the Army] and incidental expenses are apt to mount up'.[55]

Meanwhile, No. 68 (Australian) Squadrons' Avro and Sopwith training machines had been replaced by DH5 fighters. The squadron was now an active service squadron with a complement of pilots whom Watt 'personally trained ... in England before leading ... into combat'.[56] With No. 68 (Australian) Squadron now working itself up as a fighter squadron some of its pilots were sent to the School of Aerial Gunnery in Scotland and also on the Fighting Course at Spittlegate, both being considered 'finishing schools'.[57] Efforts were also made to bolster the squadron's actual combat experience by sending likely flight commanders on three- and four-week secondments to fighter squadrons in France. Among those sent out was Lieutenant Richard Howard who between May and July 1917 flew DH4s with No. 57 Squadron. Lieutenant Victor Norvill, who was attached to No. 29 Squadron flying reconnaissance patrols in Nieuport 17s was, unfortunately, shot down and taken prisoner.[58] Lieutenant George Matthews (ex-9th Light Horse and born in Stranraer, Scotland), Lieutenant Gordon Wilson and Lieutenant Henry Forrest were also sent out; Forrest flying Strutters and DH5s with No. 43 and No. 32 Squadrons.[59] Similarly, Captain Roy Phillipps, MC, who had replaced Basil Liddell Hart as the squadron's adjutant, was sent out to No. 32 Squadron to build up his DH5 experience.[60] Phillipps had already seen active service in France with the 28th Australian Infantry Battalion, where he won his MC and was severely wounded in the leg. Rather than being invalided home he transferred into the AFC to become adjutant of No. 68 (Australian) Squadron. He then successfully applied to his OC for pilot training, and after completing his training at Harlaxton, he went to France, returning to the squadron unharmed having been hit by ground fire and crashing near Ypres.

Phillipps returned to a squadron still in shock from the loss of Stanley Muir, known affectionately in the squadron as 'Little Muir', who was killed in a flying accident on 12 September 1917. The squadron *War Diary* described this incident as 'a terrible loss'.[61] Writing to his father, Major Watt wrote: 'His sad death deprives the flying service of one they can ill afford to lose. Never was an officer more truly mourned by his fellow-officers or by his men.'[62] The whole squadron was 'broken up over his death'.[63] Verner Knuckey provides a detailed account of what had happened:

> he had gone up in one of our DeH5 machines to test it, they say he gave a wonderful performance in the air and flew on his back for quite a long time when he regained his proper position he must have strained one of the struts of the machine and immediately upon gaining his proper position this strut appears to have snapped for Muir crashed to the ground, when the onlookers went to the smash the man was unrecognisable, every bone in his body must have been broken.[64]

On Friday 14 September 1917 Stanley Muir was given a funeral with full military honours:

> His body was borne on a gun carriage covered with a Union Jack and his belt on top, there was a firing party of 72 Australian Machine Gunners, a splendid Australian Military Band, quite 100 Officers from the surrounding camps and the three Squadrons of Flying Corps at Harlaxton, 44th, 54th and the 68th Australian Flying Corps. We marched about a mile to Harlaxton Church where a short service was held and then some of his brother Officers carried the Coffin out to the grave where the burial service was gone through. The grave from top to bottom was lined with flowers, you could not see an inch of bare earth and the saddest part of the whole performance was to see every Officer and man walk slowly past the open grave, stop, look down, then salute and move away making room for the next man. We formed up outside the Church yard and marched back to camp, no more work was done for that day. Harlaxton is a very pretty little old English village, he is buried in an extremely pretty and peaceful spot. I have a photo of the grave, one mass of wreaths but I suppose his friends will come and take the Coffin back to Australia.[65]

They never did, and so today Stanley Muir rests along with Stanley Rutledge and Alick Charlesworth in a quiet corner of Harlaxton churchyard but, in an inspired move to restore the squadron's morale, Watt decided it would fly together from Harlaxton to France on 21 September. In so doing, it gained the distinction of being the only squadron to achieve a one-day deployment to the Continent. In 1965, T.H. Hampshire, having trained alongside No. 68 (Australian) Squadron as 'a very junior officer in the RFC with No. 54 Squadron stationed on the same 'drome'[66] remembered seeing them:

> returning after an evening forage with pea rifles under their elbows and a brace a rabbits or such dangling from the other arm. Then suddenly one morning the whole lot were conspicuous by their absence and later on it leaked out that the whole squadron had taken off for France.[67]

Figure 39. Group portrait of pilots from 68 Squadron, posed in front of a DH5 at Harlaxton, 1917. Left to right (back row only): Unidentified; Lt Douglas George Morrison; Lt Howard; Lt Albert Griggs (of Mississippi, USA); Lt Agnew; Capt. McCloughry; Maj. Walter Oswald Watt; Lt Col. Burdett; Capt. John Bell; Capt. Wilson; Capt. Phillipps; unidentified; Lt George Campbell Matthews.

CHAPTER 7

The Aerodrome and the Armistice

In January 1918, Sir Hugh Trenchard was recalled from France to become the first Chief of the Air Staff (CAS). His place in France, as GOC in the field, was filled by Sir John Salmond. It would be Salmond who, having helped reform the method of instruction in England in 1916–17, would lead a better trained and equipped RFC (and after April 1918, RAF) to victory. By March 1918, Salmond had 63 squadrons under his command. To keep these squadrons operational the RAF needed to find an average of 550 new pilots per month.[1] Only six years earlier the target had been to train a total of 364 pilots to keep seven squadrons operational. By 1917/18, the training programme in England had been expanded to produce an estimated 17,000 pilots.[2] In 1918, the training system produced 1,200 service pilots a month. When coupled to the production of 4,300 aeroplanes and 5,300 engines per month, this was a sufficiency of men and machines capable of absorbing an average monthly operational loss of 800–900 pilots, 2,200 aeroplanes and 3,000 engines.[3] The system of producing more and better trained pilots was also subject to one last innovation namely, the conversion of all Training squadrons to the Training Depot Station (TDS) model by mid 1918. This model allowed for economies of scale and also reduced the need for new aerodromes, given that the rapid growth of the RFC's training programme was already 'taking too big a toll of agricultural land'.[4]

Squadrons were now housed together, with pupils progressing through their elementary and higher training with the same instructor, in an 'all through' system, flying a standard training machine, before graduating to flying their service machines as they were delivered to the station. As soon as 'pilots were proficient the instructors and newly qualified pilots moved, with their aircraft, to an operational airfield ready for the fray'.[5] On 15 August 1918, No. 40 TDS was formed at

Figure 40. Harlaxton aerodrome, 1918–19.

Harlaxton by bringing together Nos 20, 53 and 64 training squadrons.[6] No. 40 TDS would therefore, according to the official history of the US 165th Aero Squadron, fly aeroplanes of 'several different British types'.[7] Shortly thereafter, by the autumn, the number of types in use with No. 40 TDS had been reduced to the now standard RE8s and Avro 504a and 504j machines.[8] This simplified maintenance and training and allowed pupils to focus on practising formation flying and air-fighting, as well as strafing and bombing. The last two, especially, being integral to what had become the most significant feature of the air war by 1918, namely close ground-support or taking 'offensive action by means of machine-gun fire and bombing to assist in ground fighting'.[9] Both the Australians in No. 68 (Australian) Squadron and Brian Garrett with No. 64 Training Squadron were required to 'fly three times over a Bachelor mirror, an instrument for judging the exactitude with which bombs could be dropped'.[10] However:

> An exception must be made in the case of bombing by single-seater fighting machines from low altitude, a method of attack which has been employed with very considerable success. In this case no sight is used, and the method found by experience to give the best result is to dive the machine steeply at a point on the ground a few yards in front of the target. The lag of the bomb released from a few hundred feet on a steep

dive is very little. Individual pilots must find out by experiment exactly how far ahead they must aim.[11]

Whether this kind of experimentation was attempted in training at Harlaxton is unclear, but both low altitude bombing and strafing by the RFC were to be a feature of the Battle of Passchendaele, during which Philip Pearson Gregory of Harlaxton Manor was to win his MC.

At the battle of Cambrai in November 1917, the RFC, including J.A. Butler, continued to develop the tactics of close ground-support. This battle involved the newly arrived No. 68 (Australian) Squadron, 'brilliantly led by Major Watt, flying their DH5s often only meters above the trenches because of heavy fog ... [as they] bombed and strafed enemy troops [and] gun batteries'.[12] Given the greater exposure of pilots to fire from the ground, the squadron experienced heavy losses. By the end of their first day in action, 6 of No. 68 (Australian) Squadron's 18 aircraft had been shot down and one was missing. These losses reflected both the dangers of flying at low altitude and the readiness of the AFC and RFC pilots to do so. As a result, No. 68 (Australian) Squadron, according to Charles Bean, 'are winning themselves a magnificent name ... [under] Watt who has worked them up to this remarkably high level of conduct and general tone'.[13] Of course, as with all the other aspects of the technology and tactics of the air war, the Germans were developing their own tactical doctrine for close ground-support using specialist battle-flights or *Schlachtstaffeln* equipped with ground-attack machines such as the Halberstadt CLII. Tactically, while the German pilots were being trained to fly in waves there was no comparable evidence to suggest that in the RFC, 'tactical manoeuvres *en masse* were [being] rehearsed in the German fashion'.[14] In February the RFC noted that 'formation flying has lately been adopted for the attack of ground targets with excellent results ... [but] formation flying at low altitudes demands even more constant practice together than does formation flying at height, because fire from the ground makes continuous changes of direction and height a necessity'.[15] Unfortunately, the time for fighter squadrons in France to practise low-level formation flying was running out.

In March 1918, 38 *Schlachtstaffeln* were committed to supporting the German Army's last great attack aimed at the British Expeditionary Force. The *Schlachtstaffeln* were, in turn, supported by the *Jagdstaffeln*. Conforming perhaps to a now-ingrained tactical tradition the latter 'all too often patrolled at high altitudes and waited for their opponents to come to them, as they always had in the past'.[16] These tactics failed to lure the RFC/RAF away from their new tactical objective of trying to slow down the attacking German infantry through pitiless and relentless strafing and bombing. This meant ignoring the German scouts who could swoop down on them from above, whilst they were being assailed from below by ground fire and anti-aircraft guns.[17] As 'Harry' Cobby, flying Camels with No. 71 (Australian) Squadron, explains:

> flying under the clouds [in formation] ... shooting up the ground targets, and getting in return all the 'hate' the enemy could throw up at us with machine guns, field guns and flaming onions ... We nearly always came home with our machines shot about.[18]

The low-level fighting in March and April 1918, between fighters, ground-attack machines and artillery cooperation machines was thus confused and deadly; losses among the latter being particularly heavy given that in March the RFC had 27 squadrons concentrating on ground-attack sorties and only six squadrons screening the Corps machines with high-altitude offensive patrols.[19] However, Salmond's re-orientation of RFC and RAF fighter squadrons did the trick, helping to slow the momentum of the attacking German infantry.[20]

Subsequently, in the combined arms counter-attacks of the summer and the autumn, the RAF participated in the 'ultimate apotheosis of air-land integration'.[21] At the heart of this campaign was the system of Army air cooperation and the RAF's Corps squadrons who 'derived great benefit from the intensified tactical offensive'.[22] This was because, alongside the ongoing ground-attack role given to some fighter squadrons, Salmond had enough fighter squadrons available to return the remainder to the daily routine of offensive patrols and restore the protection formerly enjoyed by the Corps squadrons. This meant the Corps squadrons again enjoyed relative immunity from attack, 'largely unhampered by the need to defend themselves against aerial attack'.[23] Meanwhile, fighter-reconnaissance machines were keeping brigade and battalion HQs in contact with their attacking battalions and companies by flying contact patrols.[24] The return to offensive patrolling by the RAF also saw the now depleted *Jagdstaffeln* return to their preferred defensive tactical doctrine and traditions.

The *Jagdstaffeln* had suffered in the spring by going over to the offensive for two reasons. Firstly, this was 'a function for which it was unsuited, either by doctrine or tradition'.[25] Secondly, in modernising its fighter squadrons with the Sopwith Camel and Dolphin, SE5a and Bristol F2b machines, the RFC left the German air service 'operating for the first time in one and a half years at a qualitative disadvantage to its opponents'.[26] The *Jagdstaffeln* was also exposed to attack on the ground as DH4 machines bombed its aerodromes and eroded its combat effectiveness.[27] Was this the RAF's opportunity to finally overpower its opponent in the air and achieve aerial supremacy?[28] The RAF however, remained committed to its original task of providing tactical support to the Army through contact patrols, artillery-spotting and photographic reconnaissance. This meant a return to offensive patrols, to the 'LOP' and the 'DOP', to screen the work of the Corps machines and to the high offensive patrol or 'HOP' to give 'top cover' to those machines committed to strafing and bombing the enemy. These patrols attained and retained the aerial superiority necessary for the Army's sustained and ultimately successful counter-attack over the summer and autumn of 1918. Thus, the 'British air service's main contribution to victory, had come through its participation in the ground war'.[29] But in contributing to victory, the RAF had also been victorious in the air against a formidable foe.

The Germans had re-equipped their elite formations with the formidable Fokker DVII fighter to maintain their 'hard cutting edge'.[30] These *Jastas* had to be engaged by fighter pilots flying the SE5a in open or 'battle' formation.[31] These patrols were flown in formations of up to six aeroplanes, but once an enemy formation of equivalent size was engaged, the formation inevitably broke up into a series of dogfights that were 'fierce, brief and usually lethal'.[32] In these dogfights pilots were utilising the skills now being taught in training in the skies above rural England. This was because: 'Once contact was joined the flight leaders could hope for no tactical cohesion, for the fighting became at once a free-for-all, where each pilot was on his own … the whole game played with such ferocious pace and intensity that it was usually over within a few minutes.'[33] Overall, two-thirds of aerial combats occurred over the German side of the line,[34] as the Army squadrons screened the Corps squadrons doing the 'less glamorous but more significant'[35] work of aerial observation and photography. This could only occur by establishing and maintaining aerial superiority over the German air service, and this achievement rested on having a greater ability to produce enough machines and pilots in Training wings in England, Egypt, Canada and also the United States, to replace the losses in France. In 1916–17:

> aircraft production and pilot training facilities had experienced severe difficulty in keeping up with losses during periods of intensive activity. In 1918, the British were able to maintain the flow of replacements …

the output of new pilots was also equal to the demands placed on it, and … Salmond was generally able to replace casualties as they occurred, without pulling units out of action.[36]

By the Armistice, the RAF was the strongest air force in the world with a wartime strength of 30,000 officers, 261,175 other ranks and 22,647 aeroplanes in 188 service squadrons, with 99 of these stationed in France, supported by approximately 200 training squadrons.[37] The air service, having grown exponentially since the inception of the RFC six years earlier, was still considerably smaller than the other services, the British Army and the Royal Navy, of which it was now independent. Regardless of this numerical disparity, the RAF, and specifically its pilots, were better able to embody the contemporary blending together of tradition and modernity than the other two services. Berberich's analysis of Virginia Woolf's comment that on or about December 1910, human character changed, is instructive here: 'the reason for this change in human character was the intrusion of modernity into everyday life: changes in transport for instance – faster trains, new automobiles, the first aeroplanes – sped up everybody's life'.[38] The war intruded the speed of modernity into everyday life with automobiles driving through Harlaxton village and aeroplanes flying above it. In being confronted by the speed of modernity it is hardly surprising that some reassurance was sought, hence the dichotomy identified by Paris:

> The pilots, by and large members of the officer corps, were the knights, the cutting edge of the Flying Corps: mechanics and riggers the faithful squires who prepared their masters' mechanical steeds for the test of personal combat in the skies over the Western Front. For the realist, who rejected such notions of chivalry in combat, it was equally possible to see the air force as the cutting edge of technology; the ultimate means of mechanical warfare. Either interpretation was sufficient to give the RAF a special status.[39]

The officers of the RFC/RAF did not have to masquerade as an officer and a gentleman as someone with a temporary commission in the infantry might have to,[40] because in contemporary society they were the new model officers and gentlemen of a new air service who had mastered the technology of flight to win victory in the air. Of course, for the original Edwardian pilots of the RFC the appellation of an officer and a gentleman was entirely apt as most were officers and country gentlemen who had transferred into the RFC from one of the elite cavalry or infantry regiments, the latter also being expected to ride well. Indeed, while the nucleus of the Military Wing of the RFC established in 1912 was the Royal Engineer Air Battalion (established in 1911),[41] it soon attracted officers from the cavalry. As a consequence, neither the RFC nor the RAF became 'a corps of flying civilian or military engineers: it represented the bringing together of technology with the aristocratic, martial spirit. The association of piloting with horsemanship was an obvious manifestation of this combination.'[42]

In the early years of the war, the original cadre of aristocratic ex-cavalrymen was supplemented by recruits from the public school system. Thanks to them, as Mackersey states, the RFC 'was firmly public school … [and its] squadrons, at least initially, were elite establishments in which grammar-school, lower middle and, most emphatically, working class applicants found scant welcome'.[43] These pilots would have encountered the horse-riding, fox-hunting cavalry officer in France, in which context they could have easily succumbed to both Edwardian 'expectations regarding a country gentleman: as a good horseman and a passionate foxhunter',[44] and the accompanying expectations of an officer embodied by these polished individuals. Siegfried Sassoon, in his *Memoirs of a Fox-Hunting Man*, explores the self-fashioning that could occur on exposure to 'the epitome of the young sporting gentleman: perfectly attired, perfectly at ease, with the slightest hint of arrogance because he is aware of his effortless appearance … the apogee of the hunting gentleman … is [thus] somebody to be emulated'.[45]

These pilots were then rotated through a training system in England set amidst the great country house estates. This was also a training programme that was becoming ever more cosmopolitan as the RFC increasingly sought individuals with the right temperament to be pilots. And as selection placed less and less, or 'little emphasis on a candidate's cultural background or social standing',[46] the public schoolboy was joined by pupils 'from all walks of life – farmer, bank clerk, college graduate'.[47] Kennett suggests that this new openness was 'perhaps understandable in a new branch of the service lacking in tradition and unencumbered by association with any particular class'.[48] There was, however, a strong association with the original figure of the fox-hunting cavalry officer among the young pilots training in the English countryside, in 1917 and 1918, who were going to France to join the 'crack cavalry of the air'.[49] According to Arthur Gould Lee: 'At a time when to fly was the privilege of the very few, [flying was also] … a wonderful, wonderful thrill.'[50] Thus, the RAF became, to paraphrase Patrick Bishop, one vast imperial machine capable of transforming the social and self-identity of individuals from all walks of life and from across the Empire and who, having first taken to the air in England, 'were never quite the same as other earthbound men'.[51]

Then it was all over. At 11 p.m. on 11 November 1918 the bells rang out across Britain and the Empire. On hearing news of the Armistice, Leslie McNab flew with one of his pupils in an Avro 504 'to the Manners at Bassingthorpe, landing in their field ... bringing the good news in the modern manner ... [and then to] the village church where we ring the church bells pulling so hard that the rope ... break[s]'.[52] Meanwhile, back at Harlaxton aerodrome, McNab found that all were 'in the air flying very drunkenly and with many streamers of bunting, and Verey lights popping off everywhere, and several crashes [indeed] ... Many are killed all over England through foolish flying.'[53] Thereafter, the training programme in England was wound down with No. 40 TDS being disbanded in May 1919, whereupon the aerodrome was given over to their 'brother officers from overseas'.[54] RAF Harlaxton now became a repatriation camp for unemployed RAF pilots from overseas. The camp was under the command of Major J.A. Butler and while his command would only last for that summer, it represents a most remarkable expression of the RAF at the culmination of the First World War.

Describing his experiences at Harlaxton in the summer of 1919, 2nd Lieutenant H.G. Warburton, a New Zealander, wrote: 'One doubts if there was ever a more Cosmopolitan band than that gathered together and dubbed the Royal Air Force, not even excepting the notorious Foreign Legion'[55] but despite 'our various Homelands we are all at one for the Empire'.[56] This imperial air service could also be glimpsed in training. In a diary entry dated 3 November 1918, McNab described the Officers' Mess at Harlaxton, as viewed from the instructor's table, '200 or so pupils, cadets, and senior officers in training all at tables [and] ... full of all sorts. Youngsters keen as mustard just from school, drawling Canadians, and South Africans.'[57] The South African contingent in the RFC/RAF was considerable. According to Lieutenant Warburton, 'running the Canadians very close in point of numbers the South Africans easily take third place'.[58]

By contrast, as the previous chapter highlighted, 'representatives from the lands of the Southern Cross were not in large numbers, partly on account of the Australian Air Force absorbing most of the men of that country'.[59] Australians were therefore becoming a minority in a service now heavily reliant on the Canadians and the South Africans, who in 'the greatest game of all ... in the flying ranks ... took to each other [as a] ... fellow who could and would play the game for all he was worth ... [as] jolly good fellows, hail fellows well met, fighters when need be, and gentlemen without swank'.⁶⁰ They, like their Australian, New Zealand and British counterparts, would now spend their last summer in England, walking around the grounds of Harlaxton Manor. In so doing, they were walking in the footsteps of the hundreds of pilots who had arrived at Harlaxton from across the globe between 1916 and 1918. Training in the English countryside had exposed these pilots to the country house lifestyle of the original cavalry officers and country gentlemen of the Edwardian RFC. If this influenced their self-identity, and collectively the social identity of the RFC/RAF, then we can perhaps see why the English country house estate would have been a place to which they would be happy to return after flying over the fields of France. As one New Zealand pilot wrote:

> To those of us who have spent the most of the past month in and around Harlaxton, these will be remembered as halcyon days. Certain it is that placing a military camp in such surroundings savoured of sacrilege, yet we are the gainers thereby. In later days, when amid Canadian snows, in the dusty cities of the [South African] Union, on the parched plains of Australia, amidst the tussock-covered hills of New Zealand, or in the sweltering heat of the Tropics we think of the peaceful setting of Harlaxton Manor in the golden days of May, well we can realise how

Figure 41. 'Three South African boys'. Capt. Frost, 2nd Lt Nicholson and 2nd Lt Van der Riet, Harlaxton.

those banished Englishmen hunger for a glimpse of the green fields and hedgerows of the Motherland.⁶¹

Becoming familiar with the world of the English country house during training was not without its social hazards. Leslie McNab described a country house weekend, where at dinner, 'I become more and more decomposed every minute ... pass[ing] the port decanter in the wrong direction ... in spite of this I ... enjoy myself immensely and have a top-hole time.'⁶² On the Monday, he was invited to go fox-hunting and he was not overly enthusiastic, 'thinking of the hedges and fences, not yet having jumped anything on horses. I ... suggest that I am more at home on camels for fox-hunting ... Praise be! ... the hound[s] ... do not meet, and I do not go solo.' In other words, it was not necessary, for all the parallels between riding a horse and flying, for the trainee pilot officer to be actually able to ride. Nonetheless, they were living and training amidst a social elite who did, and who saw in the flying officer the modern cavalry officer of the air. And so at Christmas, in Grantham, McNab attended the local meet of the Belvoir Hunt:

> all is bustle and activity in the bright frosty morning, and the square resounding to yapping ... and the stamping of the horses ... [followed by] the Hunt Ball ... [with] many of the local gentry ... some still in their little red coats ... [and] Capt. Cross ... a Canadian ... full of ribbons and reddish hair [who] ... details himself ... to attend the Hon. Lady ____ at supper ... [and] return[ing] to the aerodrome very late that night in a RAF lorry with ... some of the WRAF's [Women's Royal Air Force] who ... assist[ed] in the supper of the Ball ... I take the risk of speaking to one, whom I find very well spoken, a maid of great beauty named 'Rose' [who assisted in the officers' mess] ... She [was] very interested in the fact that I was a Knight of the Round Table and assured me she would avail herself of my protection if ever it were needed.⁶³

The identification of the flying officer with the fairy-tale chivalric ancestors of the neighbouring fox-hunting aristocracy and gentry is, of course, now self-evident. Taken to extremes could it also become a parody? McNab's diary refers to a remarkable individual, one Captain Nutt, whom he met as the festive season approached and Harlaxton became a rendezvous for out of work flying officers:

> He and I [are] thicker than two thieves, and we ... call each other 'Horace' and 'Walter' for short. We are both in our imaginations 'Sir

Horace' and 'Sir Walter' Knights of the Round Table, and a by-word in the Squadron, and do many deeds of rescuing fair maidens, and drinking gallons of sack. Horace ... first intrigue[s] me when I see him enter the ... Royal and Angel at Grantham ... and call in a loud voice 'Prithee wench fetch the Landlord, I fain would quaff a stoup of Bass'.

He ... [is from] Leeds, and born 100 years, too late – a throw-back to some hunting ancestor – well-read but thinking the book of a man named Storrocks the only classic written. The hero of the story is a large eating, loud swearing, long drinking hunter of the hounds. Horace ... endeavour[s] at all times to follow his example so that the WRAF wenches when they serve him hot coffee on the morning after ... enquire delicately if he went hunting the night previous. This from his habit of rousing the camp on his return with 'Yoicks Ginger Tally Ho. Come away Daisy' and many other hunting cries.[64]

Figure 42. 'Season's Greetings.' RFC Christmas card, RAF Harlaxton, c. 1914–19.

Horace was in fact modelling himself on R.S. Surtees' fictional character of John Jorrocks, but in so doing was he engaged in a grand parody? Today, the most recognisable parody of the aristocratic flying officer of the First World War is the squadron commander Lord Flashheart, 'thundering in his airborne steed'.[65] But do we see parody, where today we might likewise see irony? Paul Fussell states modern understanding 'is essentially ironic; and ... it originates largely in the application of mind and memory to the events of the Great War'[66] and in particular in the writing of Robert Graves and Siegfried Sassoon. But as Philpott points out, and as we saw in the introduction, there is a marked difference between the memory of the war on the ground and in the air, where 'pilot accounts consistently reinforced the associated notions of glamour, adventure and [a] just war'.[67] Similarly, Horace is not a contemporary parody of the First World War flying officer. Rather, he is perhaps the most outrageous example of the social influence exerted over the Corps by the ex-cavalry officer and fox-hunting country gentlemen originals. Their successors from overseas were similarly gentlemen keen to embody 'that chivalry and attentiveness which English girls are good enough to remark of the Men from Overseas'.[68]

Harlaxton, like all RAF Training Depot Stations in 1918, had a complement of WRAF stationed there to provide general, domestic, technical and clerical support. The technical section included fabric workers, metal workers, fitters, riggers and aeroplane repairers, helping to relieve the pressure to find more mechanics. The technical section also included drivers for tenders and motorcycle riders, which is why women belonging to the Women's Legion of Motor Drivers (WLMD), who were already working at air stations, were invited to join the WRAF. Volunteers also came from the Women's Auxiliary Army Corps (WAAC) and the Women's Civilian Subordinates (WCS). In addition, the RFC had established its own Women's Companies that were then absorbed into the general, domestic and clerical sections of the WRAF. Private Phyllis Chambers, having previously worked in a munitions factory in Birmingham before moving to Grantham to live with her brother, was assigned to the clerical section at Harlaxton by the Grantham Labour Exchange:

> They said, with my education I could do well in the Royal Flying Corps ... They sent me to Harlaxton and gave me a uniform which wasn't measured, it just fitted where it touched and went down to our ankles. First they sent me to the pay office, and then I went to be clerk to a Captain. He was a very nice man, very quiet, he just told me what to do and that was that.

To get to Harlaxton from Grantham we had to go by lorry and they picked us up at the same place every day. We had to climb on the wheel and over the side of the lorry. The New Zealand troops who were in Grantham at the time used to congregate at the corner wanting to see a bit of leg! We used to go to the dances with them and dance the military two-step, the Lancers and waltzes. They used to write in my autograph book, decent things of course.

Then the Captain was called to the front. He said he would like to give me a little present, and he gave me a fountain pen. Then he asked me if I would like a little flight. He said we'd have to keep it a secret, or he'd get into trouble. So I said 'Yes, I'm game enough'. We went up in this little plane, I don't know what type it was but the boys had to swing the propeller and push the plane along until it connected. It was an open cockpit, the sky was coming down and the earth was coming upwards. We only just went around the airfield at Harlaxton which wasn't very far, but it was enough for me. I was glad to get out.[69]

Alongside the clerical workers were the WRAFs who assisted in the Officers' Mess, among whom, according to McNab, were:

Many pretty wenches … [who] look after us [and among whom were] … Bright Eyes and Rose, and others, all good scouts, bringing us strong coffee in the morning when they think we need it.

It is a pity we are not allowed to talk with them except to ask for food – officially. Several I have seen whispering in the moonlight, near the hedges, with young officers, but they [were] no doubt asking what is on for breakfast.[70]

Among the others was 'Bunny' Barnes, who received a postcard from her friend Gracie in France addressed to 'WRAF, Officers' Mess, RAF Harlaxton Camp'[71] in 1919. By 1919, of course, following the Armistice, Harlaxton had become a repatriation camp in which the services of Rose, 'Bright Eyes' and 'Bunny' were still needed. We can gain another glimpse of these young women in *Parti Patter*, where one evening a contributor described the following scene: 'I discover … a sewing bee … out on the Wraf hut green … There on the green: Ye Bunny, who must have put the hug in the dance: Ye Damsel of Ye Sparkling Orbs; Ye Glad(e)y(e)s and Ye Restive Rose … Restive Rose bit a thread "How's this for the back?" she enquired … "though it's all the same worn back or front".'[72] This prompted some speculation regarding the nature of the evening gown she was working on to which Rose replied, '"Can't you see, you silly ass, that it's not what you ... Oow!! Oh, he has seen!" ... It was an evening gown – that is, er – a night-gown!'[73] Sadly, the diaries and letters of these young women remain undiscovered, but their lives, in contrast to those of women serving in the neighbouring country house, had been speeded up by their proximity to modernity – to automobiles and aeroplanes. Before the war these machines had been the exclusive playthings of the aristocracy; now Phyllis Chambers had flown in an aeroplane like Lady Diana Manners, the daughter of the Duke of Rutland.

The machinery of modernity had also given the pilot officers of the RFC/RAF the opportunity to walk through the doors of England's country houses and thus the world of the original officers of the Edwardian Flying Corps. In July 1919, Charles Portal, formerly officer commanding No. 24 Training Wing, actually married into the world of the English country house, although in this regard he did have an edge over his fellow officers, as *The Times* explains:

> The marriage took place yesterday, at Denton, Grantham, of Major C.F.A. Portal, DSO, MC, RAF., son of Mr E.R. Portal, formerly Master of the Craven Hounds, of Eddington House, Hungerford, and Miss Joan

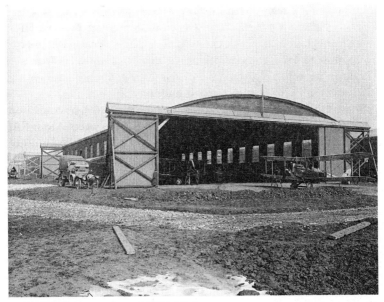

Figure 43. Hangar, tender and DH4, Harlaxton.

Margaret Welby, third and youngest daughter of Sir Charles Glynne Welby and Maria Welby, of Denton Manor. The bride, who was given away by her father, wore a gown of cream brocade velvet, with an underdress of cream chiffon, and a train of old Flemish lace, lined with cream chiffon. Her only ornament was a pearl necklace. The train-bearers were the Misses Mellora and Patsy, the little daughters of Brigadier-General and Mrs Anderson, wearing white muslin frocks with Dutch caps of lace. The best man was Lieutenant Reginald Portal, DSC, RN, brother. The service, which was choral was conducted by the Rev. Lord Manners Hervey, rector of Horringer, Suffolk, and the Rev. B.W. Keymer, OBE, RAF. As the bride and the bridegroom were leaving the church an aeroplane hovered overhead and dropped a message of congratulation near the Manor, where the reception was held.[74]

The example of the country gentleman was one that could be followed by all pilots training in rural England, whether they were Charles Portal (ex-Winchester College, and Christ Church College, Oxford), Brian Garret (ex-Bradford Technical College), Stanley Muir (ex-Melbourne Grammar School), or Alexander Klynes who trained at Harlaxton in 1917.

Klynes had already begun to change his self-identity by changing his name from Kienz to Klynes, anglicising his Germanic surname a little less dramatically than the Royal Family, who went from Saxe-Coburg-Gotha to Windsor. He also successfully transferred into the RFC from the infantry without having first obtained a field commission. His medal card records he was a sergeant in the 2/9 Hampshire Regiment before he became a flying officer in the RAF, and was photographed at Harlaxton, in his cavalry-inspired uniform, sitting at the wheel of a sports car.[75] For the young man with the individuality and confidence to sit in a glove-tight cockpit high in the sky,[76] flying was also a socially transformative opportunity to become part of a new officer and gentlemanly elite. It was though an opportunity fraught with risk, and forced a pilot to test himself to the limit, but:

> If you can trust yourself ...
> ...
> If you can force your heart and nerve and sinew
> To serve your turn long after they are gone,
> And so hold on when there is nothing in you
> Except the Will which says to them: 'Hold on!'
> ...

THE AERODROME AND THE ARMISTICE

If you can fill the unforgiving minute
With sixty seconds' worth of distance run,
Yours is the Earth and everything that's in it,
And – which is more – you'll be a Man, my son!

Rudyard Kipling.[77]

Figure 44. 'Off duty'. Klynes at the wheel of a sports car, Harlaxton.

Conclusion

The dissipation of the memory of Harlaxton aerodrome, its community, and the names of the pilots who trained and served there, was inevitable given that, in addition to the departure of the RAF personnel, the physical infrastructure of the aerodrome was also removed to allow the fields to return to their original agricultural use. The wooden hangars, huts and workshops were designed to be erected quickly to facilitate the rapid expansion of the training programme in England. This also meant that they were just as easily dismantled. Initially, the aerodrome was only to have been mothballed. In a memorandum dated 9 December 1918, Sir Frederick Sykes (having succeeded Sir Hugh Trenchard as CAS in April 1918) wrote:

> It seems improbable that for some years there will be a great war between first-class powers. It seems equally unlikely that there will be a satisfactory league of nations either than that which perhaps may be possible between the British Empire, America and France. In any case there will be a period of deep-seated disturbances throughout the world. The Commonwealth which has carried the greater share of the responsibilities of civilization during the war, must continue to bear them into more stable times. We wish to turn our swords into ploughshares, but it is in the best interests of the world that we should do so – especially in regard to the Air Force – not so fast as merely to shatter a wonderful machine nor so slowly as to allow other nations to usurp our place.[1]

To this end, he recommended that 57 squadrons and 19 wings be reduced to cadres ready to be reactivated in an emergency. RAF Spittlegate was to be home to three of these squadron cadres with RAF Harlaxton providing storage. This recommendation was ignored and over the coming months the RAF was reduced to under 30 squadrons;

CONCLUSION

indeed, given the precipitousness of this reduction, 'the Royal Air Force did not seem destined long to outlive the conflict which had brought it into being'.² In January 1919, Trenchard replaced Sykes as CAS. In a reversal of his earlier position that the RAF was simply an extension of its parent services, he was now determined to preserve what remained of an autonomous RAF. This would keep in being a cadre of officers who could continue to 'encourage and develop airmanship, or better still the air spirit'.³

In the battle to ensure this spirit was not extinguished, Trenchard won valuable support from Sir Walter Raleigh whose official history of the RAF, published in 1922, emphasised 'the original, the heroic and the successful'⁴ role played by the RAF in the war. Pilots were equally conscious of their part in this heroic story, and publicised it accordingly in their memoirs. As we see in the pages of *Parti Patter*, they were also conscious of how, through their own efforts, they had tempered themselves into something rather more than temporary officers and gentlemen.⁵ By 1919, they were a new officer elite who brought together the traditional style of the cavalry with the technical skill of the modern aviator flying a machine that was the wonder of its age.⁶ Ben Sewell for example, recalled:

> Father roused us very early in the morning to come and see aeroplanes following one another and they appeared to be flying from north to south and flying along the railway, which ran just at the end of our garden [in Grantham] ... There were a number of aeroplanes and that would be ... in the summer months of 1913. I very rarely saw an aeroplane. I remember one occasionally flying over the town ... [then] I saw an aeroplane ... flying and landing and then taking off again, and flying round and landing and taking off again ... [from the] top of Spittlegate Hill ... and there was one canvas hangar and I am not sure whether there were two or three aircraft there and this was the beginning of Spittlegate Aerodrome ... later on, the number of canvas hangars grew ... then the building people came and started to erect more permanent hangars, and eventually it developed into a full scale training aerodrome ... A little after that, another aerodrome was started on the top of the hill behind Harlaxton Manor, and that was Harlaxton Aerodrome.⁷

Back in 1914, two machines of the RFC had flown low over Grantham and landed on Spittlegate Hill; the pilots then 'went into Grantham for refreshment and at 2:00pm took off and headed south'.⁸ This is, of course, an example from the cavalier days of the Edwardian RFC when it 'attracted many cavalry officers to its ranks',[9] but as the RFC expanded, the opportunity to become a pilot was opened out to anyone possessing the right temperament. As a flight commander stated: 'The air, to the flying man, is exactly what his temperament happens to make it.'[10] On 11 August 1917, the following appeal for recruits appeared in the *Grantham Journal*:

> **Splendid Opportunity for Young Men**
>
> Recently, the age and method of enlisting Cadets for the Royal Flying Corps were somewhat altered and eligible young men are afforded an exceptional opportunity of joining this attractive branch of His Majesty's Forces. Briefly, the procedure is this: Application to joining the RFC Cadets may be made at the age of seventeen years eight months. If accepted, the applicant would join the Officers Technical Training Corps. Admission is by selection after an interview with an officer of the Royal Flying Corps, and after passing the prescribed medical examination. A Cadet will receive 1s. per day, and there will also be provided uniform, messing, and quarters. No instructional fees of any kind are required. A Cadet, during training will be considered to be on probation, and if he is found unsuitable for retention, he will be liable to serve elsewhere. Men over twenty-five are not eligible. This form of military service is one that should strongly appeal to our younger patriots, and we hope there will be a very ready response. The fullest information will be gladly given on application at the nearest Recruiting Office.[11]

On 25 August 1917, another appeal was made calling for 'the right sort of young men, with patriotic instinct ... [to] eagerly grasp this chance of serving the country'.[12] By 1919, the RAF was composed of pilots selected for their aptitude and skill, in contrast to the social exclusivity of the Edwardian Corps and its original cadre of officers recruited from the elite cavalry regiments.

In Edwardian England, as Edgerton states: 'It is not just that gentlemen wanted to fly, it was that the authorities wanted gentlemen to do the flying.'[13] This was reflected in the conclusions of the Bailhache Committee which reported in 1916 that:

> the most noteworthy feature of the Royal Flying Corps system is that now every pilot must be an officer. Either he is an officer before he joins, or he is drawn from the class of civilians from which army officers mostly come and becomes an officer on joining. Much importance is attached to

CONCLUSION

this fact by the heads of the Royal Flying Corps, who attribute the skill and initiative largely to it.[14]

In training to become a flying officer, it was also possible to become a gentleman pilot. As a consequence, in 1917 and 1918, the body of youth identified by Raleigh, whose temperament was fitted to the work of the air, was no longer composed exclusively of public school boys. This fact was highlighted in the House of Commons by Captain Wedgwood Benn in 1919:

> I believe the Air Force should be a democratic Force. You want to select your men in order to get the qualities that go to make good pilots, and you should have the whole field open for that purpose ... I understand the plan of the Air Ministry to be to select boys who have passed through public school ... because they say that public school education gives a boy a certain amount of 'savvy' or self-confidence which is requisite for the handling of machines of the air ... The history of the War has shown that ... by no means all the most brilliant pilots have been chosen from the class of boys to whom the whole thing would be restricted if such a plan were adopted.[15]

With the exigencies of war removed and the pressure to find pilots lessening, it is surprising to see how quickly the issue of social exclusivity re-emerged. This perhaps explains why so many young men from the so-called 'skilled mechanic class'[16] grasped at a fleeting opportunity to become pilots, officers and gentlemen in the RFC.

An eight-month training programme gave these officer cadets the technical knowledge to be flying officers, and also the chance to escape from 'the desk or the work-bench',[17] to permanently transform their social and self-identity and to become more than temporary officers and gentlemen. In the Schools of Aeronautics these young men learned the 'etiquette of gentleman officers'.[18] When they then went to their elementary and higher training squadrons they were also going to a social finishing school. This was because the RFC's training aerodromes were built in rural England which was home to the most polished gentlemen in the world who opened the doors of their stately homes to these pilots. Pilots at Harlaxton aerodrome were entertained at Harlaxton Manor, Denton Manor and Belvoir Castle. Similarly, pilots at Gosport were entertained by the owners of country houses in Hampshire, for whom 'the RFC was always *persona grata*'.[19] Meanwhile, in Canada, officers 'were frequently invited to the finest homes where they were entertained by the cream of society'.[20]

In considering the RFC's three most famous aces, John Keegan observed that James McCudden, 'an ex-private soldier, and [Edward] Mannock, a convinced Socialist, were cold-hearted technicians of dogfighting from backgrounds wholly at variance with the majority of public school pilots whom Albert Ball typified'.[21] Was their cold, technical efficiency in killing the enemy in the air a way to combat the class prejudices they encountered on the ground? Class prejudice did exist but, as 'the social mix of cadets gradually broadened out ... pre-war snobbery succumbed to the pragmatism required in a global conflict'.[22] The appearance of wingmen and formation flying introduced a degree of mutual dependency between pilots that would have rendered such snobbery meaningless.

The RFC that Ball typified was being superseded by a Corps in which there were pilots from all classes in Britain and all corners of the British Empire. These pilots included the Canadian ace Billy Bishop who viewed air-fighting as a 'wonderful game'.[23] Similarly, the Australian ace R.A. Little considered fighting in the air to be a 'gloriously exhilarating sport'.[24] In 1917 and 1918, while it was increasingly difficult to sustain the illusion that the relentless and deadly routine of daily offensive patrols was a sport[25] or indeed chivalrous, the ace remained a role model for new pilots by combining the technical efficiency of the airman and the recklessness of the cavalryman. More importantly, when measured by these criteria young men of the 'right sort' could be from whatever class or nation[26] and still be considered suitable candidates to become officers and gentlemen in the RFC/RAF. These pilots were shifting the air service away from an 'early public schoolboy image ... [as] high numbers of the original pilots were lost, [because, their] replacements had to be found from Other Ranks, as well as from other countries'.[27]

The belief in the dynamic power of flying to transform an individual into the ultimate man was also an illusion, but it was based upon the actions of these brave and reckless individuals who gave Britain an heroic alternative to the squalor and anonymity of the trenches.[28] The resulting adulation of the airman reached its apogee, perhaps, in the triumphant welcome given to the Australian aviation pioneer and Sopwith test-pilot Harry Hawker in May 1919. Hawker and his navigator, Kenneth Grieve, arrived in Britain having been presumed lost at sea when attempting to fly across the Atlantic. Travelling south to London, Hawker was met by his wife and Mr. and Mrs. Sopwith at Grantham with their meeting being relayed to the world 'by a small army of London Press photographers and cinema operators'.[29] The *New York Times* correspondent described how:

CONCLUSION

Grantham was determined to do its part to honour them. There was a crowd at the station ... and a still larger one outside, unable to get in. Officers from the local aerodromes at Spittlegate and Harlaxton gathered in a group to cheer, and a fleet of airplanes droned a welcome from overhead.[30]

The *Grantham Journal* reported how 'the array of camera men ... positively monopolised the situation, each bent on securing the best point of vantage ... [whilst] Overhead, several airmen engaged the attention of the crowd below ... [then as his train pulled into the station] the Band struck up "See the Conquering Hero Comes" and the assembled concourse sent forth vociferous cheers'.[31]

Earlier in the day, 'the news was abroad in the town that [Mrs. Hawker] ... had actually arrived ... and had motored to the Aerodrome at Harlaxton for lunch!'[32] This was a mistake, but it highlights the social scene that now revolved around the aerodromes as much as the local country houses. Aerodromes were now part of the locality, and there was a 'highly successful whist drive and dance ... to raise funds for the Denton Village Cricket Club ... [where the] excellent band was accompanied by the drums from Harlaxton aerodrome'.[33] The centre piece of Harlaxton aerodrome's social calendar was the annual sports day for

Figure 45. Aerial view, sports day, Harlaxton.

which a running track and sports field were specially laid out. In 1919, the Harlaxton contingent performed well across an eclectic programme of events: the high jump was won by A.M. Royston with Lieutenant Vine coming second; Royston also came second in the sack race; the long jump was won by Lieutenant Paling MC, with A.M. Royston again coming second; Lieutenant Paling came second in the hurdle race; tilting-the-bucket was won by S.M. Kirby and Sergeant Fretwell, with A.M.G. Parson and A.M. Walker coming second; Sergeant Fretwell came second in the pick-a-back fight; whilst third place in the 100 yards race went to one McCurdy; third place went to Sergeant Major Stafford in the 100 yards veterans race who went on to win the pillow-fight. The *Grantham Journal* concluded:

> It was not surprising to see such a large company at the Harlaxton aerodrome on Thursday to witness the annual athletic sports of the Royal Air Force for the weather was ideal … Previously, such events have taken place at both Spittlegate and Harlaxton, but this year it was decided to combine, and this proved a capital idea. Apart from a goodly muster of the RAF, there was also present a distinguished company of officers from the MGC [Machine Gun Corps], Grantham, and a large muster of machine gunners, in addition to a contingent from the Air Force at Cranwell … [the] President [was] Major M.G. Lee; vice-president, Major J. Butler … the band of the 1st. Battalion MGC was [also] in attendance … Through the thoughtfulness of the officers of the station, the visitors were provided with tea, al fresco … In the evening Mrs M.G. Lee very graciously distributed the awards, and … an act of thoughtfulness on the part of the Band, in expressing a desire to stay for dancing, was greatly appreciated, and the company experienced a merry time.[34]

This was the last July sports day to be held at Harlaxton and, in addition to the officers and men of No. 40 TDS (officially disbanded on 5 May 1919), it would also have included any of their 'brother officers from overseas'[35] who still remained at the repatriation camp (officially established on 3 May 1919) under the command of Major J.A. Butler. In June, Butler wrote in *Parti Patter*:

> Having been very lucky in having the good fortune to be appointed your last Commanding Officer … I take this excellent opportunity (thanks to the worthy Editor, Lieut. Howard Wallace, who I know has worked extremely hard to give you this souvenir of your sojourn at Harlaxton, in getting out this Magazine), to thank you on behalf of the Old Country,

CONCLUSION

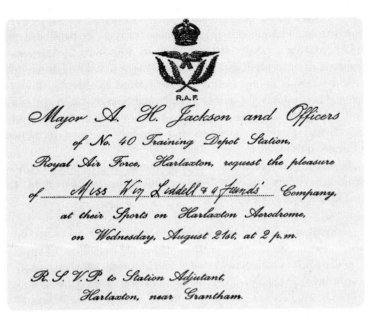

Figure 46. Invitation to Harlaxton Sports Day.

the Royal Air Force and myself … you have come from all corners of the globe … to fight shoulder to shoulder … with the boys of the Old Country … When you leave this country you will take back with you many memories … and I hope not the least will be [of] your short and final stay at Harlaxton under my command.[36]

The affection felt by Butler for his officers was reciprocated and expressed on their departure from Grantham train station:

On a day in June – the first June he had been away from the front line of battle since the battles began – a four-ribboned Major of the Air Force stood silent on the station platform, stood silent while and long after the air rang in the ears with stout Canadian and South African applauding cries. A … man, who had carried himself with courage among men since his laddy days in the Boer War remained … while the sons of men who had fought with and against him … raised his name in cheers … [as] their unanimous choice of an English gentleman and soldier … 'He is a prince!' said a braw American …[37]

If so, he was a prince among fellow 'princes of the air'[38] from all classes and nations, whose training programme in rural England had seen cadets, wearing a cavalry-inspired uniform, welcomed into the world of the cavalry and fox-hunting originals. This was still evident in 1927, with the Belvoir Hunt meeting at RAF Cranwell.[39] Indeed, the belief that the best pilot was a recycled cavalryman persisted into the 1930s, with RAF pilots being encouraged to ride horses as a way to improve their flying, given the 'deftness and dexterity in hand movements common to the good horseman and good pilot'.[40]

By 1927, RAF Harlaxton had disappeared. In December 1919, the auctioneers Escritt and Barrell, acting under instructions received from the Officers' Mess put up for sale:

> Two pianos, three gramophones and records, 80 upholstered wicker and 10 wood armchairs, 3 lounge chairs upholstered in leather, 100 chests of drawers, 73 washstands, 151 single iron bedsteads, 120 mattresses, 20 card tables, 13 upholster settees, writing and other tables, mirror, gramophone record cabinet ... carpets, mats, curtains, 107 bowls, 70 jugs, 80 Chambers, Flower pots and vases, plant stands, clocks, cash register, electric heaters, pendants and fans etc., etc.[41]

Subsequently, in February 1920, the auctioneers G.W. Golding put up for sale three full-size billiard tables, 'in capital condition, with mahogany frame, slate bed, with full complement of accessories. The tables can be viewed at any time on application to the officer commanding.'[42] He was commanding what was now an empty aerodrome that was itself about to disappear. In October 1920, the Disposal Board (Huts and Building Materials Section) of the Ministry of Munitions announced the sell-off, by public auction, of all the buildings on the site, whereupon the huts, hangars and workshops all now disappeared.[43] With the physical evidence of the aerodrome now removed, it continued to exist only in the memories of those who had served or trained there, such as William Way who had been 'a member of the RAF, Harlaxton Aerodrome during the Great War'[44] and who, in 1928, married Miss H.M. Geeson, the Sunday School teacher in Denton, who 'has always been ready to help forward every good movement in the village'.[45] In contrast, during the war, Basil Liddell Hart recalled one officer who 'got married, and on his return from a brief honeymoon amused himself in the early morning by waking up his bride with aerobatics round their house, and almost piercing its walls with his wing tips'.[46]

CONCLUSION

In Harlaxton village, today, the memory of the aerodrome survives in the poppy wreaths placed on the graves of Stanley Muir, Alick Charlesworth and Stanley Rutledge by Kevin Lawry (ex-RAF) each November. Hopefully, this book has put these young men into their proper context, at the heart of a training programme in England that was in turn adapting to the new technology and tactical systems of the world's first air war in France. This was living literally at the cutting edge of modernity. As Arthur Gould Lee states:

> The resolution needed by the airmen of World War One was of a special kind, and it was demanded from the moment you began to learn to fly. This process, with the uncertain methods of instruction of 1916–1917, was so crowded with lethal crashes that nearly as many lives were lost in training schools in England as in the warring skies of France.[47]

Similarly, in his memoir, *Into the Blue*, Norman MacMillan recalled the crudeness of even advanced training with ineffective instructors and the, 'so many needlessly killed'.[48] The losses in England compounded those being suffered in France, through to mid 1917, due to inadequate training which, in turn, contributed to shorter training times for their replacements.[49] Fortunately, by 1918, the quality of the instruction given to pupils in training was much higher and the time spent in the air was considerably longer. Accusations of insufficient training were now:

> happily, rare, and … becoming rarer, though it occasionally occurs, especially when pilots are urgently required for some special reason. It must be remembered that the instructor's job is not easy. He has to teach his pupil to fly, and gauge his nervous capacity, confidence, and judgment; to do this he must allow him complete control at all heights, and at the same time be ready at the fraction of a second's notice to take over control in the case of an error in flying or of threatened collision with an early soloist in another machine. Since most instructors in this country are in the air with pupils for about three hours a day, and are encouraged to turn out the largest possible number of soloists per month, I think it is extraordinary that crashes caused by too little instruction are as rare as they are.[50]

The cause of accidents was the subject of an analysis by H. Graeme Anderson, a surgeon attached to the RNAS in 1918. In his so-called 'V' series he studied the 58 crashes that occurred at one station over a six-month period. These represented one crash in every 155 flights whilst the 16 airmen who were injured represented one pupil injured in every 560 flights, from which figures he concluded, 'one can see that school flying is fairly safe and compares favourably with other high velocity forms of transit'.[51] In addition to the frequency of these crashes he also developed seven criteria for their causes:

1 a defect in the aeroplane;
2 an error of judgement in flying;
3 'loss of head';
4 brain fatigue or lethargy;
5 fear;
6 physical illness;
7 unavoidable causes.

Of these, the single highest cause of accidents, accounting for 42 out of 58, was an error of judgement, with 38 accidents occurring on landing and 4 on take-off. But what of fear? Significantly, when questioned, many pupils 'confess to a sense of danger lurking somewhere at the back of the head, but say that it rarely if ever asserts itself'.[52] This was because they had the right temperament for flying.[53] Indeed, after mid 1917, instructors were keen to establish whether a pupil had this temperament as quickly as possible and would take new pupils up for a 'joy-ride'. As a result, 'first flights often lead a pupil to discover he has nerves – leading him to rejoin his Regiment'.[54] Those pupils with the requisite temperament who graduated as service pilots, would then become participants:

> in the repetitive and unrelenting stress of aerial fighting [and develop] … its characteristic physiognomy: 'skeletal hands, sharpened noses, tight drawn cheek bones, the bared teeth of a rictus smile and the fixed, narrowed gaze of men in a state of controlled fear'.[55]

These men would, in turn, go home at regular intervals to work as instructors. Before they began instructing, they were now required to spend two weeks at Gosport,[56] or one of the other new schools for instructors, where they, together with their fellow trainee-instructors, were assessed on their aptitude for teaching. Only after they were assessed as competent to be an instructor in a training programme geared to teaching advanced combat flying, could they begin working with their new pupils. Their pupils would, in turn, develop a similar state of controlled fear, as they too became ever more confident in

CONCLUSION

their own ability to instinctively execute these advanced manoeuvres. Nonetheless, the willpower required to control one's fears could, sometimes, be overwhelmed, as Basil Liddell Hart witnessed during his time at Harlaxton in 1917:

> There was one incident that stands in my memory as a sidelight on the different kinds of courage. It occurred when walking across the airfield with a pilot who had won decorations for most gallant feats and gone on flying with unbroken nerve after a crash in which he had been badly injured. While we were strolling along a tractor plane from another squadron landed close to us, and in getting out its pilot stepped into the propeller before it had stopped swinging and had his head nearly severed. It was a ghastly sight, although no more than daily experience in land battle, but I was astonished to see that it completely unnerved my companion.[57]

His surprise is instructive and illustrative of the self-control and emotional imperturbability expected of a fellow officer especially as flying officers fought to preserve their standing in their own eyes and in the eyes of other units.[58] Losses were inevitable, given the RFC's relentlessly aggressive and offensive ethos; consequently, in the Officers' Mess it was 'an unwritten law for pilots to forget their sorrow and assume a cheerfulness which gave the impression of "living for the day"'.[59] This unwritten rule would have been observed in the Officers' Mess of the operational squadrons in France and the training squadrons in England where, regardless of the risks involved, a 'lonely impulse of delight', to quote Yeats, continued to inspire Raleigh's 'young gallants who were gay and reckless'.[60] They were also training above an English countryside that still belonged to the social elite of both Britain and the Empire, who introduced these pioneering pilots into their rural realms. This, in turn, facilitated the transformation of their social and self-identity from 'temporary gentlemen'[61] into the recognisable heirs of the fox-hunting country gentlemen and ex-cavalry officer originals. These were, after all, reckless fellows who saw themselves as a winged aristocracy – *Tally Ho!*

Appendix I

RFC/RAF Harlaxton (Training Squadron Station and Training Depot Station) Roll of Honour, 1917–18

See p. 151 for Notes and Abbreviations

Squadrons based at Harlaxton	Duration of posting	Fatalities	Details
44 Reserve Squadron/ Training Squadron*	13.11.1916/ 24.11.1917	13.3.1917. Leonard Murray, aged 20	Lt Pilot (f. Lancs Hussars Yeo.) 44 Res Sqn 'accidentally killed when struck by the propeller of DH4 A2125' (Hobson, *Airmen*, pp. 76, 241 and 349).
		30.5.1917. Alick Thomas Bentall Charlesworth†, aged 24	2nd Lt Pilot (f. 88/Can Inf; 7/Can Inf) 44 Res Sqn, Kwf in DH4 A2164 (Hobson, *Airmen*, pp. 28, 32, 247, 349). 'Banked steeply, spun in' (Hancock, *Traditional*, p. 3).
		4/5.9.1917. Walter Brown	AMII (1980), 44 Sqn (Hobson, *Airmen*, p. 254) in DH4 A2152 'Port wings collapsed in spin' (Hancock, *Traditional*, p. 4).
		6.10.1917. Charles Henry Walton, aged 29	AMII (83458), 44 Tr Sqn, died of meningitis (Hobson, *Airmen*, pp. 104, 257 and 349).

146

		10.10.1917. Cecil Reginald Bascombe, aged 19	2nd Lt Pilot 44 Tr Sqn, Kwf in DH4 B3959 (Hobson, *Airmen*, pp. 22, 257 and 349). 'Stalled on t/o' (Hancock, *Traditional*, p. 4).
		16.11.1917. Stanley Arthur Rutledge†, aged 26	Lt Pilot (f. 28/Can Inf) 44 Tr Sqn, Kwf in DH4 A7711, 2nd Lt J.W. Rhode. 'was injured' (Hobson, *Airmen*, pp. 89, 260 and 349). 'Hit tree on approach' (Hancock, *Traditional*, p. 4).
68 (Australian) Squadron	30.1.1917/ 21.9.1917	12.9.1917. Stanley Keith Muir, MC†, aged 25	Capt. Pilot (Aust LH) 68 Sqn, Kwf in DH5 A9275 (Hobson, *Airmen*, pp. 75, 255 and Hancock, *Traditional*, p. 4).
54 Reserve Squadron/ Training Squadron	17.3.1917/ 12.12.1917	10.7.1917. Walter Vosper Jakins, aged 20	2nd Lt Pilot (f. RE) 54 Tr Sqn, Kwf in Strutter A8204 with Lt D.D. Lockwood who was injured' (Hobson, *Airmen*, pp. 60, 250, 350 and Hancock, *Traditional*, p. 3).
		18.8.1917. Frederick William Eady, aged 20	AMI (37420), 54 Tr Sqn (Hobson, *Airmen*, pp. 42, 253 and 350).
		7.12.1917. Jack Randell Falck, aged 19	2nd Lt Pilot 54 Tr Sqn, Kwf in Pup B2246 (Hobson, *Airmen*, pp. 44, 262, 350). 'Spun in' (Hancock, *Traditional*, p. 4).
98 Squadron (nucleus of ex-44 TS)	15.8.1917/ 30.8.1917		
3 Training Depot Station (A Flight, nucleus of ex-54 TS)	22.8.1917/ 5.9.1917		

26 Training Squadron	22.9.1917/ 3.2.1918	11.11.1917. Duncan Alexander Robertson	2nd Lt Pilot 26 Tr Sqn, Kwf in MFSH/Shorthorn S11 B2009 (Hobson, *Airmen*, pp. 88, 260 and Hancock, *Traditional*, p. 4).
64 Training Squadron	12.12.1917/ 15.8.1918	24.3.1918. James Leslie Cumming, aged 19	2nd Lt Pilot 64 Tr Sqn, Kwf in RE8 A4493 (Hobson, *Airmen*, pp. 38, 270, 350 and Hancock, *Traditional*, p. 5).
		24.3.1918. G.R. Johnston	Cadet. Arty and Inf Co-Op Sch, AFC, Kwf in RE8 A4493 (Hobson, *Airmen*, p. 270 and Hancock, *Traditional*, p. 5).
		8.5.1918. Arthur Burrell Thorne, aged 23	Lt Pilot (f. RFA) 64 Tr Sqn, Kwf in RE8 B7729 (Hobson, *Airmen*, pp. 196, 277 and 378 and Hancock, *Traditional*, p. 6). See also 53 Sqn, same date.
		8.5.1918. Howard Watson, aged 18	2nd Lt Pilot 64 Tr Sqn, Kwf in RE8 B7729 (Hobson, *Airmen*, pp. 201, 277 and 378 and Hancock, *Traditional*, p. 6) See also 53 Sqn, same date.
53 Training Squadron	6.12.1917/ 15.8.1918	26.1.1918. George Henry Tufts‡	2nd Lt Pilot (f. KRRC) 53 Tr Sqn, Kwf in DH6 A9669 (Hobson, *Airmen*, pp. 101, 265, 350 and Hancock, *Traditional*, p. 5).
		27.1.1918. Edmund Barnes+, aged 18	2nd Lt Pilot 53 Tr Sqn, Kwf in DH6 C6806 (Hobson, *Airmen*, pp. 21, 265, 350 and Hancock, *Traditional*, p. 5).
		11/13.2.1918. 2nd Lt Gerald Arthur Bloomfield, aged 23	2nd Lt Pilot (f. RFA) 53 Tr Sqn Doi received 11.2.1918 in RE8 A3881 (Hobson, *Airmen*, pp. 25, 267, 350 and Hancock, *Traditional*, p. 5).

27.2.1918. Ralph Hemsworth Jarvis, MC, MiD, CG(B), aged 27		Capt. Pilot 53 Tr Sqn, Kwf in DH6 B2763 (Hobson, *Airmen*, pp. 60, 268 and 350).
27.2.1918. John James Nicholson Musgrave, aged 19		2nd Lt Pilot 53 Tr Sqn, Kwf in DH6 B2763 (Hobson, *Airmen*, pp. 76, 268 and 350).
8.5.1918. Myer Joseph Levine, aged 18		2nd Lt Pilot 53 Tr Sqn, Kwf in RE8 A4546 (Hobson, *Airmen*, pp. 161, 277, 377 and Hancock, *Traditional*, p. 6). 'Levine, Thorne and Watson collided during formation practice near Grantham' (Hobson, *Airmen*, p. 277).
22.5.1918. James Norman Clitheroe, aged 32		Lt Pilot 53 Tr Sqn, Kwf in RE8 B6669 (Hobson, *Airmen*, pp. 128, 279 and 377 and Hancock, *Traditional*, p. 6).
22.5.1918. Clarence Everard Johnson, aged 19		2nd Lt Pilot 53 Tr Sqn, Kwf in RE8 B6669 (Hobson, *Airmen*, pp. 156, 279 and 377 and Hancock, *Traditional*, p. 6).
17.7.1918. Harold Buckley		Flt Cadet (85900). Pilot 53 Tr Sqn, Kwf RE8 D4724 (Hobson, *Airmen*, pp. 123, 288, 377 and Hancock, *Traditional*, p. 7).
28.7.1918. John Arnold Sheperd		2nd Lt Pilot 53 Tr Sqn, Kwf Avro 504K D8832 (Hobson, *Airmen*, pp. 188, 289, 377 and Hancock, *Traditional*, p. 7).

20 Training Squadron	27.11.1917/ 15.8.1918	
	7.1.1918. William Kay Anderson, aged 25	Lt Pilot (f. 156/Can Inf) 20 Tr Sqn, Kwf in DH6 A9637 (Hobson, *Airmen*, pp. 19, 264, 348 and Hancock, *Traditional*, p. 4).
	7.1.1918. Arthur Charles Perryman, aged 29	2nd Lt Pilot (f. ASC; Middx Rgt) 20 Tr Sqn, Kwf in DH6 A9593 'Anderson and Perryman collided over Lincolnshire' (Hobson, *Airmen*, pp. 82, 264, 348 and Hancock. *Traditional*, p. 4).
	25.3.1918. Gordon Smith Mellis Gauld, MC+, aged 24	Lt Pilot (f. RFA) 20 Tr Sqn, Kwf in RE8 B6637 (Hobson, *Airmen*, pp. 48, 271, 348 and Hancock, *Traditional*, p. 5).
	25.3.1918. Alexander Drysdale, aged 18	2nd Lt Pilot 20 Tr Sqn, Kwf in RE8 B6637 (Hobson, *Airmen*, pp. 42, 48, 271, 348 and Hancock, *Traditional*, p. 5).
	20.4.1918. Henry Leslie Barradell, aged 18	2nd Lt Pilot (f. R. Warwicks Regt) 20 Tr Sqn, Kwf in RE8 B4067 (Hobson, *Airmen*, pp. 116, 275, 377 and Hancock, *Traditional*, p. 6).
	29.7.1918. Arthur Moulton Cross, aged 23	2nd Lt Pilot 20 Tr Sqn, Kwf in RE8 C2385 (Hobson, *Airmen*, pp. 131, 290, 377 and Hancock, *Traditional*, p. 7).
50th Aero Squadron USAS	4.2.1918/ 3.7.1918	

| 40 TDS (an amalgamation of Nos 20, 53 and 64 TS) | 15.8.1918/ 8.5.1919 | 6.9.1918. S.R. Iddon | Flt Cadet 40 T.D. S., Kwf in RE8 D4874 (Hobson, *Airmen*, p. 297 and Hancock, *Traditional*, p. 8). |
| | | 29.10.1918. A.W. Mather | Lt 40 T.D. S., Kwf in RE8 D1552 (Hobson, *Airmen*, p. 309 and Hancock, *Traditional*, p. 8). |

Source: Mick Davis and Bill Morgan, 'Gazetteer of flying sites, Part 9: Gai-Har', *Cross and Cockade International*, xliii/1(2012), GFS-72; Chris Hobson, *Airmen Died in the Great War, 1914–1918: The Roll of Honour of the British and Commonwealth Air Services of the First World War* (London, 1995); T.N. Hancock, *Aircraft Crashes in the Traditional County of Lincolnshire, 1914–2006* (Lincolnshire Library Services, 2006); Michael J.F. Bowyer, *Actions Stations Revisited: The Complete History of Britain's Military Airfields. No. 1: Eastern England* (Manchester, 2000), p. 204, and www.bcar.org.uk/world-war-one-incident-logs/.

Notes and Abbreviations

† Buried at Harlaxton
+ Buried at Grantham
‡ Buried at Attleborough
* Reserve Squadrons were re-designated Training Squadrons 31.5.1917

Acc: Accidentally killed
AFC: Australian Flying Corps
AMI/AMII: Air Mechanic, First and Second Class
ASC: Army Service Corps
Aust LH: Australian Light Horse
Can Inf: Canadian Infantry
CG(B): Croix de Guerre (Belgium)
Doi: Died of injuries
f: Formerly of

KRRC: King's Royal Rifle Corps
Kwf: Killed whilst flying
MC: Military Cross
MiD: Mentioned in Dispatches
Middx Rgt: Middlesex Regiment
MFSH: Maurice Farman Shorthorn bi-plane
RE: Royal Engineers
RFA: Royal Field Artillery

Appendix II
The Last Parade, 1919

RANK	NAME	ADDRESS	COUNTRY
2/Lt	Allen, John Donald	Peddie, Cape Province	South Africa
2/Lt	Anderson, William	Pine Street, Vernon, British Columbia	Canada
2/Lt	Annett, Francis Cris.	44A Galley Avenue, Toronto	Canada
2/Lt	Archer	Eric Court, Somerset East	South Africa
2/Lt	Arnold, Chas. Emanuel	679 Colborne St., London	Canada
2/Lt	Aspeling, Arthur Leslie Rex	Grey St., Queenstown	South Africa
Capt	Baguley, Fred Hubert	Dunedin, Florida	USA (formerly Canada)
2/Lt	Baker, Howard Russell	Warburton Avenue, Bayside, Long Island, New York City	USA
2/Lt	Ball, Ross Washington	Kelsey Wheel Co., Windsor	Canada
2/Lt	Ballentyre, Watson	1354 Wilder, Honolulu	Hawaii
2/Lt	Banham, Francis Joseph	The Grange, Beccles	USA

THE LAST PARADE, 1919

Rank	Name	Address	Country
Capt	Bannerman, Ronald Burns	Bank of N. Zealand, Dunedin	New Zealand
Lieut	Baron, Harry Krummeck	Beaufort Weir, Cape Colony	South Africa
2/Lt	Barry, Harry Edward	Wellington, Cape	South Africa
Capt	Baskerville, Milton Groves	Dominion City, Manitoba	Canada
Lieut	Beart, William	Durban, Natal	South Africa
Lieut	Beeton, Vernon	Aliwal, North Kimberley	South Africa
2/Lt	Berry, William Vivian	Hotel Peddie, Peddie	South Africa
2/Lt	Blair, John	Somerset St., Grahamstown	South Africa
2/Lt	Bradley, Lloyd Tempest	Thorold, Ontario	Canada
Lieut	Bremicker, Carl Theodore	Highlands, Wisconsin	USA
2/Lt	Brine, James Dawson	116 Colony St., Winnipeg	Canada
2/Lt	Brooks, Harold	Cornwall, Ontario	Canada
2/Lt	Brown, Edward Harold	407 Charlevoix, Montreal	Canada
2/Lt	Brown, Eric Thomas Francis	La Hortencia, Banfield, Buenos Aires	USA
2/Lt	Buchanan, William Roy	North Bay, Ontario	Canada
2/Lt	Buirski, Joseph Isaac	P.O. Box 1, Swelleindam, Cape Province	South Africa
Lieut	Burpee, Clarence Alfred	c/o C.P.R. Telegraphs, Edmonton, Alberta	Canada
2/Lt	Burran, Albert Lewis	356 John St., Quebec	Canada

Rank	Name	Address	Country
Capt	Burt, Arthur Henry	Oudtshoorn, Cape Province	South Africa
2/Lt	Butchart, Dana Lochart	Bigging, Minnesota	USA
2/Lt	Cairns, James Herbert	2104 Fifth Avenue, Vancouver	Canada
2/Lt	Campain, William Charles	La Riviere, Manitoba	Canada
Lieut	Canton, Oswald Lawrence	Winnipeg	Canada
2/Lt	Carr, Kevin Hampden	80 Unley Road, Adelaide, South Australia	Australia
2/Lt	Carswell, John Arthur	Red Deer, Alberta	Canada
Lieut	Carter, Clifford Gould	Westminster, Orange Free State	South Africa
2/Lt	Chapman, Maurice Leonard	15 Church St., Christchurch	New Zealand
2/Lt	Charlebois, Joseph Ephraim	Curran, Ontario	Canada
2/Lt	Chouler, Fred Terence	Cape Town	South Africa
Lieut	Clapp, Ross Lee	48 Lynd Avenue, Toronto	Canada
2/Lt	Clark, Ernest Sanford	Yorktown, Saskatchewan	Canada
2/Lt	Cochrane, William McGillivray	Moose Jaw, Saskatchewan	Canada
2/Lt	Comvery, Frank Eugene	202 Brock Street, Brantford	Canada
Capt	Craig, Henry Clifford	Cobourg, Ontario	Canada
2/Lt	Crane, Harry Everett	1805 Montier, Pittsburg	USA
Capt	Cross, Alfred Richard	Regina	Canada

THE LAST PARADE, 1919

Rank	Name	Address	Country
2/Lt	Davidson, Edward Henry John	786 Bruce Street, Winnipeg	Canada
2/Lt	Davis, Ammon Victor	176 Queen St. E, Toronto	Canada
2/Lt	Davis, Price Hughes	Box 2900 Johannesburg	South Africa
2/Lt	Devenish, Francis St.	Leger, Swellendam, Cape Province	South Africa
2/Lt	DeWolfe, Alex Boyd	652 Elias Street, Ontario	Canada
2/Lt	Dickson, Cecil Francis Hughes	Jagersfontein, Orange Free State	South Africa
2/Lt	Didcott, Fred. Ernest	Box 548 Durban	South Africa
2/Lt	Doble, Walter Noble	Fort Beaufort	South Africa
2/Lt	Driscoll, George Edward	Winnipeg	Canada
2/Lt	Dunseith, Harold Enos	St. Mary's, Ontario	Canada
2/Lt	Duthie, George Rex	Brenton, Kinysna	South Africa
2/Lt	Duthie, Raymond Roderick	Brenton, Kinysna	South Africa
2/Lt	Dymock, Walter Leslie	Anne St., Dundee, Natal	South Africa
2/Lt	Fenn, Egerton Dudley	Pretoria, Orange Free State	South Africa
2/Lt	Findlay, George McMurray	1342 Fifteenth Avenue, W. Calgary	Canada
2/Lt	Findlay, James H.	Caledonia, Ontario	Canada
2/Lt	Fitzsimmons, Embert Lewis	56 School St., Groveland, Mass.	USA
Lieut	Fulton, Robert Blackwood	Vernon, British Columbia	Canada

Rank	Name	Address	Country
2/Lt	Garrod, John Douglas L	478 Barlolome Mine, Buenos Aires	Argentine
2/Lt	Hallatt, George Morley	Comber, Ontario	Canada
2/Lt	Harris, Victor Tobias	Box 249, Kimberley	South Africa
2/Lt	Hawkins, Bert Percival	Kimberley	South Africa
2/Lt	Hayward, Kenneth	Sayville, Long Island, New York	USA
2/Lt	Henry, Heber Andrew	2025 Retallic St., Regina, Saskatchewan	Canada
2/Lt	Hindson, Douglas	2220 Lorne St., Regina, Saskatchewan	Canada
2/Lt	Horne, Sydney Daniel	Suva	Fiji Islands
2/Lt	Hotine, Percy	1288 Schoeman, Pretoria	South Africa
2/Lt	Howse, Walter Gordon	J.Bowen & Co., Port Elizabeth	South Africa
Lieut	Hull, Alen Herbert	21 Seventh St., Saskatoon	Canada
2/Lt	Hunt, John Alfred Paul	Darwin	Australia
2/Lt	Hunter, Charles James Gordon	Koffyfontein, Orange Free State	South Africa
2/Lt	Jacobs, Lionel Dudley	Box 3109 Jonnesburg	South Africa
2/Lt	Kleinot, Isedcre	P.O. Alberton, Transvaal	South Africa
2/Lt	Knowles, John Hillis	Lanark, Ontario	Canada
2/Lt	Lacasse, Albert Louis John	Rock Island, Quebec	Canada
Lieut	Lacasse, Alex Joseph	Rock Island	Canada

THE LAST PARADE, 1919

2/Lt	Lalonde, Gaston Le Febvre	786 Granville St., Vancouver, British Columbia	Canada
2/Lt	Lang, Chris. Donovan	Winnipeg, Manitoba	Canada
2/Lt	Laughton, William Muir	711 Ravensview Drive, Portland, Oregon	USA
2/Lt	Laver, Reg. Rayner	Inwain, Nr. Queenstown	South Africa
2/Lt	Lawson, Harold Paul	Rockville Center, Long Island, New York	USA
2/Lt	Le Grice, Alfred Charles	Cook's Avenue, Canterbury, New South Wales	Australia
2/Lt	Liebenberg, Petrus Albertus	Dieplaagte, Edenburg	South Africa
2/Lt	Lloyd, N.W.	92 Fentimen Avenue, Ottawa	Canada
2/Lt	Lofquist, Ernest	1358 Post St., San Francisco, California	USA
2/Lt	Lowe, Louis Godfrey	La Plata, Drabbel, F.C.O.	Argentine
2/Lt	MacConnell, Robert Stanley	Toronto	Canada
2/Lt	MacDougall, Douglas	628 Dallas Road, Victoria, British Columbia	Canada
2/Lt	MacDougall, Wm. Fraser	Box 533 Carleton Place, Ontario	Canada
Lieut	MacIntyre, Geoffrey Purvis	Dormey Mooseclub, Sunningdale Melbourne	Australia
Lieut	MacNab, Leslie Murdock	Warora Road, Melbourne	Australia
2/Lt	Manly, Glenn Horace	Grand Forks, British Columbia	Canada
2/Lt	Manson, James Edward	Kamloops, British Columbia	Canada
Lieut	Martin, Jas	Johnsone St., West Hill, Grahamstown	South Africa

Rank	Name	Address	Country
2/Lt	Mathews, Arnold Stan	762 Avenue Des Erables, Montreal	Canada
2/Lt	May, Newell	Irvington, New York State	USA
2/Lt	McEwen, James West	Wingham, Ontario	Canada
Lieut	McFie, Charles Stewart	W.T.Dept. G.M. Co., P.O Box 5, Knight	South Africa
2/Lt	McLeod, Carson Ross	Grand Forks, British Columbia	Canada
F/Cdt	McTurk, Edward	c/o Government sec.	British Guiana
2/Lt	Melville, James Victor	Klerksdorp, Transvaal	South Africa
2/Lt	Melvin, William	Simmereast, Germiston, Transvaal	South Africa
2/Lt	Merrington, John Leonard	Pretoria	South Africa
2/Lt	Merwe, George Murray Van Der	43 Lombard St., Bloemfontein	South Africa
2/Lt	Middleton, Arthur Edward Waring	21 Baker St., Maplewood, New Jersey	USA
2/Lt	Millar, George Andrew	Freeman, Ontario	Canada
2/Lt	Morris, William	217 P.I. Buildings, Seattle, Washington	USA
2/Lt	Mosley, Harold Millett	27 Parkway Heights, Welland, Ontario	Canada
2/Lt	Mousseau, Lawrence Joseph	55 Church Street, Windsor, Ontario	Canada
2/Lt	Mowat, Hugh Penden	2152 Broad Street, Regina	Canada
2/Lt	Muir, Archie	163 Wellington Avenue, Victoria, British Columbia	Canada
2/Lt	Munro, Jas. Grewer	21 Seper Road, Johannesburg	South Africa

THE LAST PARADE, 1919

2/Lt	Murray, Charles Rutherford	St. Boswell, Saskatchewan	Canada
Capt	Murray, George	8 Highbury Grove, East Parkran, Victoria	Australia
2/Lt	Myles, Lyness Andrew	Thornbury	Canada
2/Lt	Nelson, Frank Wright	Box 1012 Johannesburg	South Africa
2/Lt	Ney, Cecil Herman	Aurora, Ontario	Canada
2/Lt	Nicholas, David Llewellyn	Queenstown	South Africa
2/Lt	Noel, Harold Fred	1334 Merit St., Victoria, British Columbia	Canada
2/Lt	Northey, Herbert Louis	Vancouver, British Columbia	Canada
2/Lt	Nott, Robert Richard	40 Ponbrandis St., Krugersword	South Africa
2/Lt	Nuttall, George Charles	Gananocque, Ontario	Canada
2/Lt	Officer, Jack	c/o Atlas Manufacturing Co., Montreal (Home – Winnipeg)	Canada
2/Lt	Palmer, Harold James	625 Admirals Road, Esquimalt, British Columbia	Canada
2/Lt	Paton, George	Box 1024, Johannesburg	South Africa
2/Lt	Perrins, Arnold Mansfield	Vancouver, British Columbia	Canada
2/Lt	Phelan, William Lawrence	Lanarck, Ontario	Canada
2/Lt	Phoeney, Harold Henry	Halifax, Nova Scotia	Canada
Lieut	Pinkerton, Harold	Pinkerton, Ontario	Canada
2/Lt	Plamer, Geo. Henry	82 Chestnut St., Everett, Massachusetts	USA

2/Lt	Porteous, Thomas Clifford	45 Orchard Avenue, Waban, Massachusetts	USA
2/Lt	Pursel, Harry Llewellyn	Niagara Falls	Canada
2/Lt	Ramage, John	Queen Street, Outtshorn, Cape Province	South Africa
2/Lt	Richards, Robert Lamplough	35 Havelock, Port Elizabeth	South Africa
2/Lt	Riley, R. T.	24 Central Road, Bucansfield	South Africa
2/Lt	Robertson, George David R.	2 Petrolia, Ontario	Canada
2/Lt	Robinson, Roy B.	68 Chatham St., Windsor	Canada
2/Lt	Rowland, Lydall	Box 579, Port Elizabeth	South Africa
2/Lt	Rutherford, Leslie Earle	Brumley, Johannesburg	South Africa
2/Lt	Saffery, William Ambrose	Humansdorp, Cape Province	South Africa
2/Lt	Sangster, Leslie Innis	66 London St., Sherbrook, Quebec	Canada
2/Lt	Saunders, William	219 St James Street, S. St Marie, Ontario	Canada
2/Lt	Shannon, John Shand	S.A.R. Bloemfontein	South Africa
Major	Shaw, Harry Turner	Terang	Australia
2/Lt	Shipp, Leslie Fred	Station Master, East Rand Station, Transvaal	South Africa
2/Lt	Simon, Herbert	Box 195, Pretoria	South Africa
2/Lt	Smith, Arthur Burton	1104 Grant Avenue West, Collingwood, New Jersey	USA
2/Lt	Smith, Ernest Edward	Benoni	South Africa

THE LAST PARADE, 1919

2/Lt	Snee, Bernard	Vancouver	Canada
2/Lt	Spencer, William Arcourt	4 Kimberly Terrace, East London	South Africa
2/Lt	Staples, Walter Gordon	26 Memorial Road	South Africa
Lieut	Stead, Ivan Oliver	c/o Cox & Co., Pretoria	South Africa
2/Lt	Steeds, Eric Herbert	Box 1198, Johannesburg	South Africa
2/Lt	Stephens, Jas. Russel	24 St Arnant S., Mabyern, Johannesburg	South Africa
2/Lt	Stroud, George Levi	Woodville, Ontario	Canada
2/Lt	Sutton, John George	Barberton, Transvaal	South Africa
2/Lt	Sweeney, William P.	917 Hornby St., Vancouver	Canada
2/Lt	Tainton, Cecil John S.	Nahoon, East London	South Africa
2/Lt	Tarr, Raymond Kimball	Wenham, Massachusetts	USA
2/Lt	Taylor, Douglas Norton	Alui, Cape Province	South Africa
Lieut	Thornton, Charles Price	Moose Jaw, Saskatchewan	Canada
2/Lt	Thurman, Percy Clement	Fairview, Via Maclear	South Africa
2/Lt	Tilney, Robert John	Bredasthorpe, Cape Province	South Africa
2/Lt	Vanderburgh, Alfred Wharron	Summerland, British Columbia	Canada
2/Lt	Vaughan, Gerald	Mount Pleasant, Pearl	South Africa
2/Lt	Villis, Thomas Alfred	Stapleton, New York City	USA

2/Lt	Waddell, Henry Rex	Port Lambton, Ontario		Canada
2/Lt	Wallace, Howard Vincent	297 Chebucto Road, Halifax		Canada
2/Lt	Warburton, Herbert George	10 Hutcheson St., Christchurch		New Zealand
2/Lt	Waters, Albert Victor	111 Rainsford Road, Toronto, Ontario		Canada
Capt	Watkins, Arthur Bernard	Sydney, New South Wales		Australia
2/Lt	Watt, Maitland	Vinemouth, Ontario		Canada
2/Lt	Wayland, Douglas Charles	Fort Richmond, Belmont, Cape Province		South Africa
2/Lt	Weeding, John	Toronto		Canada
2/Lt	Whiskin, Frank	Regina		Canada
2/Lt	Whitehouse, Arthur George	Livingstone, New Jersey		USA
2/Lt	Wilcox, James Furnival	133 Milton, Nanaimo, British Columbia		Canada
2/Lt	Woodhouse, Walter Leonard	1043 St. Patrick St., Victoria, British Columbia		Canada
2/Lt	Wrigglesworth, George Albert	Didsbury, Alberta		Canada
2/Lt	Wright, Arthur	19 Quinn St.		South Africa
2/Lt	Wright, Cecil Wynne	Box 12, Koffyfontein		South Africa

Notes

Introduction

1. See Maryam Philpott, *Air and Sea Power in World War I: Combat and Experience in the Royal Flying Corps and the Royal Navy* (London, 2013), pp. 173–4.
2. Ralph Barker, *The Royal Flying Corps in France: From Bloody April 1917 to Final Victory* (London, 1995), p. 235.
3. Sir Walter Raleigh, *The War in the Air: Being the Story of the Part Played in the Great War by the Royal Air Force*, Vol. 1 (London, 1922), pp. 446–7. The Royal Flying Corps, as constituted in 1912, had a Military Wing and a Naval Wing but when the latter was renamed the Royal Naval Air Service (RNAS) by the Admiralty, the Military Wing gained the Corps appellation. The original Military and Naval Wings would be reunited when the RFC and the RNAS were combined to form the Royal Air Force in 1918.
4. W.B. Yeats, 'An Irish Airman Foresees His Death', in *The Wild Swans at Coole* (New York, 1919).
5. Malcolm Cooper, *The Birth of Independent Air Power: British Air Policy in the First World War* (London, 1986), p. 71.
6. See Mark Bostridge, *The Fateful Year: England 1914* (London, 2014), p. 111.
7. Lord Hugh Cecil, 'The Royal Flying Corps: The work and training of the Royal Flying Corps', *The London Illustrated News* (London, 1918), p. 5.
8. Joshua Levine, *On a Wing and a Prayer: The Untold Story of the Pioneering Aviation Heroes of WWI, in Their Own Words* (London, 2008), p. 63.
9. Enacted by the 1931 Statute of Westminster.
10. In July 1917, Sir David Henderson had made a similar recommendation: 'It is difficult to indicate any method of overcoming the present illogical situation of divided responsibility in aeronautics, except by the formation of a complete department and a complete united service dealing with all operations in the air.' Centre for Air Power Studies, 'Appendix I: Memorandum on the organization of the Air Services', *Air Power Review*, Special Edition, Spring (2013), pp. 138–9.

NOTES

11 In response to the raids on London by German Gotha bombers in 1917, it was envisaged that the RAF would become a bomber force capable of mounting retaliatory raids on Germany. See John James, *The Paladins: A Social History of the RAF up to the Outbreak of World War II* (London, 1990), pp. 61–5; David Lloyd George, *War Memoirs of David Lloyd George*, Vol. 2 (London, 1933), p. 1108; and Michael Paris, 'The rise of the airmen: The origins of air force elitism, c. 1890–1918', *Journal of Contemporary History* xxviii/1 (1993), pp. 123–4.
12 Malcolm Cooper, 'Blueprint for confusion: The administrative background to the formation of the Royal Air Force, 1912–1919', *Journal of Contemporary History* xxii/3 (1987), p. 447.
13 Lieutenant Stanley A. Rutledge, *Pen Pictures from the Trenches* (Toronto, 1918), https://archive.org/stream/penpicturesfromt00rutluoft#page/n5/mode/2up, p. 135. See also 'Canada, Ledgers of CEF Officers Transferring to Royal Flying Corps, 1915–1919', www.ancestry.co.uk.
14 'Mr. Lloyd George on his task', *The Times*, 25 November 1918, p. 13.
15 Mark David Sheftall, *Altered Memories of the Great War: Divergent Narratives of Britain, Australia, New Zealand and Canada* (London, 2009), p. 3.
16 'Ave, Frater, Atque Vale!', in 2nd Lieutenant Howard Wallace (ed.), *Parti Patter: Being Serious and Smiling Chatter about a Number of Globe Trotters Awaiting the Word to Race for Home* (Grantham, 1919), p. 2.
17 Quoting the Roman poet Horace: 'It is sweet and fitting to die for one's country.'
18 See Philpott, *Combat and Experience*, pp. 174–5 and p. 173.
19 Paris, 'Elitism', p. 124.
20 Paris, 'Elitism', p. 124.
21 Philpott, *Combat and Experience*, p. 171.
22 Christine Berberich, *The Image of the English Gentleman in Twentieth Century Literature: Englishness and Nostalgia* (Aldershot, 2007), p. 8.
23 Martin Petter, 'Temporary gentlemen in the aftermath of the Great War: Rank, status and the ex-officer problem', *Historical Journal* xxxvii/1 (1994), p. 131.
24 Chester Kirby, *The English Country Gentleman: A Study of Nineteenth Century Types* (London, 1937), p. 221.
25 Berberich, *English Gentleman*, p. 54. See also David Edgerton, *England and the Aeroplane: Militarism, Modernity and Machines* (London, 2013), p. 18.
26 'Valedictory', *Parti Patter*, p. 1.
27 Elizabeth O'Kiely, *Gentleman Air Ace: The Duncan Bell-Irving Story* (Madeira Park, 1992), p. 63.
28 Joshua Levine, *Fighter Heroes of WWI: The Extraordinary Story of the Pioneering Airmen of the Great War* (London, 2009), p. 186.
29 Kirby, *English Country Gentleman*, pp. 250–1.
30 Rutledge, *Pen Pictures*, pp. 146 and 147.
31 Cecil, 'Flying Corps', p. 4.
32 Levine, *Fighter Heroes of WWI*, p. 186, and Paris, 'Elitism', p. 125.

NOTES

33 See Hildebidle quoted in Berberich, *English Gentleman*, p. 54.
34 Patrick Bishop, *Wings: The RAF at War, 1912–2012* (London, 2013), p. 28.
35 See Peter Parker quoted in Berberich, *English Gentleman*, p. 54.
36 Berberich, *English Gentleman*, p. 54.
37 Bishop, *Wings*, p. 63.
38 'The Ladies – God Bless 'Em!', *Parti Patter*, p. 22.
39 Peter G. Cooksley, *Royal Flying Corps Handbook, 1914–1918* (Stroud, 2007), p. ix.
40 Alan Rowe, 'The RE8 controversy revisited', *The '14-'18 Journal* (2001), p. 68.
41 F.D. Tredrey, *Pioneer Pilot: The Great Smith Barry Who Taught the World How to Fly* (London, 1976), p. 7, and Ralph Barker, *The Royal Flying Corps in France: From Mons to the Somme* (London, 1994), p. 212.
42 Denis Richards, *Portal of Hungerford: The Life of Marshal of the Royal Air Force Viscount Portal of Hungerford* (London, 1977), pp. 71–2.
43 Richards, *Portal*, p. 72.
44 'Harlaxton Manor', *Parti Patter*, p. 7. Sadly, none of Thomas Pearson Gregory's personal papers for the period 1914–18 have been found by the author and are presumed lost.
45 'A glance in the mirror. While affixing that civvy tie', *Parti Patter*, p. 21. Lady Diana Manners having flown before the war. See Bostridge, *Fateful Year*, p. 106. The aerodrome at Harlaxton would have been visible from Belvoir Castle.
46 'Harlaxton', *Parti Patter*, p. 7.
47 A.H. Cobby, *High Adventure* (Melbourne, 1981), p. 35.
48 'A Princely CO', *Parti Patter*, p. 14.

Chapter 1: Poor Bloody Observers and Aerial Reconnaissance

1 David Lloyd George, *War Memoirs of David Lloyd George*, Vol. 2 (London, 1933), p. 1105, and Kenneth Munson, *Bombers, 1914–1919: Patrol and Reconnaissance Aircraft* (London, 1972), pp. 104–5. Hence the call for an independent air service to fly retaliatory bombing raids against Germany.
2 'Aeroplanes in war: The government's scheme', *The Times*, 13 April 1913, p. 7.
3 Centre for Air Power Studies, 'Training Manual, Royal Flying Corps, Part II [Military Wing]', *Air Power Review*, Special Edition, Spring (2013), p. 109.
4 James McCudden, VC, *Flying Fury: Five Years in the Royal Flying Corps* (Elstree, 1987), p. 18.
5 Centre for Air Power Studies, 'Training Manual', p. 110.
6 Denis Richards, *Portal of Hungerford: The Life of Marshal of the Royal Air Force Viscount Portal of Hungerford* (London, 1977), p. 39.

NOTES

7   Munson, *Bombers*, p. 130. See also Peter Fearon, 'The formative years of the British aircraft industry, 1913–1924', *The Business History Review* xliii/4 (1969), p. 481.
8   Alistair Smith, *Images of War: Royal Flying Corps: Rare Photographs from Wartime Archives* (Barnsley, 2002), p. 10. The Royal Aircraft Factory also developed the 'SE' or Scouting Experimental series which would culminate in the superb SE5a.
9   Mark Bostridge, *The Fateful Year: England 1914* (London, 2014), p. 111.
10 'Aeroplanes in war', p. 7.
11 'Aeroplanes in war', p. 7.
12 'Royal Flying Corps. The Military Wing', *The Times*, 16 April 1912, p. 5.
13 'Aeroplanes in war', p. 7.
14 'Aeroplanes in war', p. 7, and Sir Walter Raleigh, *The War in the Air: Being the Story of the Part Played in the Great War by the Royal Air Force*, Vol. 1 (London, 1922), pp. 203–4.
15 'Dispatch received by the Secretary of State for War from the Field-Marshal Commanding-in-Chief, British Forces in the Field', *The London Gazette*, 8 September 1914, p. 7192, https://www.thegazette.co.uk/London/issue/28897/supplement/7189 and Raleigh, *War in the Air*, p. 323.
16 Richards, *Portal*, p. 39.
17 Patrick Bishop, *Wings: The RAF at War, 1912–2012* (London, 2013), p. 56.
18 Bishop, *Wings*, p. 56 and p. 69. Between March and November 1915, five wings were formed.
19 Robert F. Grattan, *The Origins of Air War: The Development of Military Air Strategy in the First World War* (London, 2009), pp. 26–7.
20 Michael Armitage, *The Royal Air Force: An Illustrated History* (London, 1993), p. 13.
21 Armitage, *Illustrated History*, p. 13.
22 Grattan, *Origins*, p. 35.
23 Raleigh, *War in the Air*, p. 234.
24 Centre for Air Power Studies, 'Training Manual', p. 110.
25 David Stevenson, *With Our Backs to the Wall: Victory and Defeat* (London, 2011), p. 178, and David Stevenson, *1914–1918: The History of the First World War* (London, 2005), p. 190.
26 Centre for Air Power Studies, 'Training Manual', p. 110.
27 Centre for Air Power Studies, 'Training Manual', p. 114.
28 See McCudden, *Flying Fury*, p. 55. Oswald Watt (see Chapter 6) flew a Maurice Farman 'Shorthorn' with an observer armed with a rifle. Portal flew a Morane which was unable to carry both a Lewis Gun, 'and me and in consequence I always went up with a stripped rifle and 100 rounds of .303', Richards, *Portal*, p. 42.
29 Centre for Air Power Studies, 'Training Manual', p. 114.
30 See Bishop, *Wings*, p. 69; Joshua Levine, *Fighter Heroes of WWI: The Extraordinary Story of the Pioneering Airmen of the Great War* (London, 2009), p. 168; and McCudden, *Flying Fury*, pp. 69–70.

NOTES

31 Munson, *Bombers*, p. 130. See also Kenneth Munson, *Fighters, 1914–1919: Attack and Training Aircraft* (London, 1971), p. 13. Airframe production was relatively easy to expand as any firm working with wood could follow the drawing provided, but throughout the war 'there was a bottleneck in [aero] engine production'. Fearon, 'Formative years', p. 484.
32 Ralph Barker, *The Royal Flying Corps in France: From Bloody April 1917 to Final Victory* (London, 1995), p. 36, and Munson, *Bombers*, p. 134. Concerns regarding the handling qualities of the RE8 are discussed in a subsequent chapter.
33 'Wing Adjutant' (W.T.B.), *The Royal Flying Corps in the War* (London, 1918), p. 6.
34 © AWM, Frederic Cutlack, 'Appendix No. 5, AFC Training in England', in *Official History of Australia in the War of 1914–1918. Vol. 8: The Australian Flying Corps in the Western and Eastern Theatres of War, 1914–1918* (11th edition, 1941), www.awm.gov.au/histories/first_world_war/AWMOHWW1/AIF/Vol8, p. 431.
35 Lord Hugh Cecil, 'The Royal Flying Corps: The work and training of the Royal Flying Corps', *The London Illustrated News* (London, 1918), p. 6.
36 Lieutenant Colonel William A. Bishop, *Winged Warfare* (London, 1975), p. 24.
37 Bishop, *Winged Warfare*, pp. 24–5.
38 Cecil, 'Flying Corps', p. 6, and Geoffrey Norris, *The Royal Flying Corps: A History* (London, 1965), p. 115. The recreated front line at Harlaxton may also have played a role in the development of Artillery Training Maps. See reference to Harlaxton in Peter Chasseud, 'Artillery Training Maps of the U.K. 1914–1918, Part II: The 1:20,000 Series (GSGS 2748)', *Sheetlines*, Nos 11 to 14 (undated), p. 13.
39 © AWM, Cutlack, 'Training in England', p. 431. This involved passing an additional test in 'Buzzing': Sending and receiving eight words a minute on a buzzer.
40 Raleigh, *War in the Air*, p. 350.
41 Stevenson, *Backs to the Wall*, p. 208. See also Stevenson, *1914–1918*, pp. 190–1.
42 Albert P. Palazzo, 'The British Army's Counter-Battery Staff Office and control of the enemy in World War I', *The Journal of Military History* lxiii/1 (1999), p. 57 and p. 62.
43 'UK, Citations of the Distinguished Conduct Medal, 1914–1920' and 'All British Army WWI Service Records, 1914–1920', www.ancestry.co.uk.
44 Barker, *April 1917 to Final Victory*, p. 190. See also Stevenson, *Backs to the Wall*, p. 174.
45 Royal Flying Corps, *Royal Flying Corps Technical Notes, 1916* (Reprinted, London, 1968), pp. 7–8.
46 Centre for Air Power Studies, 'Training Manual', p. 110.
47 Centre for Air Power Studies, 'Training Manual', p. 110.
48 Richards, *Portal*, p. 47; Raleigh, *War in the Air*, p. 447; Norris, *Royal Flying Corps*, p. 146. The arrival, in 1916, of new fighters grouped together into

specialist fighter squadrons, coupled to the phasing out of general, multi-purpose squadrons, with their mix of aeroplanes, allowed for changing tactics with the faster fighting-scouts patrolling in mutually supporting pairs above the slower reconnaissance machines. See Maryam Philpott, *Air and Sea Power in World War I: Combat and Experience in the Royal Flying Corps and the Royal Navy* (London, 2013), p. 112, and Armitage, *Illustrated History*, p. 16.

49 Armitage, *Illustrated History*, p. 13.
50 Grattan, *Origins*, p. 147.
51 Sir Robert Thompson, *The Royal Flying Corps: Per Ardua ad Astra* (London, 1968), p. 107.
52 Barker, *April 1917 to Final Victory*, p. 126.
53 Barker, *April 1917 to Final Victory*, p. 126, which is why, in 1918, signalling, photography and artillery-spotting were all included in Brian Garrett's pilot training at Harlaxton. Captain B.F. Garrett, 'Pilot's Flying Log Book' (unpublished), pp. 8–9. Extracts quoted with the kind permission of Roger Bragger.
54 Cecil, 'Flying Corps', p. 6.
55 'Alexander Griffiths, Interview 18th January 1993', Acc.No. S01644/ Australian War Memorial, www.awm.gov.au/transcripts/s01644_tran.htm.
56 Barker, *April 1917 to Final Victory*, p. 125 and p. 123.
57 A.G.J. Whitehouse, *Hell in the Heavens: The Adventures of an Aerial Gunner in the Royal Flying Corps* (London, 1938), pp. 47–8. See also Michael Paris, *Winged Warfare: The Literature and Theory of Aerial Warfare in Britain, 1859–1917* (Manchester, 1992), p. 224. A notable exception being Major James McCudden VC, who joined the RFC as a mechanic.
58 Elizabeth O'Kiely, *Gentleman Air Ace: The Duncan Bell-Irving Story* (Madeira Park, 1992), p. 62.
59 O'Kiely, *Gentleman Air Ace*, p. 61.
60 Sergeant Gunner/Observer Albert Curtis, 'Record of Service' (unpublished). Extracts quoted with the kind permission of Phyllis E. Bujak.
61 Curtis, 'Record of Service' (unpublished).
62 David Edgerton, *England and the Aeroplane: Militarism, Modernity and Machines* (London, 2013), p. 80, and C.G. Jefford, *Observers and Navigators and Other Non-Pilot Aircrew in the RFC, RNAS and RAF* (Shrewsbury, 2001), p. 97.
63 Jefford, *Observers and Navigators*, p. 98.
64 Rutledge, *Pen Pictures*, p. 87.
65 Jefford, quoting Major K.R. Park, OC No. 48 Squadron, *Observers and Navigators*, p. 100. See also p. 98.
66 Ian Mackersey, *No Empty Chairs: The Short and Heroic Lives of the Young Aviators Who Fought and Died in the First World War* (London, 2012), pp. 190–1.
67 Raleigh, *War in the Air*, p. 204.
68 Mackersey, *No Empty Chairs*, p. 190.
69 George Jones, *From Private to Air Marshal: The Autobiography of Air Marshal Sir George Jones* (Richmond, Australia, 1988), p. 14. In the early

years of the Corps it often helped to have acquired, privately, a Royal Aero Club ticket: Mackersey, *No Empty Chairs*, p. 58.
70. If an observer was killed or wounded, the pilot usually got home, but if the pilot was killed or wounded the chances of an observer/gunner getting home were 100:1 against: Whitehouse, *Hell in the Heavens*, pp. 46–7.
71. Grattan, *Origins*, p. 249.
72. John Sweetman, *Cavalry of the Clouds: Air War over Europe, 1914–1918* (Stroud, 2010), p. 10, quoting Cecil Lewis.
73. Curtis, 'Record of Service' (unpublished).
74. Curtis, 'Record of Service' (unpublished).
75. Philpott, *Combat and Experience*, p. 110.

Chapter 2: Reckless Fellows and Aerial Superiority

1. Sir Walter Raleigh, *The War in the Air: Being the Story of the Part Played in the Great War by the Royal Air Force*, Vol. 1 (London, 1922), p. 293.
2. Norman Franks, *Dog-Fight: Aerial Tactics of the Aces of WWI* (London, 2003), p. 54.
3. Robert F. Grattan, *The Origins of Air War: The Development of Military Air Strategy in World War One* (London, 2009), p. 26.
4. Raleigh, *War in the Air*, p. 436 and p. 449.
5. Malcolm Cooper, *The Birth of Independent Air Power: British Air Policy in the First World War* (London, 1986), p. 148. However, given the RFC's pursuit of the offensive, Cooper has calculated that whilst the number of Corps squadrons plateaued in 1917, by 1918, the number of Army squadrons had doubled.
6. Raleigh, *War in the Air*, p. 436.
7. Raleigh, *War in the Air*, p. 436.
8. Raleigh, *War in the Air*, p. 434.
9. Peter Gray, 'The Air Ministry and the formation of the Royal Air Force', in Gary Sheffield and Peter Gray (eds), *Changing War: The British Army, The Hundred Days Campaign and the Birth of the Royal Air Force, 1918* (London, 2013), p. 137, and Grattan, *Origins*, p. 34. The Ministry of Munitions also took over the Royal Aircraft Factory at Farnborough.
10. David Lloyd George, *War Memoirs of David Lloyd George*, Vol. 2 (London, 1933), p. 1103. See also John Sweetman, 'Crucial months for survival: The Royal Air Force, 1918–1919', *Journal of Contemporary History* xix/iii (1984), p. 529; Malcolm Cooper, 'Blueprint for confusion: The administrative background to the formation of the Royal Air Force, 1912–1919', *Journal of Contemporary History* xxii/3 (1987), p. 443; and John James, *The Paladins: A Social History of the RAF up to the Outbreak of World War II* (London, 1990), pp. 61–2.

NOTES

11 See Christopher Luck, 'The Smuts Report: Interpreting and misinterpreting the promise of air power', in Gary Sheffield and Peter Gray (eds), *Changing War: The British Army, The Hundred Days Campaign and the Birth of the Royal Air Force, 1918* (London, 2013), p. 157.
12 Lloyd George, *War Memoirs*, p. 1103, and Ralph Barker, *The Royal Flying Corps in France: From Bloody April 1917 to Final Victory* (London, 1995), p. 5.
13 Barker, *April 1917 to Final Victory*, p. 201.
14 Kenneth Munson, *Fighters, 1914–1919: Attack and Training Aircraft* (London, 1971), p. 99, and Maryam Philpott, *Air and Sea Power in World War I: Combat and Experience in the Royal Flying Corps and the Royal Navy* (London, 2013), p. 110.
15 William Philpott, *Bloody Victory: The Sacrifice on the Somme* (London, 2009), p. 268; Kenneth Munson, *Bombers, 1914–1919: Patrol and Reconnaissance Aircraft* (London, 1972), pp. 134–6; and Munson, *Fighters*, p. 13.
16 This was a far more effective tactic than having a 'cluster of escorts for each reconnaissance flight': Bishop, *Wings*, p. 77.
17 Philpott, *Combat and Experience*, p. 111.
18 Philpott, *Combat and Experience*, p. 110.
19 Philpott, *Combat and Experience*, p. 111.
20 Raleigh, *War in the Air*, p. 441.
21 Philpott, *Combat and Experience*, p. 111.
22 David Stevenson, *1914–1918: The History of the First World War* (London, 2005), p. 191.
23 Peter Dye, 'The genesis of modern warfare: The contribution of aviation logistics', in Gary Sheffield and Peter Gray (eds), *Changing War: The British Army, the Hundred Days Campaign and the Birth of the Royal Air Force, 1918* (London, 2013), p. 186.
24 Philpott, *Bloody Victory*, p. 268. Although, according to Stevenson, in the opening phases of the battle the RFC was committed to driving the Germans out of their airspace, 'even if this meant neglecting the defence of British spotter aircraft and accepting punishing casualties': Stevenson, *1914–1918*, p. 191.
25 Philpott, *Bloody Victory*, p. 268.
26 Vincent Orange, 'Trenchard, Hugh Montague, first Viscount Trenchard [1873–1956]', *Oxford Dictionary of National Biography* (Oxford, 2004; Online Edition 2011), www.oxforddnb.com/view/article/36552.
27 Stevenson *1914–1918*, p. 191.
28 Peter Hart, *Somme Success: The Royal Flying Corps and the Battle of the Somme, 1916* (Barnsley, 2001), p. 222.
29 Lieutenant Stanley A. Rutledge, *Pen Pictures from the Trenches* (Toronto, 1918), https://archive.org/stream/penpicturesfromt00rutluoft#page/n5/mode/2up/, pp. 45–7.
30 Christopher Shores, Norman Franks and Russell Guest, *Above the Trenches: A Complete Record of the Fighter Aces and Units of the British Empire*

NOTES

    Air Forces, 1915–1920 (Stoney Creek, Ontario, 1990), p. 16. See also Munson, *Fighters*, pp. 100, 113 and 116–17.

31 Raleigh, *War in the Air*, p. 450, and Christopher Cole (ed.), *Royal Flying Corps, 1915–1916* (London, 1969), p. 334 and p. 312.
32 Cole, *Flying Corps*, p. 334, and Grattan, *Origins*, p. 26.
33 Barker, *April 1917 to Final Victory*, p. 6 and p. 201. See also Peter Hart, *Bloody April: Slaughter in the Skies over Arras, 1917* (London, 2005), p. 101.
34 Munson, *Fighters*, pp. 144 and 146.
35 Arthur Gould Lee, *No Parachute: A Classic Account of War in the Air in WWI in Letters Written in 1917 by Lieutenant A.S.G. Lee, Sherwood Foresters, Attached Royal Flying Corps* (London, 2013), p. 18.
36 Barker, *April 1917 to Final Victory*, p. 7. The 'Pup', with one machine gun, was out-gunned by the twin machine guns of the Albatros. By contrast, the SE5a mounted a forward-firing Vickers machine gun and a Lewis machine gun on the top wing, whilst the Camel had twin forward-firing Vickers machine guns.
37 John Keegan, *The First World War* (London, 1999), p. 386.
38 Barker, *April 1917 to Final Victory*, p. 50.
39 Shores, Franks and Guest, *Above the Trenches*, p. 17.
40 Lee, *No Parachute*, p. 22.
41 Lee, *No Parachute*, p. 22, and Franks, *Dog-Fight*, pp. 149–50.
42 Raleigh, *War in the Air*, p. 451.
43 Christine Berberich, *The Image of the English Gentleman in Twentieth Century Literature: Englishness and Nostalgia* (Aldershot, 2007), p. 54.
44 Berberich, *English Gentleman*, p. 54.
45 Lee, *No Parachute*, p. 3.
46 Barker, *April 1917 to Final Victory*, p. 48.
47 Denis Richards, *Portal of Hungerford: The Life of Marshal of the Royal Air Force Viscount Portal of Hungerford* (London, 1977), p. 60.
48 Rutledge, *Pen Pictures*, p. 132.
49 Michael Paris, 'The rise of the airmen: The origins of air force elitism, c. 1890–1918', *Journal of Contemporary History* xxviii/1 (1993), p. 124.
50 Rutledge, *Pen Pictures*, p. 134.
51 Rutledge, *Pen Pictures*, pp. 132–3.
52 Michael Armitage, *The Royal Air Force: An Illustrated History* (London, 1993), p. 17, and Robert Thompson, *The Royal Flying Corps: Per Ardua ad Astra* (London, 1968), p. 106.
53 Lord Hugh Cecil, 'The Royal Flying Corps: The work and training of the Royal Flying Corps', *The London Illustrated News* (London, 1918), p. 4.
54 Geoffrey Norris, *The Royal Flying Corps: A History* (London, 1965), p. 241; five 'kills' conferred the title of 'ace': Terry Treadwell and Alan C. Wood, *The Royal Flying Corps* (Stroud, 2000), p. 66.
55 Norris, *Flying Corps*, p. 241.
56 'Heroes of the Air', *The West Australian*, 10 June 1919, http://trove.nla.gov.au/ndp/del/article/27607366.

NOTES

57 'Heroes of the Air', trove.nla.gov.au/27607366, and Norman Franks, *SE5/5a Aces of World War I* (Oxford, 2007), p. 43. See also Norman Franks, *Sopwith Camel Aces of World War One* (Oxford, 2003), p. 72.
58 Grattan, *Origins*, p. 35. For details of the training programme in Canada, see C.W. Hunt, *Dancing in the Sky: The Royal Flying Corps in Canada* (Toronto, 2009), pp. 109–28.
59 Elizabeth O'Kiely, *Gentleman Air Ace: The Duncan Bell-Irving Story* (Madeira Park, 1992), pp. 179–80.
60 'Canada, Soldiers of the First World War, 1914–1918', www.ancestry.co.uk, having joined up in 1915.
61 O'Kiely, *Gentleman Air Ace*, p. 179.
62 O'Kiely, *Gentleman Air Ace*, p. 179.
63 Ian Mackersey, *No Empty Chairs: The Short and Heroic Lives of the Young Aviators Who Fought and Died in the First World War* (London, 2012), p. 58.
64 John H. Morrow, *The Great War in the Air: Military Aviation from 1909 to 1921* (Shrewsbury, 1993), p. 241.
65 Morrow, *War in the Air*, pp. 240 and 241.
66 Ralph Barker, *A Brief History of the Royal Flying Corps in WWI* (London, 2002), p. 21.
67 'A Unique Career', *Parti Patter*, p. 17 and 'British Army Medal Rolls Index Cards, 1914–1920', www.ancestry.co.uk. The date of his field commission was 14 January 1915. According to *Parti Patter* he attained the rank of regimental sergeant major (RSM) in the Royal Irish Fusiliers.
68 *Parti Patter* states that No. 16 Squadron was based at Harlaxton.
69 'A Princely C.O.', *Parti Patter*, p. 14.
70 'His Send Off to Us', *Parti Patter*, p. 15.
71 Lee Kennett, *The First Air War, 1914–1918* (New York, 1991), p. 119, and Berberich, *Literary Gentleman*, p. 54.
72 Mackersey, *No Empty Chairs*, p. 58.
73 Morrow, *War in the Air*, p. 241.
74 Kennett, *Air War*, p. 119.
75 Rutledge, *Pen Pictures*, p. 137, and Bishop, *Wings*, p. 110.
76 Rutledge, *Pen Pictures*, p. 137.
77 'His Send Off to Us', *Parti Patter*, p. 15.
78 Patrick Bishop, *Wings: The RAF at War, 1912–2012* (London, 2013), p. 110, and Kennett, *Air War*, p. 136.
79 'His Send Off to Us', *Parti Patter*, p. 15.
80 Philpott, *Combat and Experience*, p. 182, and Morrow, *War in the Air*, p. 241.
81 Cecil, 'Flying Corps', pp. 4–5.
82 Lloyd George, *War Memoirs*, p. 1115.
83 Morrow, *War in the Air*, p. 241.
84 Morrow, *War in the Air*, p. 241.
85 Morrow, *War in the Air*, p. 241. See also John Sweetman, *Cavalry of the Clouds: Air War over Europe, 1914–1918* (Stroud, 2010), p. 11.

NOTES

86 David Edgerton, *England and the Aeroplane: Militarism, Modernity and Machines* (London, 2013), p. 83.
87 Raymond Collishaw quoted in Morrow, *War in the Air*, p. 242.
88 See Joanna Bourke, *Dismembering the Male: Men's Bodies, Britain and the Great War* (London, 1996), p. 28.
89 Arthur Gould Lee quoted in Morrow, *War in the Air*, 241.
90 Morrow, *War in the Air*, p. 241.
91 Bishop, *Wings*, p. 30.
92 Leslie McNab, 'Diary' (unpublished). Extracts quoted with the kind permission of the McNab family.
93 Raleigh, *War in the Air*, p. 443.
94 Raleigh, *War in the Air*, p. 441.

Chapter 3: Young Icarus and Flight Training

1 Courtesy of Mick Davis. See also T.N. Hancock, *Bomber County: A History of the Royal Air Force in Lincolnshire* (Lincoln, 1978), p. 118. N.B. The designation Reserve Squadron was adopted in January 1916, previously, training units were designated Reserve aeroplane squadrons. See also Michael J.F. Bowyer, *Actions Stations Revisited: The Complete History of Britain's Military Airfields. No. 1: Eastern England* (Manchester, 2000), p. 204, and Leslie Hunt, 'Flying round Grantham', *Lincolnshire Life*, September 1998, p. 22.
2 Courtesy of Mick Davis and Hancock, *Bomber County*, p. 118.
3 Courtesy of Mick Davis. See also George Jones, *From Private to Air Marshal: The Autobiography of Air Marshal Sir George Jones* (Richmond, Australia, 1988), pp. 13–14, who also refers to Henri Farmans being used in training. Hancock also indicates the squadron used RE8, DH4, FK3, BE2 and DH6 machines: Hancock, *Bomber Country*, p. 118.
4 Geoffrey Norris, *The Royal Flying Corps: A History* (London, 1965), p. 202, and Robert F. Grattan, *The Origins of Air War: The Development of Military Air Strategy in World War One* (London, 2009), p. 35. See also Ray Sturtivant and John Hamlin, *Royal Air Force Flying Training and Support Units since 1912* (Trowbridge, 2007), p. 6.
5 Ray Sturtivant, *The History of Britain's Military Training Aircraft* (Yeovil, 1987), p. 22, and Peter G. Cooksley, *Royal Flying Corps Handbook, 1914–1918* (Stroud, 2007), p. 22.
6 Ralph Barker, *The Royal Flying Corps in France: From Bloody April 1917 to Final Victory* (London, 1995), p. 6. In January 1917, this was raised to 97 Reserve squadrons: Sturtivant and Hamlin, *Training and Support*, p. 6.
7 Cooksley, *Handbook*, p. 23.
8 Sturtivant and Hamlin, *Training and Support*, p. 6, Geoff Gardiner, *Airfield Focus 17: Spittlegate* (Peterborough, 1994), p. 3, and Grattan, *Origins*,

NOTES

p. 36. The Group Commands were, in turn, divided into 3 or 4 Reserve wings: Sturtivant, *Military Training*, p. 22.

9 Mike Osborne, *Defending Lincolnshire: A Military History from Conquest to Cold War* (Stroud, 2010), p. 127.

10 Hancock, *Bomber County*, p. 11.

11 Hancock, *Bomber County*, p. 13, and Gardiner, *Spittlegate*, p. 3. In 1918, Harlaxton and No. 24 Wing became part of the new No. 12 (Training) Group in No. 3 Area (which replaced the Northern Training Brigade). This became the Midland Area Command in May 1918. Gardiner, *Spittlegate*, p. 4, and Sturtivant and Hamlin, *Training and Support*, p. 7. In January 1918, Robert Smith Barry was given the temporary rank of Brigadier-General and given command of the Northern Training Brigade, which included Cranwell, Spittlegate, Harlaxton, South Carlton, Scampton and Waddington, each aerodrome being commanded by a brigadier: F.D. Tredrey, *Pioneer Pilot: The Great Smith Barry Who Taught the World How to Fly* (London, 1976), pp. 79 and 81. He relinquished this command in February 1918.

12 Leslie McNab, 'Diary' (unpublished). Extracts quoted with the kind permission of the McNab family.

13 'Ministry of Munitions. By direction of the Disposal Board (Huts and Building Materials Section)', *Grantham Journal*, October 30 1920, p. 3. Water was piped to the aerodrome along a new water main running along Gorse Lane and The Great North Road to Thompson's Malting in Grantham: 'Grantham Town Council', *Grantham Journal*, 5 February 1921, p. 8, and 'Grantham Rural District Council', *Grantham Journal*, 7 October 1922, p. 8.

14 Mick Davis and Bill Morgan, 'Gazetteer of flying sites, Part 9. Gai-Har', *Cross and Cockade International* xliii/1 (2012), GFS-72 and Osborne, *Defending Lincolnshire*, p. 127.

15 Davis and Morgan, 'Gai-Har', GFS-72.

16 Patrick Offer, *Lincolnshire Airfields in the Second World War* (Newbury, 1996), p. 81.

17 'Wing Adjutant' (W.T.B.), *The Royal Flying Corps in the War* (London, 1918), pp. 9–10.

18 Arthur Gould Lee, *Open Cockpit: A Pilot of the Royal Flying Corps* (London, 1969; Reprinted 2013), p. 33.

19 Patrick Bishop, *Wings: The RAF at War, 1912–2012* (London, 2013), p. 29. See also 'Royal Aero Club Aviator's Certificate', rafmuseum.org.uk, and John Blake, 'A Brief History of the Royal Aero Club', www.royal-aeroclub.co.uk.

20 Nigel Steel and Peter Hart, *Tumult in the Clouds: The British Experience of the War in the Air, 1914–1918* (London, 1997), p. 87.

21 Elizabeth O'Kiely, *Gentleman Air Ace: The Duncan Bell-Irving Story* (Madeira Park, 1992), pp. 59–60.

22 'Wing Adjutant', *Royal Flying Corps*, p. 11.

23 Sturtivant, *Military Training*, p. 21.

NOTES

24 No. 3 School of Military Aeronautics was formed at Abu Qir (Aboukir) in Egypt in 1916, with No. 4 School being formed at Toronto in 1917: Sturtivant and Hamlin, *Training and Support*, p. 6.
25 Michael Molkentin, *Fire in the Sky: The Australian Flying Corps in the First World War* (Crows Nest, 2010), p. 180.
26 Peter Wright, *The Royal Flying Corps, 1912–1918, in Oxfordshire* (Oxford, 1985), p. 19. This was the course attended by George Jones. Coincidentally, Portal was an alumnus of Christ Church College.
27 'Wing Adjutant', *Royal Flying Corps*, pp. 7–8, and Wright, *Flying Corps*, p. 19.
28 Wright, *Flying Corps*, pp. 20–1.
29 Wright, *Flying Corps*, p. 19; Molkentin, *Fire in the Sky*, p. 182; and R.J. Brownell, *From Khaki to Blue: The Autobiography of Air Commodore R.J. Brownell* (Canberra, 1978), p. 129. However, Alderson suggests that 'newly gazetted officers to the RFC [were] drafted to one of the ground schools': A.G.D. Alderson, *The First War in the Air, 1914–1918* (England, c. 1990), p. 1. By 1918, according to Jefford, a cadet was gazetted as a 2nd lieutenant only after the completion of Stage 'B' of his training programme at a training depot station: C.G. Jefford, *Observers and Navigators and Other Non-Pilot Aircrew in the RFC, RNAS and RAF* (Shrewsbury, 2001), p. 41. This would explain why William Leedham is still wearing the distinctive white flash of the 'Gentleman Cadet' in the photograph taken of him at Harlaxton.
30 Lieutenant Stanley A. Rutledge, *Pen Pictures from the Trenches* (Toronto, 1918), https://archive.org/stream/penpicturesfromt00rutluoft#page/n5/mode/2up/, p. 135.
31 Sturtivant, *Military Training*, p. 22. In the new training environment of 1918, training in 'all through' squadrons was reinstated. See Chapter 7.
32 Central Flying School, *Training Manual, Royal Flying Corps, Part I (Provisional), 1914* (London, 1914), pp. 101–2.
33 *Training Manual*, 1914, pp. 101–2.
34 Sir Walter Raleigh, *The War in the Air: Being the Story of the Part Played in the Great War by the Royal Air Force*, Vol. 1 (London, 1922), p. 441.
35 © IWM (80000015/Reel 1), sound recording of Eric John Furlong.
36 Patrick Bishop, *Wings: The RAF at War, 1912–2012* (London, 2013), p. 73.
37 Michael Paris, *Winged Warfare: The Literature and Theory of Aerial Warfare in Britain, 1859–1917* (Manchester, 1992), p. 220.
38 Paris, *Winged Warfare*, p. 220.
39 Raleigh, *War in the Air*, p. 443.
40 Ralph Barker, *The Royal Flying Corps in France: From Mons to the Somme* (London, 1994), p. 221.
41 Raleigh, *War in the Air*, pp. 441–2. Eventually, the 'folly of committing such inexperience to war was realized' and pilots were not permitted to cross the enemy line until they had built up a number of hours in the air in France: Grattan, *Origins*, pp. 34–5.

NOTES

42 Ian Mackersey, *No Empty Chairs: The Short and Heroic Lives of the Young Aviators Who Fought and Died in the First World War* (London, 2012), p. 121.
43 Ralph Barker, *The Royal Flying Corps in France: From Bloody April 1917 to Final Victory* (London, 1995), p. 6.
44 Robert Thompson, *The Royal Flying Corps: Per Ardua ad Astra* (London, 1968), p. 106, and F.D. Tredrey, *Pioneer Pilot: The Great Smith Barry Who Taught the World How to Fly* (London, 1976), p. 101.
45 Peter Hart, *Bloody April: Slaughter in the Skies over Arras, 1917* (London, 2005), p. 101.
46 Sturtivant, *Military Training*, p. 22.
47 Philip S. Meilinger, 'Salmond, Sir John Maitland [1881–1968]', *Oxford Dictionary of National Biography* (Oxford, 2004; Online Edition 2011), www.oxforddnb.com/view/article/35915.
48 Jefford, *Observers and Navigators*, p. 39; Alderson, *War in the Air*, p. 2; and © AWM, Frederic Cutlack, 'Appendix No. 5, AFC Training in England', in *Official History of Australia in the War of 1914–1918. Vol. 8: The Australian Flying Corps in the Western and Eastern Theatres of War, 1914–1918* (11th edition, 1941), www.awm.gov.au/histories/first_world_war/AWMOHWW1/AIF/Vol8/, p. 431.
49 T.N. Hancock, *Bomber County: A History of the Royal Air Force in Lincolnshire*, Vol. 2 (Lincoln, 1985), p. 33. Having removed these tree stumps Harlaxton served as a night landing ground for No. 38 (HD) Squadron and No. 90 (HD) Squadron between November 1916 and June 1919: Davis and Morgan, 'Gai-Har', GFS-72.
50 Tredrey, *Pioneer Pilot*, p. 51.
51 Paris, *Winged Warfare*, p. 219.
52 John James, *The Paladins: A Social History of the RAF up to the Outbreak of World War II* (London, 1990), p. 72; Jefford, *Observers and Navigators*, p. 39; and Sturtivant, *Military Training*, p. 22.
53 Tredrey, *Pioneer Pilot*, p. 51; Paris, *Winged Warfare*, p. 219; Jefford, *Observers and Navigators*, p. 41; Grattan, *Origins*, p. 36; and Sturtivant, *Military Training*, p. 22.
54 Arthur Gould Lee, *No Parachute: A Classic Account of War in the Air in WWI in Letters Written in 1917 by Lieutenant A.S.G. Lee, Sherwood Foresters, Attached Royal Flying Corps* (London, 2013), p. 4.
55 © AWM, Cutlack, 'Training in England', p. 431. A pupil was required to complete a total of five hours solo on an elementary machine, 'including as many landings as possible', p. 430. Pupils also had to let out a wireless aerial five times: Brownell, *Khaki to Blue*, p. 138.
56 Tredrey, *Pioneer Pilot*, p. 51; Grattan, *Origins*, p. 36; and © AWM, Cutlack, 'Training in England', p. 431. In May, a War Office order had also authorized 'trick flying' and the practising of flying manoeuvres: Sturtivant, *Military Training*, p. 22.
57 © AWM, Cutlack, 'Training in England', p. 431.
58 'Wing Adjutant', *Royal Flying Corps*, p. 13.

NOTES

59 'Wing Adjutant', *Royal Flying Corps*, pp. 12–13.
60 Sturtivant, *Military Training*, p. 22.
61 Letter dated 27 December 1965, Liddell Hart Papers/8/140. Extracts quoted with the kind permission of the Trustees of the Liddell Hart Centre for Military Archives.
62 Jefford, *Observers and Navigators*, p. 41, and Lee Kennett, *The First Air War, 1914–1918* (New York, 1991), p. 122. In 1918, pilots were arriving in France with an average of 50 hours' flying time: Tredrey, *Pioneer Pilot*, p. 101.
63 © IWM (80000015/Reel 3), sound recording of Eric John Furlong.
64 © IWM (80000015/Reel 2), sound recording of Eric John Furlong.
65 © IWM (80000015/Reel 3).
66 © IWM (80000015/Reel 3).
67 © IWM (80000015/Reel 3).
68 © IWM (80000015/Reel 3). See also Bruce Lewis, *A Few of the First: The True Stories of the Men Who Flew in and before the First World War* (Barnsley, 1997), pp. 91–2; Joshua Levine, *On a Wing and a Prayer: The Untold Story of the Pioneering Aviation Heroes of WWI, in Their Own Words* (London, 2008), p. 70; and Joshua Levine, *Fighter Heroes of WWI: The Extraordinary Story of the Pioneering Airmen of the Great War* (London, 2009), p. 70. See also Lee, *Open Cockpit*, pp. 23–4, and © AWM, Cutlack, 'Training in England', p. 430.
69 'Wing Adjutant', *Royal Flying Corps*, p. 9.
70 Alderson, *War in the Air*, p. 3.
71 Paul R. Hare, *Fokker Fodder: The Royal Aircraft Factory BE2c* (Fonthill, 2012), p. 136.
72 Rutledge, *Pen Pictures*, pp. 151–2.
73 © IWM (80000015/Reel 4), sound recording of Eric John Furlong.
74 Rutledge, *Pen Pictures*, p. 144.
75 Rutledge, *Pen Pictures*, p. 145.
76 'Wing Adjutant', *Royal Flying Corps*, p. 13.
77 Rutledge, *Pen Pictures*, p. 151.
78 Captain B.F. Garrett, 'Pilot's Flying Log Book' (unpublished). Extracts quoted with the kind permission of Roger Bragger, p. 11. By mid 1918, a cadet had to pass a three-stage training programme: Stage 'A', or basic flight training on an Avro 504; Stage 'B', or cross-country, cloud and formation flying and air-to-ground firing (when he received his commission); and Stage 'C' or, 'specialist instruction appropriate to a particular operational role'. Only after graduating Stage 'C' could he put on his wings: Jefford, *Observers and Navigators*, p. 41. See also Chapter 4.
79 © IWM (80000015/Reel 4). N.B. Rutledge graduated 'A' on a Martinsyde Scout which would suggest that pilots had a proficiency test on each machine.
80 © IWM (80000015/Reel 4).
81 Lord Hugh Cecil, 'The Royal Flying Corps: The work and training of the Royal Flying Corps', *The London Illustrated News* (London, 1918), p. 5.
82 Rutledge, *Pen Pictures*, p. 150.
83 Rutledge, *Pen Pictures*, pp. 146–8.

84　Tredrey, *Pioneer Pilot*, p. 51.
85　Lee, *Open Cockpit*, p. 33.
86　Tredrey, *Pioneer Pilot*, frontispiece.

Chapter 4: Gosport and the Flight Instructor

1. F.D. Tredrey, *Pioneer Pilot: The Great Smith Barry Who Taught the World How to Fly* (London, 1976), p. 64.
2. Michael Paris, *Winged Warfare: The Literature and Theory of Aerial Warfare in Britain, 1859–1917* (Manchester, 1992), p. 220.
3. 'Wing Adjutant' (W.T.B.), *The Royal Flying Corps in the War* (London, 1918), p. 8.
4. Arthur Gould Lee, *Open Cockpit: A Pilot of the Royal Flying Corps* (London, 1969; Reprinted 2013), p. 30.
5. Philip Brereton Townsend, *Eye in the Sky, 1918: Recollections of Air-to-Ground Co-Operation by a World War One Pilot* (Private, 1986), p. 8.
6. 'Aeroplanes in war: The government's scheme', *The Times*, 13 April 1913, p. 7.
7. C.G. Jefford, *Observers and Navigators and Other Non-Pilot Aircrew in the RFC, RNAS and RAF* (Shrewsbury, 2001), p. 39. See also Patrick Bishop, *Wings: The RAF at War, 1912–2012* (London, 2013), p. 69.
8. Jefford, *Pilots and Navigators*, p. 38. See also Sir Walter Raleigh, *The War in the Air: Being the Story of the Part Played in the Great War by the Royal Air Force*, Vol. 1 (London, 1922), pp. 430–1.
9. Peter Dye, 'The genesis of modern warfare: The contribution of aviation logistics', in Gary Sheffield and Peter Gray (eds), *Changing War: The British Army, The Hundred Days Campaign and the Birth of the Royal Air Force, 1918* (London, 2013), pp. 179–80.
10. Dye, 'Aviation logistics', p. 180.
11. 'Wing Adjutant', *Royal Flying Corps*, p. 8.
12. Ralph Barker, *The Royal Flying Corps in France: From Mons to the Somme* (London, 1994), p. 212.
13. Alan Stephens, *The Royal Australian Air Force* (Oxford, 2001), p. 17.
14. Jefford, *Observers and Navigators*, p. 39.
15. James Fitz Morris papers, www.falkirkcommunitytrust.org/heritage/archives/finding-aids/docs/family_papers/Family_and_personal_papers_D-F.pdf.
16. A.H. Cobby, *High Adventure* (Melbourne, 1981), p. 35.
17. Tredrey, *Pioneer Pilot*, p. 54.
18. Cobby, *High Adventure*, p. 35.
19. Jefford, *Observers and Navigators*, p. 39. But as Barker points out, perhaps 'the last men you wanted as instructors … were those to whom flying had come easily': Barker, *Somme*, p. 213.
20. © IWM (80000015/Reel 4).

NOTES

21 Central Flying School, *Hints for Young Instructors on How to Instruct in Flying, Issued by the Central Flying School, Royal Flying Corps, September 1916* (London, 1916), p. 3. Author's italics.
22 Lee Kennett, *The First Air War, 1914–1918* (New York, 1991), pp. 122–3.
23 Philip S. Meilinger, 'Salmond, Sir John Maitland [1881–1968]', *Oxford Dictionary of National Biography* (Oxford, 2004; Online Edition 2011), www.oxforddnb.com/view/article/35915/.
24 Lee, *Open Cockpit*, p. 33.
25 Ray Sturtivant, *The History of Britain's Military Training Aircraft* (Yeovil, 1987), p. 23.
26 'Salmond', *Oxford Dictionary of National Biography*/article/35915, and Paris, *Winged Warfare*, pp. 220–1.
27 Lee, *Open Cockpit*, p. 33.
28 Tredrey, *Pioneer Pilot*, p. 95.
29 Geoffrey Norris, *The Royal Flying Corps: A History* (London, 1965), pp. 205–6.
30 Tredrey, *Pioneer Pilot*, p. 54.
31 Tredrey, *Pioneer Pilot*, p. 54.
32 Elizabeth O'Kiely, *Gentleman Air Ace: The Duncan Bell-Irving Story* (Madeira Park, 1992), p. 146.
33 Jefford, *Observers and Navigators*, p. 39. See also Peter G. Cooksley, *Royal Flying Corps Handbook, 1914–1918* (Stroud, 2007), p. 25.
34 John James, *The Paladins: A Social History of the RAF up to the Outbreak of World War II* (London, 1990), p. 72.
35 Sturtivant, *Military Training*, p. 25, and Tredrey, *Pioneer Pilot*, p. 95.
36 O'Kiely, *Gentleman Air Ace*, p. 145, and Tredrey, *Pioneer Pilot*, p. 72.
37 Nigel Steel and Peter Hart, *Tumult in the Clouds: The British Experience of the War in the Air, 1914–1918* (London, 1997), p. 91.
38 Norris, *Royal Flying Corps*, p. 136.
39 Leslie McNab, 'Diary' (unpublished). Extracts quoted with the kind permission of the McNab family.
40 McNab, 'Diary' (unpublished).
41 McNab, 'Diary' (unpublished).
42 McNab, 'Diary' (unpublished).
43 McNab, 'Diary' (unpublished).
44 Lieutenant Stanley A. Rutledge, *Pen Pictures from the Trenches* (Toronto, 1918), https://archive.org/stream/penpicturesfromt00rutluoft#page/n5/mode/2up/, pp. 146–8. Cobby records that after completing his higher training with No. 68 (Australian) Squadron, 'a pilot's graduation did not take place until a "finishing school" had been completed for service qualifications': Cobby, *High Adventure*, p. 33. By 1917, there were also specialist schools of aerial gunnery in England, in Egypt, and in Scotland at Turnberry: Ray Sturtivant and John Hamlin, *Royal Air Force Flying Training and Support Units since 1912* (Trowbridge, 2007), p. 6.
45 McNab, 'Diary' (unpublished).
46 Jefford, *Observers and Navigators*, p. 42. Another novel approach was the 'rocking nacelle'. This was a ground-based training system in which pilots

NOTES

fired a machine gun at a target whilst being rocked and tilted in a mock-up of an aeroplane's cockpit. See William E. Chajkowsky, *Royal Flying Corps: Borden to Texas to Beamsville* (Ontario, 1979), p. 38.

47 See Alan Rowe, 'The RE8 controversy revisited', *The '14–'18 Journal* (2001), pp. 64–70.
48 Rowe, 'RE8 controversy', p. 68.
49 Rutledge, *Pen Pictures*, p. 152.
50 McNab, 'Diary' (unpublished).
51 McNab, 'Diary' (unpublished).
52 O'Kiely, *Gentleman Air Ace*, p. 143.
53 McNab, 'Diary' (unpublished).
54 McNab, 'Diary' (unpublished).
55 Letter dated 27th December, 1965, Liddell Hart Papers/8/140. Extracts quoted with the kind permission of the Trustees of the Liddell Hart Centre for Military Archives.
56 McNab, 'Diary' (unpublished).
57 Tredrey, *Pioneer Pilot*, p. 95. According to Brownell, the 200 pupils on the fortnight-long course practised firing from the cockpit of an FE 'pusher' at a target towed by another aeroplane and firing at ground targets from the air; they also used photographic guns, before being tested in both aerial and ground gunnery: R.J. Brownell, *From Khaki to Blue: The Autobiography of Air Commodore R.J. Brownell* (Canberra, 1978), p. 139. See also Sturtivant, *Military Training*, p. 22.
58 Tredrey, *Pioneer Pilot*, pp. 72 and 80.
59 Norris, *Royal Flying Corps*, p. 207.
60 McNab, 'Diary' (unpublished).
61 McNab, 'Diary' (unpublished).
62 McNab, 'Diary' (unpublished).
63 McNab, 'Diary' (unpublished).
64 Raleigh, *War in the Air*, pp. 441–2.
65 James McCudden, V.C., *Flying Fury: Five Years in the Royal Flying Corps* (Elstree, 1987), p. 135.
66 McCudden, *Flying Fury*, p. 135.
67 McCudden, *Flying Fury*, pp. 135–6.
68 Kennett, *First Air War*, p. 73.
69 Raleigh, *War in the Air*, pp. 446–7.
70 Kennett, *First Air War*, p. 73.
71 Michael Armitage, *The Royal Air Force: An Illustrated History* (London, 1993), p. 16.
72 Robert F. Grattan, *The Origins of Air War: The Development of Military Air Strategy in World War One* (London, 2009), pp. 244 and 250; Lee, *Open Cockpit*, p. 139; and Maryam Philpott, *Air and Sea Power in World War I: Combat and Experience in the Royal Flying Corps and the Royal Navy* (London, 2013), p. 112. The machines in each flight in France were numbered one to six, with each flight having red, blue or yellow coloured wheels: Arthur Gould Lee, *No Parachute: A Classic Account of War in the*

Air in WWI in Letters Written in 1917 by Lieutenant A.S.G. Lee, Sherwood Foresters, Attached Royal Flying Corps (London, 2013), p. 14.
73 Grattan, *Origins*, p. 162.
74 Lee, *Open Cockpit*, p. 114.
75 Lee, *No Parachute*, p. 22, and Grattan, *Origins*, p. 250.
76 Grattan, *Origins*, p. 249.
77 Grattan, *Origins*, pp. 249–50.
78 Michael Molkentin, *Fire in the Sky: The Australian Flying Corps in the First World War* (Crows Nest, 2010), p. 232. See also p. 258.
79 Lord Hugh Cecil, 'The Royal Flying Corps: The work and training of the Royal Flying Corps', *The London Illustrated News* (London, 1918), p. 3.
80 Cobby, *High Adventure*, p. 35.
81 Molkentin, *Fire in the Sky*, p. 233.
82 Cecil, 'Royal Flying Corps', p. 3.
83 Paris, *Winged Warfare*, p. 221.
84 McNab, 'Diary' (unpublished).

Chapter 5: Airmen and their American Mechanics

1 Michael Molkentin, *Fire in the Sky: The Australian Flying Corps in the First World War* (Crows Nest, 2010), p. 186. Quoting from Denis Winter, *The First of the Few: Fighter Pilots of the First World War* (London, 1982), p. 36.
2 Arthur Gould Lee, *Open Cockpit: A Pilot of the Royal Flying Corps* (London, 1969; Reprinted 2013), pp. 30–1. In one training squadron, the convention developed whereby each pupil paid 2s. 6d. into a wreath fund: Molkentin, *Fire in the Sky*, p. 187.
3 Alan Stephens, *The Royal Australian Air Force* (Oxford, 2001), p. 17.
4 Molkentin, *Fire in the Sky*, p. 186.
5 Lieutenant Stanley A. Rutledge, *Pen Pictures from the Trenches* (Toronto, 1918), https://archive.org/stream/penpicturesfromt00rutluoft#page/n5/mode/2up/, pp. 152–3.
6 Rutledge, *Pen Pictures*, p. 155.
7 Rutledge, *Pen Pictures*, p. 155.
8 'The Ladies – God Bless 'Em!', *Parti Patter*, p. 22.
9 'A Base Fabrication', *Parti Patter*, p. 16.
10 'Swimmers of the air: The late Capt. Stanley K. Muir', *The Euroa Advertizer*, Friday, 16 November 1917, http://trove.nla.gov.au, p. 3.
11 Maryam Philpott, *Air and Sea Power in World War I: Combat and Experience in the Royal Flying Corps and the Royal Navy* (London, 2013), p. 173.
12 Philpott, *Combat and Experience*, p. 173.
13 Philpott, *Combat and Experience*, p. 173.
14 Arthur Gould Lee, *No Parachute: A Classic Account of War in the Air in WWI in Letters Written in 1917 by Lieutenant A.S.G. Lee, Sherwood*

Foresters, Attached Royal Flying Corps (London, 2013), p. 89. See also pp. 113 and 118.
15 Philpott, *Combat and Experience*, p. 132.
16 Rutledge, *Pen Pictures*, p. 159.
17 'Second Lieutenant Alick Thomas Bentall Charlesworth', www.canadiangreatwarproject.com/.
18 *University of Toronto, Roll of Service, 1914–1918* (Toronto, 1921), http://archive.org/stream/torontorollservic00unknuoft/torontorollservic00unknuoft_djvu.txt, p. 49; 'Gordon Smith Mellis Gauld', www.veterans.gc.ca/eng/remembrance/memorials/canadian-virtual-war-memorial/detail/379896; and 'Canada, Soldiers of the First World War, 1914–1918', www.ancestry.co.uk.
19 *Toronto, Roll of Service*, p. 49. He was buried in Grantham cemetery. See Gordon Smith Mellis Gauld, 'Commonwealth War Graves Commission', www.cwgc.org/search.
20 'Wing Adjutant' (W.T.B.), *The Royal Flying Corps in the War* (London, 1918), p. 9.
21 Leslie McNab, 'Diary' (unpublished). Extracts quoted with the kind permission of the McNab family.
22 Lord Hugh Cecil, 'The Royal Flying Corps: The work and training of the Royal Flying Corps', *The London Illustrated News* (London, 1918), p. 3.
23 A.G.D. Alderson, *The First War in the Air, 1914–1918* (England, c.1990), p. 4.
24 Philpott, *Combat and Experience*, p. 176.
25 McNab, 'Diary' (unpublished).
26 'Wing Adjutant', *Royal Flying Corps*, pp. 5–6.
27 'For Sale', *Grantham Journal*, 2 September 1922, p. 5.
28 Geoff Gardiner, *Airfield Focus 17: Spittlegate* (Peterborough, 1994), p. 3, and Mike Osborne, *Defending Lincolnshire: A Military History from Conquest to Cold War* (Stroud, 2010), p. 127.
29 *Secret: HM Office of Works, Etc. Report for fortnight ended 16th August, 1918, for the information of the Prime Minister*, TNA/CAB/24/61.
30 See Barker, *April 1917 to Final Victory*, p. 177.
31 James McCudden, VC, *Flying Fury: Five Years in the Royal Flying Corps* (Elstree, 1987), pp. 18–19.
32 John Bennett, *Highest Traditions: The History of No. 2 Squadron RAAF* (Canberra, 1995), p. 28.
33 Ralph Barker, *The Royal Flying Corps in France: From Bloody April 1917 to Final Victory* (London, 1995), p. 177. A shortage of technically qualified recruits began to be felt as early as mid 1916: Robert F. Grattan, *The Origins of Air War: The Development of Military Air Strategy in World War One* (London, 2009), p. 36.
34 Peter Dye, 'The genesis of modern warfare: The contribution of aviation logistics', in Gary Sheffield and Peter Gray (eds), *Changing War: The British Army, The Hundred Days Campaign and the Birth of the Royal Air Force, 1918* (London, 2013), p. 184.

NOTES

35 'Royal Flying Corps', *Grantham Journal*, 15 September 1917, p. 5.
36 Philip S. Meilinger, 'Salmond, Sir John Maitland [1881–1968]', *Oxford Dictionary of National Biography* (Oxford, 2004; Online Edition 2011), www.oxforddnb.com/view/article/35915.
37 *Memorandum of Arrangement between the British and United States Governments*, 5 December 1917, TNA/CAB/24/36, pp. 2–3. To attain this figure, 4,000 mechanics were sent to England in December 1917, 5,000 in January 1918 and a further 6,000 in February. Thereafter, the US kept the total number of mechanics training in England at a constant figure of 15,000.
38 *Arrangement between British and United States Governments on Training and Supply of Personnel for the Air Forces of Both Countries*, 19 December 1917, TNA/CAB/24/36.
39 *Copy of Letter No. 0153/2847 (O.1.) from Secretary of War Office to Secretary of State for Foreign Affairs*, 13 December 1917, TNA/CAB/24/36, p. 2.
40 *Copy of Cablegram from the American Military Authorities in Paris to the United States Government*, 5 December 1917, TNA/CAB/24/36, p. iv.
41 *Cablegram*, 5 December 1917, p. iv, in contrast to the pilot training programme.
42 *Copy of Letter*, 13 December 1917, p. 2.
43 Daniel P. Morse, *The History of the 50th Aero Squadron* (New York, 1920), p. 18.
44 'The History of the 165th Aero Squadron', *Gorrell's History of the American Expeditionary Forces Air Service, 1917–1919*, www.fold3.com, p. 81.
45 Alfred C. Beardslee, personal papers. Extracts quoted with the kind permission of his granddaughters.
46 Morse, *50th Aero*, p. 19.
47 Morse, *50th Aero*, p. 19.
48 Morse, *50th Aero*, pp. 19–20. Between May and 2 July 1918, 1st Lieutenant E.A. Waters, of the 104th Squadron, was in charge of the American troops at Spittlegate and Harlaxton: 'The 104th Aero Squadron (Observation)', *Gorrell's History of the American Expeditionary Forces Air Service, 1917–1919*, www.fold3.com, p. 4.
49 'History of the 638th Aero Squadron (Pursuit), Fifth Pursuit Group, Second Army', *Gorrell's History of the American Expeditionary Forces Air Service, 1917–1919*, www.fold3.com, p. 15.
50 '9th Aero Squadron', *Gorrell's History of the American Expeditionary Forces Air Service, 1917–1919*, www.fold3.com, p. 7.
51 Michael Sewell, *The Joiners Tale: Some Memories of Grantham*, www.cl.cam.ac.uk/~pes20/MJSewell/JoinersTale.pdf.
52 '85th Aero Squadron (Observation). Army Observation, Second Army', *Gorrell's History of the American Expeditionary Forces Air Service, 1917–1919*, www.fold3.com, p. 43.
53 '85th Aero Squadron', p. 43.
54 Morse, *50th Aero*, p. 20.
55 '165th Aero Squadron', p. 83.

NOTES

56 McNab, 'Diary' (unpublished).
57 '85th Aero Squadron', p. 43. See also 'AEF Air Service Station Lists 1–50, Feb 1918-Jan 1919', *Gorrell's History of the American Expeditionary Forces Air Service, 1917–1919*, www.fold3.com, p. 98.
58 Alfred C. Beardslee, personal papers. Extracts quoted with the kind permission of his granddaughters.
59 'Ye Candid Critic', *Parti Patter*, p. 19; Christopher Shores, Norman Franks and Russell Guest, *Above the Trenches: A Complete Record of the Fighter Aces and Units of the British Empire Air Forces, 1915–1920* (Stoney Creek, Ontario, 1990), p. 24; and C.W. Hunt, *Dancing in the Sky: The Royal Flying Corps in Canada* (Toronto, 2009), p. 104. Between 900 and 1,100 US citizens, coming through the RFC's training programmes in Canada and England, flew with the RFC before most transferred to the AEF's Air Service: Roger G. Miller, 'The tail to tooth ratio: Royal Flying Corps and air service co-operation in maintenance training during World War One', *Royal Air Force Historical Society* xxxii (2004), p. 11. For details of the reciprocal training programme that subsequently developed between the Air Service in the US and the RFC in Canada, see p. 17.
60 James Salter, 'The most wonderful sport', Review of Samuel Hynes, *The Unsubstantial Air: American Fliers in the First World War*, *London Review of Books* xxxvi/21 (2014), p. 5. See also Shores, Franks and Guest, *Above the Trenches*, pp. 24–5.
61 Salter, 'Wonderful sport', p. 5.
62 Salter, 'Wonderful sport', p. 5.

Chapter 6: An Australian Odyssey from Egypt to England

1 John Bennett, *Highest Traditions: The History of No. 2 Squadron RAAF* (Canberra, 1995), p. 13, and N.M. Parnell and C.A. Lynch, *Australian Air Force since 1911* (London, 1976), p. 25. A fourth squadron was raised in Australia in October 1916; designated No. 71 (Australian) Squadron it became No. 4 Squadron, AFC, in January 1918. All three squadrons were sent to England for training. No. 2 Squadron (AFC) trained at Harlaxton (24th Training Wing, RFC); No. 3 Squadron (AFC) trained at South Carlton in Lincolnshire (23th Training Wing, RFC) and No. 4 Squadron (AFC) trained at Castle Bromwich, near Birmingham (25th Training Wing, RFC): © Australian War Memorial, Frederic Cutlack, *Official History of Australia in the War of 1914–1918. Vol. 8: The Australian Flying Corps in the Western and Eastern Theatres of War, 1914–1918* (11th edition, 1941), www.awm.gov.au/histories/first_world_war/AWMOHWW1/AIF/Vol8/, p. 175.
2 Alan Stephens, *The Royal Australian Air Force* (Oxford, 2001), p. 20.
3 Stephens, *Australian*, p. 20.
4 Bennett, *Highest Traditions*, p. 14.

NOTES

5 Bennett, *Highest Traditions*, p. 16, and Michael Molkentin, *Fire in the Sky: The Australian Flying Corps in the First World War* (Crows Nest, 2010), p. 178.
6 Molkentin, *Fire in the Sky*, p. 180.
7 'Transcript diary of Verner Gladders Knuckey, 1917, Book 5', RCDIG0000471, www.awm.gov.au/collection/PR03193/, pp. 9–10.
8 Molkentin, *Fire in the Sky*, p. 178.
9 Bennett, *Highest Traditions*, pp. 3–4.
10 Bennet, *Highest Traditions*, p. 12, and Stephens, *Australian Air Force*, pp. 18–19.
11 Knuckey, 'Book 5', p. 10.
12 Knuckey, 'Book 5', p. 12.
13 Knuckey, 'Book 5', p. 14.
14 Knuckey, 'Book 5', p. 15; 2nd Lieutenant T.H. Hampshire, who was training with No. 54 Training Squadron at Harlaxton, alongside No. 68 (Australian) Squadron, considered Colonel Burdett to be a 'quite approachable man considering the high rank he held in my youthful eyes of those days'. Letter, undated, Liddell Hart Papers/8/140. Extracts quoted with the kind permission of the Trustees of the Liddell Hart Centre for Military Archives. Colonel Burdett appears on the photograph of the squadron taken prior to its departure for France.
15 Basil Liddell Hart, *The Memoirs of Captain Liddell Hart*, Vol. 1 (London, 1965), pp. 27–8.
16 T.H. Hampshire, letter dated 27 December 1965, Liddell Hart Papers/8/140. See also Charles Schaedel, *Men and Machines of the Australian Flying Corps, 1914–1919* (Dandenong, Victoria, 1972), p. 37.
17 Knuckey, 'Book 5', p. 17.
18 Molkentin, *Fire in the Sky*, p. 68; 'First World War Embarkation Rolls', www.awm.gov.au/people/rolls/R2026534; 'British Army WWI Medal Rolls Index Cards', www.ancestry.co.uk; and 'Great Britain, Royal Aero Club Aviators Certificates, 1910–1950', www.ancestry.co.uk.
19 'Honours and Awards (Recommendation)', www.awm.gov.au/people/rolls/R1564731. A shorter version of this recommendation was published in the *Edinburgh Gazette*, 'For conspicuous gallantry in action. He carried out a daring bombing raid and was largely instrumental in shooting down a hostile machine. On another occasion he pursued two enemy machines and succeeded in bringing one of them down': 'Temp. 2nd Lieutenant [temp. Lieutenant] Stanley Keith Muir, Gen. List and RFC', *The Edinburgh Gazette*, 6 March 1917, www.thegazette.co.uk/Edinburgh/issue/13061/page/495, p. 495.
20 'Transcript diary of Verner Gladders Knuckey, 1917, Book 6', RCDIG0000473, www.awm.gov.au/collection/PR03193/, p. 6. For more details of their respective service careers see: Captain Stanley Keith Muir, General List, TNA/WO 339/47360, and Captain William James Yule Guilfoyle, Royal Flying Corps, TNA/WO 339/3121.
21 'Temp. Capt. William James Yule Guilfoyle', *The London Gazette*, 2 March 1917, www.thegazette.co.uk/London/issue/29968/supplement/2193,

NOTES

      p. 2193. See also 'Great Britain Royal Aero Club Aviators' Certificates, 1910–1950', www.ancestry.co.uk; 'British Army WWI Medal Rolls Index Cards, 1914–1920', www.ancestry.co.uk; and Bennett, *Highest Traditions*, p. 27. He left No. 68 (Australian) Squadron in August 1917 to take command of an RFC Training Squadron.
22 Molkentin, *Fire in the Sky*, p. 183.
23 Cobby, *High Adventure*, pp. 28–9.
24 Molkentin, *Fire in the Sky*, pp. 205 and 204.
25 A.H. Cobby, *High Adventure* (Melbourne, 1981), p. 29.
26 Cobby, *High Adventure*, pp. 27, 29 and 31, and Bennett, *Highest Traditions*, p. 20. Intriguingly, Jones states: 'Our squadron started training pilots on Horace Farman biplanes, and later Avro 504 planes' which suggests the Australian squadrons in training in England supervised both elementary flight training as well as higher flight training: George Jones, *From Private to Air Marshal: The Autobiography of Air Marshal Sir George Jones* (Richmond, Australia, 1988), pp. 13–14.
27 Stephens, *Australian*, p. 20. George Jones, who served with Cobby in No. 71 (Australian) Squadron, described him as a man of good humour and ready wit, who, 'repeatedly sought out enemy aircraft': Cobby, *High Adventure*, p. 5. See also Dennis Newton, *Australian Air Aces* (Fyshwick, 1996), p. 27.
28 Stephens, *Australian*, p. 13.
29 Molkentin, *Fire in the Sky*, p. 187.
30 Molkentin, *Fire in the Sky*, p. 186.
31 Cobby, *High Adventure*, p. 27.
32 Cobby, *High Adventure*, pp. 27–8.
33 Cobby, *High Adventure*, p. 28.
34 Cobby, *High Adventure*, p. 28. One imagines Major Watt and Major Butler would have been kindred spirits.
35 Cobby, *High Adventure*, p. 28.
36 Cobby, *High Adventure*, p. 28.
37 Cobby, *High Adventure*, p. 28.
38 Cobby, *High Adventure*, p. 29.
39 Cobby, *High Adventure*, p. 29.
40 Cobby, *High Adventure*, p. 29.
41 Cobby, *High Adventure*, p. 29.
42 Cobby, *High Adventure*, p. 29.
43 Cobby, *High Adventure*, p. 29.
44 Molkentin, *Fire in the Sky*, p. 185.
45 Cobby, *High Adventure*, pp. 29–30.
46 Cobby, *High Adventure*, p. 35.
47 Cobby, *High Adventure*, p. 35.
48 Cobby, *High Adventure*, p. 35.
49 Lord Macauley, 'Horatius', in *Lays of Ancient Rome* (New York, 1888), p. 47.
50 Schaedel, *Men and Machines*, p. 37.

NOTES

51 © AWM, Cutlack, *Official History*, pp. 175–6. See also Frederic Cutlack, 'Appendix No. 5, AFC Training in England', in *Official History of Australia in the War of 1914–1918. Vol. 8: The Australian Flying Corps in the Western and Eastern Theatres of War, 1914–1918* (11th edition, 1941), www.awm.gov.au/histories/first_world_war/AWMOHWW1/AIF/Vol8/, p. 431.
52 Molkentin, *Fire in the Sky*, p. 187.
53 Molkentin, *Fire in the Sky*, p. 187.
54 Molkentin, *Fire in the Sky*, pp. 185–6.
55 Lieutenant Stanley A. Rutledge, *Pen Pictures from the Trenches* (Toronto, 1918), https://archive.org/stream/penpicturesfromt00rutluoft#page/n5/mode/2up/, pp. 145–6.
56 Stephens, *Australian Air Force*, p. 19. T.H. Hampshire recalled Watt wore 'his leggings like the rest of his officers, though he did sport his Sam-Browne, except when in the Mess or ante-room': Letter dated 27 December 1965, Liddell Hart Papers/8/140.
57 Bennett, *Highest Traditions*, p. 26, and Ron Blake, Mike Hodgson and Bill Taylor, *The Airfields of Lincolnshire Since 1912* (Leicester, 1984), p. 95.
58 Bennett, *Highest Traditions*, pp. 27–8, and © AWM, Cutlack, *Official History*, p. 177.
59 Bennett, *Highest Traditions*, p. 28, and © AWM, Cutlack, *Official History*, p. 177.
60 Bennett, *Highest Traditions*, p. 27; © AWM, Cutlack, *Official History*, p. 177; and Franks, *SE5a*, pp. 42–3 and p. 53. See also: Letter from Director of Air Organisation, Air Board Office, War Office, dated 19 March 1917, Liddell Hart Papers/8/137.
61 'No. 2 Squadron, Australian Flying Corps, September, 1917', www.awm.gov.au/collection/records/ AWM4/8/5/2.
62 'Obituary Notice', in *War Services of Old Melburnians 1914–18* courtesy of Stewart Brook, Alumni Manager, Melbourne Grammar School.
63 *Old Melburnians*.
64 Knuckey, 'Book 6', p. 6.
65 Knuckey, 'Book 6', pp. 6–7.
66 Letter dated 27 December, 1965, Liddell Hart Papers/8/140.
67 Letter dated 27 December, 1965, Liddell Hart Papers/8/140.

Chapter 7: The Aerodrome and the Armistice

1 Peter Dye, 'The genesis of modern warfare: The contribution of aviation logistics', in Gary Sheffield and Peter Gray (eds), *Changing War: The British Army, The Hundred Days Campaign and the Birth of the Royal Air Force, 1918* (London, 2013), p. 180, and Brereton Greenhous, 'Evolution of a close ground-support role for aircraft in World War I', *Military Affairs* xxxix/1 (1975), p. 26. See also John James, *The Paladins: A Social History of the RAF up to the Outbreak of World War II* (London, 1990), pp. 70 and 243. At the

NOTES

Armistice, there were 86 RAF squadrons in France. This total comprised 29 fighter squadrons, 20 bomber squadrons, 14 fighter-reconnaissance squadrons, 21 corps squadrons and 2 night-fighter squadrons: Robert F. Grattan, *The Origins of Air War: The Development of Military Air Strategy in World War One* (London, 2009), p. 26. At the beginning of the year there had been 54 squadrons in France: Ralph Barker, *The Royal Flying Corps in France: From Bloody April 1917 to Final Victory* (London, 1995), p. 201.

2   Roy Conyers Nesbit, *An Illustrated History of the RAF* (Godalming, 1990), p. 18. According to the Training Divisions' statistics, 6,000 pupils were in training at the end of 1917, to produce 5,000 pilots for the front line in early 1918, with an estimated 12,000 pupils entering training during 1918: F.D. Tredrey, *Pioneer Pilot: The Great Smith Barry Who Taught the World How to Fly* (London, 1976), p. 78.

3   Dye, 'Aviation logistics', p. 184.

4   Ray Sturtivant, *The History of Britain's Military Training Aircraft* (Yeovil, 1987), p. 23, and Ray Sturtivant and John Hamlin, *Royal Air Force Flying Training and Support Units since 1912* (Trowbridge, 2007), p. 7.

5   T.N. Hancock, *Bomber County: A History of the Royal Air Force in Lincolnshire* (Lincoln, 1978), p. 12. As No. 68 (Australian) Squadron had done in 1917.

6   Michael J.F. Bowyer, *Actions Stations Revisited: The Complete History of Britain's Military Airfields. No. 1: Eastern England* (Manchester, 2000), p. 204. See, however, Geoff Gardiner, *Airfield Focus 17: Spittlegate* (Peterborough, 1994), p. 4.

7   'The History of the 165th Aero Squadron', *Gorrell's History of the American Expeditionary Forces Air Service, 1917–1919*, www.fold3.com, p. 83. The variety of types referred to included DH6, RE8, Martinsyde Scout, Curtiss JN4, BE2e and FK3 machines: Courtesy of Mick Davis. See also Hancock, *Bomber County*, p. 118. For more details of the FK3 machines flown at Harlaxton by No. 20 TS and No. 64 TS, see Gordon Page and Jim Halley, 'Armstrong Whitworth FK3', *Air-Britain, Aeromilitaria* xxxvi/144 (2010), p. 164.

8   Courtesy of Mick Davis.

9   Greenhous, 'Ground-support', p. 22.

10 © AWM, Frederic Cutlack, 'Appendix No. 5, AFC Training in England', in *Official History of Australia in the War of 1914–1918. Vol. 8: The Australian Flying Corps in the Western and Eastern Theatres of War, 1914–1918* (11th edition, 1941), www.awm.gov.au/histories/first_world_war/AWMOHWW1/AIF/Vol8/, p. 431, and Captain B.F. Garrett, 'Pilot's Flying Log Book' (unpublished). Extracts quoted with the kind permission of Roger Bragger, p. 9.

11 Grattan, *Origins*, p. 244.

12 Alan Stephens, *The Royal Australian Air Force* (Oxford, 2001), p. 18.

13 Susan Johnston, 'Watt, Walter Oswald [1878–1921]', Australian Dictionary of National Biography, Vol. 12 (1990), http:/adb.anu.edu.au/biography/watt-walter-oswald-1010. Given his excellent leadership skills, in February 1918 Lieutenant Colonel Watt was given command of the four

NOTES

squadrons (Nos 5, 6, 7 and 8) of the Australian Training Wing at Tetbury in Gloucestershire.
14 Greenhous, 'Ground-support', p. 25.
15 Grattan, *Origins*, p. 253.
16 Greenhous, 'Ground-support', p. 26 and p. 27. See Hilary St George Saunders, *Per Ardua: The Rise of British Air Power, 1911–1939* (London, 1944), p. 263, and David Stevenson, *With Our Backs to the Wall: Victory and Defeat* (London, 2011), p. 193. See also Barker, *April 1917 to Final Victory*, p. 209.
17 Saunders, *Per Ardua*, p. 261, and Peter Hart, *Aces Falling: War above the Trenches, 1918* (London, 2007), pp. 110 and 113.
18 Michael Molkentin, *Fire in the Sky: The Australian Flying Corps in the First World War* (Crows Nest, 2010), pp. 233–4. As V.M. Yeates states: 'They practise this on the aerodrome, having a target marked out on the ground.': V.M. Yeates, *Winged Victory* (London, 1934; Reprinted 2008), p. 31.
19 Malcolm Cooper, *The Birth of Independent Air Power: British Air Policy in the First World War* (London, 1986), p. 147, and Hart, *Aces Falling*, p. 119.
20 See Hew Strachan, *The First World War: A New Illustrated History* (London, 2006), p. 307.
21 David Jordan, 'The genesis of modern air power: The RAF in 1918', in Gary Sheffield and Peter Gray (eds), *Changing War: The British Army, the Hundred Days Campaign and the Birth of the Royal Air Force, 1918* (London, 2013), p. 191, and Strachan, *First World War*, p. 307.
22 Cooper, *Independent Air Power*, p. 147.
23 Greenhous, 'Ground-support', p. 26, and Cooper, *Independent Air Power*, pp. 147 and 150. With the SE5a's providing 'top cover' for the Camels. For a discussion of fighter 'sweeps', see Charles Schaedel, *Men and Machines of the Australian Flying Corps, 1914–1919* (Dandenong, Victoria, 1972), p. 40, and Arthur Gould Lee, *Open Cockpit: A Pilot of the Royal Flying Corps* (London, 1969; Reprinted 2013), pp. 139–40.
24 Simon Coningham, 'The Battle of Amiens: Air-ground co-operation and its implications for imperial policing', in Gary Sheffield and Peter Gray (eds), *Changing War: The British Army, the Hundred Days Campaign and the Birth of the Royal Air Force, 1918* (London, 2013), pp. 212–13 and p. 210, and Grattan, *Origins*, pp. 150–1.
25 Cooper, *Independent Air Power*, p. 144.
26 Cooper, *Independent Air Power*, p. 144.
27 Hart, *Aces Falling*, p. 119, and Cooper, *Independent Air Service*, p. 147.
28 Cooper, *Independent Air Power*, p. 148 and p. 150.
29 Cooper, *Independent Air Power*, p. 150.
30 Cooper, *Independent Air Power*, p. 150, and Michael Armitage (ed.), *Classic RAF Battles from WWI to the Present* (London, 1995), p. 24.
31 See Norman Franks, *SE5/5a Aces of World War I* (Oxford, 2007), p. 6.
32 Lee, *Open Cockpit*, p. 140.
33 Lee, *Open Cockpit*, p. 140. N.B. Prior to March 1918, RFC scout squadrons had been increased in strength to 24 machines, with unit

NOTES

commanders, formerly restricted to 'flying a desk', also being given permission to fly into action: Christopher Shores, Norman Franks and Russell Guest, *Above the Trenches: A Complete Record of the Fighter Aces and Units of the British Empire Air Forces, 1915–1920* (Stoney Creek, Ontario, 1990), p. 23.

34 Stevenson, *Backs to the Wall*, p. 192.
35 David Stevenson, *1914–1918: The History of the First World War* (London, 2005), p. 192.
36 Cooper, *Independent Air Power*, pp. 145–6.
37 Between 1914 and 1918, Britain also produced 55,093 airframes and 41,034 engines. For comparison, Germany, up to January 1919, produced 47,637 airframes and 40,449 engines, and had 20,000 aircraft on its strength at the Armistice: Centre for Air Power Studies, 'Synopsis of British air effort during the War, 1914–1918', *Air Power Review*, Special Edition, Spring (2013), p. 196. According to James the figures were 27,333 officers, 263,827 other ranks and 22,847 aeroplanes on charge: James, *The Paladins*, p. 73. According to Bishop, the wartime strength of the RAF was 280 Squadrons: Patrick Bishop, *Wings: The RAF at War, 1912–2012* (London, 2013), p. 136.
38 Christine Berberich, *The Image of the English Gentleman in Twentieth Century Literature: Englishness and Nostalgia* (Aldershot, 2007), p. 47.
39 Michael Paris, 'The rise of the airmen: The origins of air force elitism, c. 1890–1918', *Journal of Contemporary History* xxviii/1 (1993), p. 137. See also p. 124.
40 See Berberich, *English Gentleman*, p. 54.
41 See Richard Cavendish, 'Royal Flying Corps founded', *History Today* lxii/4 (2012).
42 David Edgerton, *England and the Aeroplane: Militarism, Modernity and Machines* (London, 2013), p. 81.
43 Ian Mackersey, *No Empty Chairs: The Short and Heroic Lives of the Young Aviators Who Fought and Died in the First World War* (London, 2012), p. 58.
44 Berberich, *English Gentleman*, p. 55.
45 Berberich, *English Gentleman*, p. 57.
46 Lee Kennett, *The First Air War, 1914–1918* (New York, 1991), p. 119.
47 A.H. Cobby, *High Adventure* (Melbourne, 1981), p. 35.
48 Kennett, *First Air War*, p. 119.
49 Arthur Gould Lee, *No Parachute: A Classic Account of War in the Air in WWI in Letters Written in 1917 by Lieutenant A.S.G. Lee, Sherwood Foresters, Attached Royal Flying Corps* (London, 2013), p. 13.
50 Lee, *Open Cockpit*, p. 22.
51 Kennett, *First Air War*, p. 131.
52 Leslie McNab, 'Diary' (unpublished). Extracts quoted with the kind permission of the McNab family.
53 McNab, 'Diary' (unpublished).
54 'His Send Off to Us', *Parti Patter*, p. 15.

NOTES

55 2nd Lieutenant H.G. Warburton, 'Ye Candid Critic Gets Busy', *Parti Patter*, p. 18.
56 'Ye Candid Critic', *Parti Patter*, p. 19.
57 McNab, 'Diary' (unpublished), among whom was one Captain Blonk, 'a very bright lad' who was awarded the Air Force Cross. He had also looped both a DH6 and an RE8, which in McNab's opinion was worth a medal!
58 'Ye Candid Critic', *Parti Patter*, p. 19.
59 'Ye Candid Critic', *Parti Patter*, p. 19.
60 'Camaraderie', *Parti Patter*, p. 13. Except when needed, after all, one of the benefits of being in the RFC, the premier service in the Army, was giving a bit of swank to officers in other corps. See Molkentin, *Fire in the Sky*, p. 182, and Morrow, *War in the Air*, p. 239.
61 'A Reminder of England', *Parti Patter*, p. 23.
62 McNab, 'Diary' (unpublished).
63 McNab, 'Diary' (unpublished).
64 McNab, 'Diary' (unpublished).
65 Ben Elton and Richard Curtis, 'Plan D: Private Plane', *Blackadder Goes Forth*, episode 4 (1989).
66 Paul Fussell, *The Great War and Modern Memory* (Oxford, 2000), p. 35.
67 Maryam Philpott, *Air and Sea Power in World War I: Combat and Experience in the Royal Flying Corps and the Royal Navy* (London, 2013), p. 171.
68 'The Ladies – God Bless 'Em!', *Parti Patter*, p. 22.
69 Max Arthur, *Lost Voices of the Royal Air Force* (London, 1993), p. 3. Members of the WRAF were divided into 'mobile' and 'immobile'. The latter worked from home, whilst the former were prepared to move and live in a women's hostel on the air station.
70 McNab, 'Diary' (unpublished). In 1919, when the rules on fraternisation had relaxed a little, couples would meet, 'above the Gregory Grove': 'On Civvy Suits', *Parti Patter*, p. 6.
71 'Miss Bunny Barnes', www.warcovers.co.uk/shop/1919-PPC-FRANCE-to-WRAF-Officers-Mess-RAF-Harlaxton-Camp.html.
72 'On Civvy Suits', *Parti Patter*, p. 6.
73 'On Civvy Suits', *Parti Patter*, p. 6.
74 'Marriages: Major C.F.A. Portal, DSO, MC, and Miss Welby', *The Times*, 23 July 1919, p. 15. In announcing their engagement in December 1918, *The Times* gave Portal's rank as Lieutenant Colonel, which at that time would have accorded with his command of No. 24 Training Wing.
75 'British Army WWI Medal Rolls Index Cards, 1914–1920', www.ancestry.co.uk. The medal card also indicates that in 1922 he was with No. 8 Squadron stationed at RAF Hinaidi, Baghdad, Iraq.
76 Arthur Gould Lee, quoted in Philpott, *Combat and Experience*, p. 92.
77 Rudyard Kipling, 'If', in *Rewards and Fairies* (New York, 1910).

NOTES

Conclusion

1. *Memorandum by the Chief of the Air Staff on Air Power Requirements of the Empire*, 9 December 1918, TNA/CAB/24/71, p. 1; see also p. 290.
2. Malcolm Cooper, 'Blueprint for confusion: The administrative background to the formation of the Royal Air Force, 1912–1919', *Journal of Contemporary History* xxii/3 (1987), p. 437. See also Patrick Bishop, *Wings: The RAF at War, 1912–2012* (London, 2013), p. 136.
3. Bishop, *Wings*, p. 138 and p. 137. In April 1919, *The Times* reported that 116 of the 337 aerodromes in existence in November 1918 had already been, 'relinquished for purposes of cultivation'. Allowing for about 100 being 'required for the time being by the Royal Air Force', that left about 120 aerodromes available for civilian aviation. Harlaxton aerodrome was now earmarked as one of the possible 'stations' on a proposed London to Scotland aerial route: 'Civilian flying: Official air routes and stations', *The Times*, 25 April 1919, p. 10.
4. Michael Paris, 'The rise of the airmen: The origins of air force elitism, c. 1890–1918', *Journal of Contemporary History* xxviii/1 (1993), p. 138.
5. See 'The Ladies – God Bless 'Em!', *Parti Patter*, p. 22. For a discussion of their memoirs, see Maryam Philpott, *Air and Sea Power in World War I: Combat and Experience in the Royal Flying Corps and the Royal Navy* (London, 2013), p. 171, and Paris, 'Elitism', p. 137.
6. See Paris, 'Elitism', p. 124.
7. Michael Sewell, *The Joiners Tale: Some Memories of Grantham*, www.cl.cam.ac.uk/~pes20/MJSewell/JoinersTale.pdf, p. 7.
8. Geoff Gardiner, *Airfield Focus 17: Spittlegate* (Peterborough, 1994), p. 3.
9. David Edgerton, *England and the Aeroplane: Militarism, Modernity and Machines* (London, 2013), p. 81.
10. 'Flight Commander', *Cavalry of the Air* (London, 1918), p. 127. See also pp. 247–8.
11. 'Royal Flying Corps cadets', *Grantham Journal*, 11 August 1917, p. 4.
12. 'Royal Flying Corps cadets', *Grantham Journal*, 25 August 1917, p. 4.
13. Edgerton, *Aeroplane*, p. 81.
14. Edgerton, *Aeroplane*, p. 81.
15. Hansard, 'Pay, etc., of the Air Force', *House of Commons Debates*, Vol. 123, 15 December 1919, cc. 87–147.
16. Edgerton, *Aeroplane*, p. 80.
17. 'The Ladies – God Bless 'Em!', *Parti Patter*, p. 22.
18. Michael Molkentin, *Fire in the Sky: The Australian Flying Corps in the First World War* (Crows Nest, 2010), p. 182. See also © AWM, Frederic Cutlack, *Official History of Australia in the War of 1914–1918. Vol. 8: The Australian Flying Corps in the Western and Eastern Theatres of War, 1914–1918* (11th edition, 1941), www.awm.gov.au/histories/first_world_war/AWMOHWW1/AIF/Vol8/, p. 175.
19. F.D. Tredrey, *Pioneer Pilot: The Great Smith Barry Who Taught the World How to Fly* (London, 1976), p. 99.

NOTES

20 C.W. Hunt, *Dancing in the Sky: The Royal Flying Corps in Canada* (Toronto, 2009), p. 129. Major Cuthbert Gurney Hoare, the RFC Officer Commanding the RFC training programme in Canada, a member of the East Anglian landed gentry, and Major Dermott Allen, who had transferred into the RFC from the Royal Irish Fusiliers in 1913, and who became Hoare's chief of staff, were frequent guests of the Governor General, Lord Devonshire, Hoare sharing Devonshire's 'interest in farming and country sports': Hunt, *Dancing*, p. 129; see also p. 130.
21 John Keegan, *The First World War* (London, 1999), p. 386.
22 Peter Hart, *Bloody April: Slaughter in the Skies over Arras, 1917* (London, 2005), p. 102.
23 John H. Morrow, *The Great War in the Air: Military Aviation from 1909 to 1921* (Shrewsbury, 1993), p. 239.
24 Morrow, *War in the Air*, p. 239.
25 Morrow, *War in the Air*, p. 239.
26 Keegan, *First World War*, p. 386.
27 Michael Foley, *Pioneers of Aerial Combat: Air Battles of the First World War* (Barnsley, 2013), p. 133.
28 Paris, 'Elitism', p. 124. See also Bourke, *Men's Bodies*, p. 28.
29 'Hawker and Grieve at Grantham: Enthusiastic welcome', *Grantham Journal*, 31 May 1919, p. 8.
30 'London gives airmen an uproarious welcome', *New York Times*, 28 May 1919, p. 4.
31 'Hawker and Grieve at Grantham', p. 8.
32 'Hawker and Grieve at Grantham', p. 8.
33 'Denton. Social', *Grantham Journal*, 17 May 1919, p. 2.
34 'RAF sports at Harlaxton. A delightful afternoon', *Grantham Journal*, 12 July 1919, p. 2.
35 'His Send Off To Us', *Parti Patter*, p. 15.
36 'Send Off', *Parti Patter*, p. 15.
37 'A Princely C.O.', *Parti Patter*, p. 14.
38 Bishop, *Wings*, p. 136.
39 'Hunting notes: The Belvoir', *Grantham Journal*, 19 February 1927, p. 9. See also Centre for Air Power Studies, 'Formation of the Royal Air Force: Air Ministry Weekly Orders, 10 April 1918', *Air Power Review*, Special Edition, Spring (2013), p. 172.
40 Lee Kennett, *The First Air War, 1914–1918* (New York, 1991), p. 116.
41 'Harlaxton Aerodrome', *Grantham Journal*, 13 December 1919, p. 4.
42 'Harlaxton Aerodrome', *Grantham Journal*, 24 January 1920, p. 4.
43 'Ministry of Munitions', *Grantham Journal*, 30 October 1920, p. 3. The last of the miscellaneous stores – tables, stools, trestles, wood and iron cupboards, carpenters' benches, wood desks, chests of drawers, iron and wood bedsteads, wood store bins, wooden trays, stoves, a field boiler and steamer, fire extinguishers, buckets, electric lights, quality Morse paper, French chalk, cartridge cases, wood and iron pulley wheels, a horse-pulled broom, two hand carts,

three tons of steel bars (round, flat and angle), and scrap iron, steel and aluminium, aero wings and struts – were sold off in 1921: 'By direction of the Disposal Board', *Grantham Journal*, 17 September 1921, p. 4.
44 'Harlaxton', *Grantham Journal*, 18 August 1928, p. 5.
45 'Harlaxton' (1928), p. 5.
46 Basil Liddell Hart, *The Memoirs of Captain Liddell Hart*, Vol. 1 (London, 1965), p. 28.
47 Arthur Gould Lee, *Open Cockpit: A Pilot of the Royal Flying Corps* (London, 1969; Reprinted 2013), p. 69.
48 Morrow, *War in the Air*, p. 238.
49 Morrow, *War in the Air*, p. 238.
50 J. Eaton Lascelles, 'Loss of head in aeroplane accidents', *The British Medical Journal* i/2993 (1918), p. 535. Lascelles also suggests that the best training in how to 'grasp a situation and act immediately (almost reflexly) for the best [was] driving a car through traffic or sailing on a crowded river': Lascelles, 'Loss of head', p. 535.
51 H. Graeme Anderson, 'The medical aspects of aeroplane accidents', *The British Medical Journal* i/2977 (1918), p. 73.
52 Anderson, 'Aeroplane accidents', p. 74; see also p. 73. Lascelles attributed 'loss of head' to: (1) Lack of confidence; (2) lack of mental training; (3) congenital tendency; (4) mental fatigue; (5) the influence of ill-advised conversation; (6) insufficient instruction; (7) Fear or 'pure funk': Lascelles, 'Loss of Head', p. 535.
53 Kennett, *First Air War*, p. 116.
54 'Wing Adjutant' (W.T.B.), *The Royal Flying Corps in the War* (London, 1918), p. 9 and p. 8.
55 Keegan, *First World War*, pp. 386–7.
56 Morrow, *War in the Air*, p. 238.
57 Liddell Hart, *Memoirs*, 1, p. 28.
58 Morrow, *War in the Air*, p. 239.
59 Morrow, *War in the Air*, p. 239.
60 Raleigh, quoted in Paris, 'Elitism', p. 138.
61 Tredrey, *Pioneer Pilot*, p. 81.

Bibliography

Primary sources

Beardslee, Alfred C., personal papers. Extracts quoted with the kind permission of his granddaughters.
Curtis, Albert (Sergeant Gunner/Observer), 'Record of Service' (unpublished). Extracts quoted with the kind permission of Phyllis E. Bujak.
Garrett, B.F. (Captain), 'Pilot's Flying Log Book' (unpublished). Extracts quoted with the kind permission of Roger Bragger.
Hansard, 'Pay, etc., of the Air Force', *House of Commons Debates*, Vol. 123, 15 December 1919, cc. 87–147.
Liddell Hart, B., Papers/8/130–40. Extracts quoted with the kind permission of the Trustees of the Liddell Hart Centre for Military Archives, King's College London.
McNab, Leslie, 'Diary' (unpublished). Extracts quoted with the kind permission of the McNab family.
Wallace, 2nd Lieutenant Howard (ed.), *Parti Patter: Being Serious and Smiling Chatter about a Number of Globe Trotters Awaiting the Word to Race for Home* (Grantham, 1919):
    2nd Lieutenant H.G. Warburton, 'Ye Candid Critic Gets Busy'
    'A Base Fabrication'
    'A Glance in the Mirror. While Affixing That Civvy Tie'
    'A Princely CO'
    'A Reminder of England'
    'A Unique Career'
    'Ave, Frater, Atque Vale!'
    'Camaraderie'
    'Harlaxton Manor'
    'His Send Off to Us'
    'On Civvy Suits'
    'The Girls, Glorious Girls!'
    'The Ladies – God Bless 'Em!'
    'Valedictory'

BIBLIOGRAPHY

War Services of Old Melburnians 1914–18, Obituary notice, courtesy of Stewart Brook, Alumni Manager, Melbourne Grammar School.

Online sources

www.ancestry.co.uk:
  'All British Army WWI Service Records, 1914–1920'.
  'British Army Medal Rolls Index Cards, 1914–1920'.
  'Canada, Soldiers of the First World War, 1914–1918'.
  'Canada, Ledgers of CEF Officers Transferring to Royal Flying Corps, 1915–1919'.
  'Great Britain, Royal Aero Club Aviators Certificates, 1910–1950'.
  'UK, Citations of the Distinguished Conduct Medal, 1914–1920'.
Australian Dictionary of National Biography (http:/adb.anu.edu.au/biography/):
  Johnston, Susan, 'Watt, Walter Oswald [1878–1921]', *Australian Dictionary of National Biography*, Vol. 12 (1990), http:/adb.anu.edu.au/biography/watt-walter-oswald-1010.
Australian War Memorial (www.awm.gov.au/):
  'No. 2 Squadron, Australian Flying Corps, September, 1917', www.awm.gov.au/collection/records/AWM4/8/5/2.
  © AWM, Frederic Cutlack, *Official History of Australia in the War of 1914–1918. Vol. 8: The Australian Flying Corps in the Western and Eastern Theatres of War, 1914–1918* (11th edition, 1941), www.awm.gov.au/histories/first_world_war/AWMOHWW1/AIF/Vol8/.
  © AWM, Frederic Cutlack, 'Appendix No. 5, AFC Training in England', in *Official History of Australia in the War of 1914–1918. Vol. 8: The Australian Flying Corps in the Western and Eastern Theatres of War, 1914–1918* (11th edition, 1941), www.awm.gov.au/histories/first_world_war/AWMOHWW1/AIF/Vol8/.
  'First World War Embarkation Rolls', www.awm.gov.au/people/rolls/R2026534/.
  'Alexander Griffiths, Interview 18th January 1993', Acc.No. S01644/ Australian War Memorial, www.awm.gov.au/transcripts/s01644_tran.htm/.
  'Honours and Awards (Recommendation)', www.awm.gov.au/people/rolls/R1564731/.
  'Transcript diary of Verner Gladders Knuckey, 1917, Book 5', RCDIG0000471, www.awm/gov.au/collection/PR03193/.
  'Transcript diary of Verner Gladders Knuckey, 1917, Book 6', RCDIG0000473, www.awm/gov.au/collection/PR03193/.
British Newspaper Archive (www.britishnewspaperarchive.co.uk):
  'By direction of the Disposal Board', *Grantham Journal*, 17 September 1921.
  'Denton. Social', *Grantham Journal*, 17 May 1919.

BIBLIOGRAPHY

'For sale', *Grantham Journal*, 2 September 1922.
'Grantham Rural District Council', *Grantham Journal*, 7 October 1922.
'Grantham Town Council', *Grantham Journal*, 5 February 1921.
'Harlaxton', *Grantham Journal*, 18 August 1928.
'Harlaxton Aerodrome', *Grantham Journal*, 13 December 1919.
'Harlaxton Aerodrome', *Grantham Journal*, 24 January 1920.
'Hawker and Grieve at Grantham: Enthusiastic welcome', *Grantham Journal*, 31 May 1919.
'Hunting notes: The Belvoir', *Grantham Journal*, 19 February 1927.
'Ministry of Munitions', *Grantham Journal*, 30 October 1920.
'Ministry of Munitions: By direction of the Disposal Board (Huts and Building Materials Section)', *Grantham Journal*, 30 October 1920.
'R.A.F. sports at Harlaxton. A delightful afternoon', *Grantham Journal*, 12 July 1919.
'Royal Flying Corps', *Grantham Journal*, 15 September 1917.
'Royal Flying Corps Cadets', *Grantham Journal*, 11 August 1917.
'Royal Flying Corps Cadets', *Grantham Journal*, 25 August 1917.

Gorrell's History of the American Expeditionary Forces Air Service, 1917–1919, (www.fold3.com):
- '9th Aero Squadron'.
- '85th Aero Squadron (Observation). Army Observation, Second Army'.
- 'AEF Air Service Station Lists 1–50, Feb 1918 – Jan 1919'.
- 'History of the 638th Aero Squadron (Pursuit), Fifth Pursuit Group, Second Army'.
- 'The 104th Aero Squadron (Observation)'.
- 'The History of the 165th Aero Squadron'.

Imperial War Museum (www.iwm.org.uk):
- © IWM (80000015/Reel 1), sound recording of Eric John Furlong.
- © IWM (80000015/Reel 2), sound recording of Eric John Furlong.
- © IWM (80000015/Reel 3), sound recording of Eric John Furlong.
- © IWM (80000015/Reel 4), sound recording of Eric John Furlong.

Internet Archive (https://archive.org/):
Rutledge, Lieutenant Stanley A., *Pen Pictures from the Trenches* (Toronto, 1918), https://archive.org/stream/penpicturesfromt00rutluoft#page/n5/mode/2up/.
University of Toronto, Roll of Service, 1914–1918 (Toronto, 1921), http://archive.org/stream/torontorollservic00unknuoft/torontorollservic00unknuoft_djvu.txt/.

The National Archives (www.nationalarchives.gov.uk/):
Arrangement between British and United States Governments on Training and Supply of Personnel for the Air Forces of Both Countries, 19 December 1917, TNA/CAB/24/36.
Copy of Cablegram from the American Military Authorities in Paris to the United States Government, 5 December 1917, TNA/CAB/24/36.
Copy of Letter No. 0153/2847 (O.1.) from Secretary of War Office to Secretary of State for Foreign Affairs, 13 December 1917, TNA/CAB/24/36.

BIBLIOGRAPHY

H.M. Office of Works. Report for Fortnight Ended 16th August, 1918, for the Information of the Prime Minister, TNA/CAB/24/61.
Memorandum of Arrangement between the British and United States Governments, 5 December 1917, TNA/CAB/24/36.
Memorandum by the Chief of the Air Staff on Air Power Requirements of the Empire, 9 December 1918, TNA/CAB/24/71.
Oxford Dictionary of National Biography (www.oxforddnb.com/view/article/):
  Meilinger, Philip S., 'Salmond, Sir John Maitland [1881–1968]', *Oxford Dictionary of National Biography* (Oxford, 2004; Online Edition 2011), www.oxforddnb.com/view/article/35915/.
  Orange, Vincent, 'Trenchard, Hugh Montague, first Viscount Trenchard [1873–1956]', *Oxford Dictionary of National Biography* (Oxford, 2004; Online Edition 2011), www.Oxforddnb.com/view/article/36552/.
The Times Digital Archive (http://infotrac.galegroup.com):
  'Aeroplanes in war: The government's scheme', *The Times*, 13 April 1913.
  'Civilian flying: Official air routes and stations', *The Times*, 25 April 1919.
  'Marriages: Major C.F.A. Portal, DSO, MC, and Miss Welby', *The Times*, 23 July 1919.
  'Mr. Lloyd George on his task', *The Times*, 25 November 1918.
  'Royal Flying Corps: The military wing', *The Times*, 16 April 1912.

Other online sources

Blake, John, 'A Brief History of the Royal Aero Club', www.royalaeroclub.co.uk/.
'Dispatch received by the Secretary of State for War from the Field-Marshal Commanding-in-Chief, British Forces in the Field', *The London Gazette*, 8 September 1914, https://www.thegazette.co.uk/London/issue/28897/supplement/7189/.
Gauld, Gordon Smith Mellis, 'Commonwealth War Graves Commission', www.cwgc.org/.
'Gordon Smith Mellis Gauld', www.veterans.gc.ca/eng/remembrance/memorials/canadian-virtual-war-memorial/.
'Heroes of the air', *The West Australian*, 10 June 1919, http://trove.nla.gov.au/ndp/del/article/27607366/.
James Fitz Morris papers, www.falkirkcommunitytrust.org/heritage/archives/finding-aids/docs/family_papers/Family_and_personal_papers _ D-F.pdf/.
'London gives airmen an uproarious welcome', *New York Times*, 28 May 1919, http://query.nytimes.com/mem/archive-free/pdf/.
'Miss Bunny Barnes', www.warcovers.co.uk/shop/1919-PPC-FRANCE-to-WRAF-Officers-Mess-RAF-Harlaxton-Camp.html/.
'Royal Aero Club Aviator's Certificate', rafmuseum.org.uk.

'Second Lieutenant Alick Thomas Bentall Charlesworth', www.canadiangreatwarproject.com/.
Sewell, Michael, *The Joiners Tale: Some Memories of Grantham*, www.cl.cam. ac.uk/~pes20/MJSewell/JoinersTale.pdf/.
'Swimmers of the air. The late Capt. Stanley K. Muir', *The Euroa Advertizer*, Friday, 16 November 1917, http://trove.nla.gov.au/.
'Temp. 2nd Lt. [temp. Lt] Stanley Keith Muir, Gen. List and R.F.C.', *The Edinburgh Gazette*, 6 March 1917, www.thegazette.co.uk/Edinburgh/issue/13061/page/495/.
'Temp. Capt. William James Yule Guilfoyle', *The London Gazette*, 2 March 1917, www.thegazette.co.uk/ London/issue/29968/supplement/2193/.

Secondary sources

Alderson, A.G.D., *The First War in the Air, 1914–1918* (England, c. 1990).
Anderson, H. Graeme, 'The medical aspects of aeroplane accidents', *The British Medical Journal* i/2977 (1918), pp. 73–6.
Armitage, Michael, *The Royal Air Force: An Illustrated History* (London, 1993).
Armitage, Michael (ed.), *Classic RAF Battles from WWI to the Present* (London, 1995).
Arthur, Max, *Lost Voices of the Royal Air Force* (London, 1993).
Barker, Ralph, *The Royal Flying Corps in France: From Mons to the Somme* (London, 1994).
────── *The Royal Flying Corps in France: From Bloody April 1917 to Final Victory* (London, 1995).
────── *A Brief History of the Royal Flying Corps in WWI* (London, 2002).
Bennett, John, *Highest Traditions: The History of No. 2 Squadron RAAF* (Canberra, 1995).
Berberich, Christine, *The Image of the English Gentleman in Twentieth Century Literature: Englishness and Nostalgia* (Aldershot, 2007).
Bishop, Patrick, *Wings: The RAF at War, 1912–2012* (London, 2013).
Bishop, William A., *Winged Warfare* (London, 1975).
Blake, Ron, Mike Hodgson and Bill Taylor, *The Airfields of Lincolnshire since 1912* (Leicester, 1984).
Bostridge, Mark, *The Fateful Year: England 1914* (London, 2014).
Bourke, Joanna, *Dismembering the Male: Men's Bodies, Britain and the Great War* (London, 1996).
Bowyer, Michael J.F., *Actions Stations Revisited: The Complete History of Britain's Military Airfields. No. 1: Eastern England* (Manchester, 2000).
Brownell, R.J., *From Khaki to Blue: The Autobiography of Air Commodore R.J. Brownell* (Canberra, 1978).
Cavendish, Richard, 'Royal Flying Corps founded', *History Today* lxii/4 (2012), p. 8.

BIBLIOGRAPHY

Cecil, Lord Hugh, 'The Royal Flying Corps: The work and training of the Royal Flying Corps', *The London Illustrated News* (London, 1918).

Central Flying School, *Training Manual, Royal Flying Corps, Part I (Provisional), 1914* (London, 1914).

────── *Hints for Young Instructors on How to Instruct in Flying, Issued by the Central Flying School, Royal Flying Corps, September 1916* (London, 1916).

Centre for Air Power Studies, 'Appendix I: Memorandum on the organization of the air services', *Air Power Review*, Special Edition, Spring (2013).

────── 'Formation of the Royal Air Force: Air Ministry Weekly Orders, 10th April 1918', *Air Power Review* special edition, Spring (2013).

────── 'Synopsis of British air effort during the war, 1914–1918', *Air Power Review*, Special Edition, Spring (2013).

────── 'Training Manual, Royal Flying Corps, Part II [Military Wing]', *Air Power Review*, Special Edition, Spring (2013).

Chajkowsky, William E., *Royal Flying Corps: Borden to Texas to Beamsville* (Ontario, 1979).

Chasseud, Peter, 'Artillery Training Maps of the UK 1914–1918, Part II: The 1:20,000 Series (GSGS 2748)', *Sheetlines*, Nos 11 to 14 (undated).

Cobby, A.H., *High Adventure* (Melbourne, 1981).

Cole, Christopher (ed.), *Royal Flying Corps, 1915–1916* (London, 1969).

Coningham, Simon, 'The Battle of Amiens: Air-ground co-operation and its implications for imperial policing', in Gary Sheffield and Peter Gray (eds), *Changing War: The British Army, the Hundred Days Campaign and the Birth of the Royal Air Force, 1918* (London, 2013).

Cooksley, Peter G., *Royal Flying Corps Handbook, 1914–1918* (Stroud, 2007).

Cooper, Malcolm, *The Birth of Independent Air Power: British Air Policy in the First World War* (London, 1986).

────── 'Blueprint for confusion: The administrative background to the formation of the Royal Air Force, 1912–1919', *Journal of Contemporary History* xxii/3 (1987), pp. 437–53.

Davis, Mick and Bill Morgan, 'Gazetteer of flying sites, Part 9. Gai-Har', *Cross and Cockade International* xliii/1 (2012), GFS-72.

Dye, Peter, 'The genesis of modern warfare: The contribution of aviation logistics', in Gary Sheffield and Peter Gray (eds), *Changing War: The British Army, The Hundred Days Campaign and the Birth of the Royal Air Force, 1918* (London, 2013).

Edgerton, David, *England and the Aeroplane: Militarism, Modernity and Machines* (London, 2013).

Elton, Ben and Richard Curtis, 'Plan D: Private Plane', *Blackadder Goes Forth*, episode 4 (1989).

Fearon, Peter, 'The formative years of the British aircraft industry, 1913–1924', *The Business History Review* xliii/4 (1969), pp. 476–95.

'Flight Commander', *Cavalry of the Air* (London, 1918).

Foley, Michael, *Pioneers of Aerial Combat: Air Battles of the First World War* (Barnsley, 2013).

Franks, Norman, *Dog-Fight: Aerial Tactics of the Aces of WWI* (London, 2003).

BIBLIOGRAPHY

―――― *Sopwith Camel Aces of World War One* (Oxford, 2003).
―――― *SE5/5a Aces of World War I* (Oxford, 2007).
Fussell, Paul, *The Great War and Modern Memory* (Oxford, 2000).
Gardiner, Geoff, *Airfield Focus 17: Spittlegate* (Peterborough, 1994).
Grattan, Robert F., *The Origins of Air War: The Development of Military Air Strategy in the First World War* (London, 2009).
Gray, Peter, 'The Air Ministry and the formation of the Royal Air Force', in Gary Sheffield and Peter Gray (eds), *Changing War: The British Army, The Hundred Days Campaign and the Birth of the Royal Air Force, 1918* (London, 2013).
Greenhous, Brereton, 'Evolution of a close ground-support role for aircraft in World War I', *Military Affairs* xxxix/1 (1975), pp. 22–8.
Hancock, T.N., *Bomber County: A History of the Royal Air Force in Lincolnshire* (Lincoln, 1978).
―――― *Bomber County: A History of the Royal Air Force in Lincolnshire*, Vol. 2 (Lincoln, 1985).
Hare, Paul R., *Fokker Fodder. The Royal Aircraft Factory BE2c* (Fonthill, 2012).
Hart, Peter, *Somme Success: The Royal Flying Corps and the Battle of the Somme, 1916* (Barnsley, 2001).
―――― *Bloody April: Slaughter in the Skies over Arras, 1917* (London, 2005).
―――― *Aces Falling: War above the Trenches, 1918* (London, 2007).
Hunt, C.W., *Dancing in the Sky: The Royal Flying Corps in Canada* (Toronto, 2009).
Hunt, Leslie, 'Flying round Grantham', *Lincolnshire Life*, September (1998), pp. 22–4.
James, John, *The Paladins: A Social History of the RAF up to the Outbreak of World War II* (London, 1990).
Jefford, C.G., *Observers and Navigators and Other Non-Pilot Aircrew in the RFC, RNAS and RAF* (Shrewsbury, 2001).
Jones, George, *From Private to Air Marshal: The Autobiography of Air Marshal Sir George Jones* (Richmond, Australia, 1988).
Jordan, David, 'The genesis of modern air power: The RAF in 1918', in Gary Sheffield and Peter Gray (eds), *Changing War: The British Army, The Hundred Days Campaign and the Birth of the Royal Air Force, 1918* (London, 2013).
Keegan, John, *The First World War* (London, 1999).
Kennett, Lee, *The First Air War, 1914–1918* (New York, 1991).
Kipling, Rudyard, 'If', in *Rewards and Fairies* (New York, 1910).
Kirby, Chester, *The English Country Gentleman: A Study of Nineteenth Century Types* (London, 1937).
Lascelles, J. Eaton, 'Loss of head in aeroplane accidents', *The British Medical Journal* i/2993 (1918).
Lee, Arthur Gould, *Open Cockpit: A Pilot of the Royal Flying Corps* (London, 1969; Reprinted 2013).
―――― *No Parachute: A Classic Account of War in the Air in WWI in Letters Written in 1917 by Lieutenant A.S.G. Lee, Sherwood Foresters, Attached Royal Flying Corps* (London, 2013).

BIBLIOGRAPHY

Levine, Joshua, *On a Wing and a Prayer: The Untold Story of the Pioneering Aviation Heroes of WWI, in Their Own Words* (London, 2008).

——— *Fighter Heroes of WWI: The Extraordinary Story of the Pioneering Airmen of the Great War* (London, 2009).

Lewis, Bruce, *A Few of the First: The True Stories of the Men Who Flew in and before the First World War* (Barnsley, 1997).

Liddell Hart, Basil, *The Memoirs of Captain Liddell Hart*, Vol. 1 (London, 1965).

Lloyd George, David, *War Memoirs of David Lloyd George*, Vol. 2 (London, 1933).

Luck, Christopher, 'The Smuts Report: Interpreting and misinterpreting the promise of air power', in Gary Sheffield and Peter Gray (eds), *Changing War: The British Army, The Hundred Days Campaign and the Birth of the Royal Air Force, 1918* (London, 2013).

Macauley, Lord 'Horatius', *Lays of Ancient Rome* (New York, 1888).

Mackersey, Ian, *No Empty Chairs: The Short and Heroic Lives of the Young Aviators Who Fought and Died in the First World War* (London, 2012).

McCudden, James, V.C., *Flying Fury: Five Years in the Royal Flying Corps* (Elstree, 1987).

Miller, Roger G., 'The tail to tooth ratio: Royal Flying Corps and air service co-operation in maintenance training during World War One', *Royal Air Force Historical Society* xxxii (2004), pp. 8–27.

Molkentin, Michael, *Fire in the Sky: The Australian Flying Corps in the First World War* (Crows Nest, 2010).

Morrow, John H., *The Great War in the Air: Military Aviation from 1909 to 1921* (Shrewsbury, 1993).

Morse, Daniel P., *The History of the 50th Aero Squadron* (New York, 1920).

Munson, Kenneth, *Fighters, 1914–1919: Attack and Training Aircraft* (London, 1971).

——— *Bombers, 1914–1919: Patrol and Reconnaissance Aircraft* (London, 1972).

Nesbit, Roy Conyers, *An Illustrated History of the RAF* (Godalming, 1990).

Newton, Dennis, *Australian Air Aces* (Fyshwick, 1996).

Norris, Geoffrey, *The Royal Flying Corps: A History* (London, 1965).

Offer, Patrick, *Lincolnshire Airfields in the Second World War* (Newbury, 1996).

O'Kiely, Elizabeth, *Gentleman Air Ace: The Duncan Bell-Irving Story* (Madeira Park, 1992).

Osborne, Mike, *Defending Lincolnshire: A Military History from Conquest to Cold War* (Stroud, 2010).

Page, Gordon and Jim Halley, 'Armstrong Whitworth FK3', *Air-Britain, Aeromilitaria* xxxvi/144 (2010), pp. 160–5.

Palazzo, Albert P., 'The British Army's Counter-Battery Staff Office and control of the enemy in World War I', *The Journal of Military History* lxiii/1 (1999), pp. 55–74.

Paris, Michael, *Winged Warfare: The Literature and Theory of Aerial Warfare in Britain, 1859–1917* (Manchester, 1992).

―― 'The rise of the airmen: The origins of air force elitism, c. 1890–1918', *Journal of Contemporary History* xxviii/1 (1993), pp. 123–41.
Parnell, N.M. and C.A. Lynch, *Australian Air Force since 1911* (London, 1976).
Petter, Martin, 'Temporary gentlemen in the aftermath of the Great War: Rank, status and the ex-officer problem', *Historical Journal* xxxvii/1 (1994), pp. 127–52.
Philpott, Maryam, *Air and Sea Power in World War I: Combat and Experience in the Royal Flying Corps and the Royal Navy* (London, 2013).
Philpott, William, *Bloody Victory: The Sacrifice on the Somme* (London, 2009).
Raleigh, Walter, *The War in the Air: Being the Story of the Part Played in the Great War by the Royal Air Force*, Vol. 1 (London, 1922).
Richards, Denis, *Portal of Hungerford: The Life of Marshal of the Royal Air Force Viscount Portal of Hungerford* (London, 1977).
Rowe, Alan, 'The RE8 controversy revisited', *The '14–'18 Journal* (2001), pp. 64–70.
Royal Flying Corps, *Royal Flying Corps Technical Notes, 1916* (Reprinted, London, 1968).
Salter, James, 'The most wonderful sport', Review of Samuel Hynes, *The Unsubstantial Air: American Fliers in the First World War*, *London Review of Books* xxxvi/21 (2014), 5–6.
Saunders, Hilary St George, *Per Ardua: The Rise of British Air Power, 1911–1939* (London, 1944).
Schaedel, Charles, *Men and Machines of the Australian Flying Corps, 1914–1919* (Dandenong, Victoria, 1972).
Sheftall, Mark David, *Altered Memories of the Great War: Divergent Narratives of Britain, Australia, New Zealand and Canada* (London, 2009).
Shores, Christopher, Norman Franks and Russell Guest, *Above the Trenches: A Complete Record of the Fighter Aces and Units of the British Empire Air Forces, 1915–1920* (Stoney Creek, Ontario, 1990).
Smith, Alistair, *Images of War: Royal Flying Corps: Rare Photographs from Wartime Archives* (Barnsley, 2002).
Steel, Nigel and Peter Hart, *Tumult in the Clouds: The British Experience of the War in the Air, 1914–1918* (London, 1997).
Stephens, Alan, *The Royal Australian Air Force* (Oxford, 2001).
Stevenson, David, *1914–1918: The History of the First World War* (London, 2005).
―― *With Our Backs to the Wall: Victory and Defeat* (London, 2011).
Strachan, Hew, *The First World War: A New Illustrated History* (London, 2006).
Sturtivant, Ray, *The History of Britain's Military Training Aircraft* (Yeovil, 1987).
Sturtivant, Ray, and John Hamlin, *Royal Air Force Flying Training and Support Units since 1912* (Trowbridge, 2007).
Sweetman, John, 'Crucial months for survival: The Royal Air Force, 1918–1919', *Journal of Contemporary History* xix/iii (1984), pp. 529–47.
―― *Cavalry of the Clouds: Air War over Europe, 1914–1918* (Stroud, 2010).
Thompson, Robert, *The Royal Flying Corps: Per Ardua ad Astra* (London, 1968).

BIBLIOGRAPHY

Townsend, Philip Brereton, *Eye in the Sky, 1918: Recollections of Air-to-Ground Co-Operation by a World War One Pilot* (Private, 1986).

Treadwell, Terry and Alan C. Wood, *The Royal Flying Corps* (Stroud, 2000).

Tredrey, F.D., *Pioneer Pilot: The Great Smith Barry Who Taught the World How to Fly* (London, 1976).

Whitehouse, A.G.J., *Hell in the Heavens: The Adventures of an Aerial Gunner in the Royal Flying Corps* (London, 1938).

'Wing Adjutant' (W.T.B.), *The Royal Flying Corps in the War* (London, 1918).

Wright, Peter, *The Royal Flying Corps, 1912–1918, in Oxfordshire* (Oxford, 1985).

Yeates, V.M., *Winged Victory* (London, 1934; Reprinted 2008).

Yeats, W.B., 'An Irish Airman Foresees His Death', in *The Wild Swans at Coole* (New York, 1919).

Index

This index covers RFC/RAF training at Harlaxton, primarily under different headings, in chapters and notes. Terms are indexed by abbreviation. A page number in *italics* indicates a figure; 'n.' after a page number indicates a note, and 't.' a table.

Aboukir aerodrome 69
ace pilots 40 *see also individual names*
AFC *see* Australian forces
air shows 53
Albatros aircraft 36
alcohol 99
Amria aerodrome 69
Anderson, H. Graeme 143–4
Anderson, William, Lieutenant 88
aristocracy *see* elite classes
Armistice 125, 186 n.1
Arras (battle) 37–8, 54
ARS (Aircraft Repair Section) 90–1
artillery-spotting 4, 16, 21, 22, 23–4
Australian forces 8, 41, 100, 103–4, *104*, 108, 110–11, 115, *117*, 125–6, 183 n.1
  bombing 120
  casualty and 116–17
  confidence 111
  crashes 111
  delayed participation 111–12
  discipline and 105
  discreteness and 100
  drill 104–5
  experience and 114, 115
  graduation 115
  horsemanship 100–2
  journey home and 40–1
  journey to Harlaxton 102, 103
  landings 111
  mascot *109*
  one-day deployment 116–17
  rabbit shooting 105
  recognition 40
  risk and 114
  skill 114
  strafing 105, 120, 121
  stunt flying 85, 86
  welcome to 102, 103
Aviator's Certificate 51, 58
Avro 504 75–6, *76*, 107, 112–13

Barnes, Bunny 131
Bascombe, Cecil, Lieutenant 88
'A Base Fabrication' 84
Bayeux-Armentières sector 10–11
BE aircraft 16
BE2 series 73
BE2c 20, *97*
BE2d 58
BE2e *16*, 58, *59*
Beardslee, Alfred, Mechanic 94, 98–9
Beech, A.H., Lieutenant 86
BEF (British Expeditionary Force) 18
Bell, John, Captain 111

205

INDEX

Bell-Irving, Duncan 10
Belvoir Castle 45, *46*
Belvoir Hunt 127
Benn, William Wedgwood, Air Commodore 137
Billiard Room *31*
Bir Saba 108
Bishop, Billy, Air Marshal 138
Bloomfield, Gerald, Lieutenant 88
Boelcke, Oswald, Hauptmann 20
bombing 119–21
Brancker, Sefton, Air Vice-Marshal 29
Brigade of Guards 91
brigades 18–19
Brown, Walter, Mechanic 81
Buckley, Harold 88
Burdett, Lieutenant Colonel 104–5, 184–5 n.14
Butler, James, Major 43, 140–1

Cambrai (battle) 120
camera guns 72
Canadian forces 7, 28, 41, *41*, 125–6, 141
Canteen 98–9
CAS (Chief of the Air Staff) position 6
Caudron aircraft 57
CBSO (Counter-Battery Staff Office) 24
Cecil, Hugh 13, 40, 44, 61, 79
CFS (Central Flying School) 15, 47, 67
Chambers, Phyllis 130
Charlesworth, Alick, Lieutenant 87, 143
chivalry 43, 44, 45, 123, 127–9
class issues 28–9, 42, 43, 45, 124–5, 138 *see also* elite classes
clay pigeon shooting 72, 73, *73*
cloud flying 79
Cobby, Harry, Air Commodore 40, 65–6, 79, 110, 111–14, 121
communication systems 23–4, 79
concert 98
confidence 67–8, 84, 111, 138
crashes *16*, 50, *57*, 59, *70*, *76*, *82*, *101*, 144

blame and 58
casualties *see* deaths and injuries
overcoming 111
risk and 120
scale 81–3, 143–4
Cross, Arthur, Lieutenant 88
Curtis, Albert, Sergeant 29, 31
Cutlack, Frederic 114

Dalziel, William, Lieutenant *59*
deaths and injuries 5–6, 26–7, 31, *82*, 83, 84, 87, 88, *89*, *99*, 116
controlled fear and 145
disillusionment and 7–8
funeral 116
grief and 116
ground accidents 89, 145
hidden feelings 88–9, 145
mementoes 27
morale and 116–17
post-combat 125
recognition and 83–4, 86
remembrance 143
replacement and 122–3
risk and 38–40, 86, 89, 113–14
routineness and 81
scale 35, 38–40, 53–4, 64, 79, 81, 88, 143
suddenness and 88, 114
Denton Manor 13, *14*, 131–2
DH2 34
DH5 59, 61–2, 73, 83, 89
DH6 37, *82*, 88, *101*, 105, 116
dogfighting 71–2, *72*, 86, 108, 122
drill 104–5
Drysdale, Alexander, Lieutenant 88
'Dulce Et Decorum Est' (Owen) 8

education 12, 43, 124, 132, 137
Egypt 69, 100
elite classes 6, 126, 137
chivalry 45
daring 145
disillusionment and 7
education and 43, 124, 132, 137
equality and 6, 136

206

INDEX

friendships 9–10
horsemanship 42, 124, 127
parties and dances 127
see also officers
everyday and modern life 123

Falck, Jack, Lieutenant 87
FE aircraft 16
FE2b 34
Fitz Morris, James, Captain 65
FK8 *72*
Fokker aircraft 20, 25, 33–4
Fokker E-type 5
fox hunting 11, 124, 127–9
freedom 107–8
French, John, Field Marshal 18
friendships 9–10, 114
Frost, Captain *126*
funeral 116
Furlong, Eric 56–8, 59, 60–1, 66–7, 82–3

Gauld, Gordon, Lieutenant 87–8
General Methods of Teaching Scout Pilots (Smith Barry) 69
Gosport 63, 67–8, 69
Gough, Hubert, General 35
Grant, Tom 107
Grantham 138–9
Grantham (station) 103, 141
grief 116
Griffiths, Alexander, Wireless Operator 26–7
Guilfoyle, William, Captain 110, 111

Hampshire, T.H., Lieutenant 117
hangars *49*, 50
Harlaxton *3*
Harlaxton aerodrome 6, 48, 50, *54*, *90*, *119*, *129*
 ARS 90–1
 auctioning off 142, 192 n.43
 Canteen 98–9
 Christmas card *128*
 constructing 50, 103–4
 dismantling 134, 142

hangars *49*, 50
infrastructure 89–91
Machine Gun Lecture Room *26*
mothballing and 134–5
Officers' Mess 28, *31*, 125, 130–1
repatriation camp 2, 7, 125, 131, 140
requisitioned land *48*, 50
sports days *139*, 139–40, *141*
Harlaxton Manor 6, *9*, 94, 126–7
Harlaxton Photographic Section 21–2, *22*
Hawker, Harry 138–9
hedge-hopping 89
Henderson, David, Lieutenant-General 162 n.10
Hewson, Tommy 111–12, 114
HF Rumpety 73
Hints for Young Instructors on How to Instruct in Flying (CFS) 67
Hoare, Cuthbert, Brigadier-General 191 n.20
Hoeppner, Ernst von, General 3
horsemanship 2, 7, 10, 100–2, 123–4, 142
 daring and 3, 42
 hunting 10–11, 124, 127–9
 non-transferability 42
 reconnaissance and 3–4
 skill and 11, 12–13, 42
 stunt flying and 86
horseplay 71, 97
hunting 10–11, 72–3, 124, 127–9

Iddon, S.R. *89*
'If' (Kipling) 132–3
Immelmann, Max, Oberleutnant 20
'In Memoriam, Lieut. S.A. Rutledge' (Stewart) 87
injuries *see* deaths and injuries
Into the Blue (MacMillan) 143

Jackson, Albert 29
Jagdstaffeln (Jastas) 36, 37, 121–2
James, Jimmy, Lieutenant 71
Jenkins, Major 83–4, *106*

INDEX

Jones, Fred 31
Jones, George, Air Marshal (CAS) 30
Jones, O.J. 111–12

keeping station 77–9
Kipling, Rudyard 132–3
Klynes, Alexander 132, *133*
Knuckey, Verner, Wireless Operator 102, 103–5, 107, 108, 110, 116

landings 50
    forced 58–9, 70–1, 75–6, 82–3, 111
    night-time 55, 70–1
    risk 50
    see also crashes
Lawry, Kevin 143
Lee, Arthur, Air Vice-Marshal 44–5, 64, 67, 68, 81, 143
Leedham, William, Mechanic 28
Levine, Myer, Lieutenant 79
Lewis, Cecil 45
Lewis machine guns 19–20, 34
Liddell Hart, Basil, Captain 105, 142, 145
Lincolnshire 48
Lincolnshire Cliff 48
Little, R.A., Captain 138
Lloyd George, David 15
looping the loop 112–13
Lyon Williams, B.S., Captain 75

Machine Gun Corps Training Centre 21
Machine Gun Lecture Room *26*
machine guns 19–21, *23*, 34, 71
    innovations 20
    skill 26
    strafing 26–7, 70, 105, 119, 120–1
MacMillan, Norman, Wing Commander 143
manliness 2, 86
Mannock, Mick, Major 138
markings (aircraft) 18
marriages 131–2, 142
Martinsyde aircraft 61

mascot *109*
Mather, A.W., Lieutenant *99*
Matthews, George, Lieutenant 111
McCudden, James, Major 77, 138
McNab, Leslie 45, 50, 69, 75, 76, 80, 127, 130–31
    on Armistice 125
    graduation 69–70
    on horsemanship 127–9
    on horseplay 97
    on landings 70–1, 75–6, 82–3
    on multinational forces 125
    on photography 72
    on strafing 70
Measures, Arthur, Bombardier 24, 35
mechanic rank 17, 27–8, 89–91, 92–3, 94–5, 97, *97*
    horseplay 97
    numbers 91–2
    promotion and 28–9, 30, 91
    recognition 91
    rotation and 96
    school squadrons 93–4, 95–7
    skill 91
Memoirs of a Fox-Hunting Man (Sassoon) 124
MF Shorthorn *57*, 73
MF8 Longhorn 57–8
monkey (mascot) *109*
Mons (battle) 18
Morse, Daniel, Captain 95
Morse code 23–4
motoring *133*
Muir, Stanley, Captain 91, 108, *109*, 110, 111
    death and 116–17, 143
    recognition 108, 184 n.19
    skill 108
    on stunt flying 85–6, 108
multinational forces 43–4, 99, 125
Murray, Leonard, Lieutenant 89

NCOs (non-commissioned officers) 17–18, 29–10
Nicholson, Lieutenant *126*
Nieuport 12 34

INDEX

night-time landings 55, 70–1
Notes on Aeroplane Fighting in Single Seat Scouts (RFC) 77
'Notes on Teaching Flying for the Instructor's Courses' (Smith Barry) 69

offensive patrols 4, 32, 37, 77, 121, 122
  scale 35, 78
  stunt flying 122
officers 2–3, 9, 30, *44*, 115, 135, 136–7
  casualties 145
  chivalry 123
  commissions and 17–18, 29–30, 42
  confidence 111
  discreteness and 93
  education 12
  equality and 12, 28, 131–2, 137
  graduation 51, 115
  horsemanship 2, 3, 7, 10–11, 12–13, 42, 123–4, 127–9
  mimicry and 11
  modernity and 8, 12–13
  numbers 9, 12
  parties and dances 13
  promotion and 28–9, 30
  rabbit shooting 105
  risk 132–3
  role models and 8–9, 12, 13
  success and 8, 79–80
  uniforms and 52
  see also individual names
Officers' Mess *28*, *31*, 125, 130–1, 145
Owen, Wilfred 8

parties and dances 13, 127
Passchendaele (battle) 120
Pearson Gregory, Philip, Major 9
Perryman, Arthur, Lieutenant 88
Phillipps, Roy, Major 40, 115–16
photography 21–2, *22*, 23–4, 72
Portal, Charles, Marshal (CAS) 13, 131–2
Portal (née Welby), Joan 13, 131–2

propeller accidents 89, 145
public school 12, 43, 124, 137
pusher design 16, 20, 34

rabbit shooting 105
RAF (Royal Air Force) 6–7, 123, 134–5, 188 n.37, 190 n.3
ragtime songs 98
RE aircraft 16
RE8 69, 73–4, *74*
  casualties 79, 88, *89*, 99
  reconnaissance 20–1, 26–7
reconnaissance 3–5, 15, 16, 21, 24, 26, 27–8, 32, 35
  arming 19–21, 26–7
  balance 27
  casualties 31
  escorts 5, 24, 25, 34, 122
  evasive flying 18
  local knowledge 32
  numbers 18
  photography 21–2, *22*, 23–4, 72
  promotion and 28–9
  recognition and 22
  risk and 5, 19, 20, 22, 24, 30
  skill 21
  success 18
  unescorted and 30–1
relationships 97, *98*, 140–1
  casualties and 31
  crashes and 58
  experience and 31
  friendships 9–10, 114
  horseplay 97
  multinational forces 43–4, 99, 125
repatriation camp 2, 7, 125, 131, 140
rest 65–6
RFA (Royal Field Artillery) 4, 24
RFC (Royal Flying Corps) 7, 24–5, 32–4, 37, 38, 162 n.3
  daring and 6, 44–5
  enlisting age 136
  equality and 41–2, 43–4, 135–6
  inception 3–4
  limitations 33
  risk to 38–40

INDEX

straight and level flying 4, 15
tactical fighting 34
RNAS (Royal Naval Air Service) 162 n.3
Rowe, H.J.N., Lieutenant 13
Royal Aero Club 51
Royal Aircraft Factory 16
Royal Engineers 91
Royston, A.M. 140
Rutledge, Stanley, Lieutenant 11, 35–6, 38, *39*, 41, 60–1
  on cross-country flying 60
  on daring 83
  death and 83–4, 86–7, 143
  graduation and 60
  on landings 59, 82–3
  on stunt flying 61–2, 71–2
Rutledge, Wilfred, Lieutenant 38

Saint, Captain *82*
Salmond, John, Marshal (CAS) 55, 92, 118, 121
sappers 91
Sassoon, Siegfried 124
Schlachtstaffeln 120–1
school squadrons 93–4, 95–7
SE5a 40, 79
sergeant rank 17
Sewell, Ben 135
Smith Barry, Robert, Major 62, 63, 67–8, 69, 74–5, 173–3 n.11
smoking 98–9
Smuts, Jan 6
social pastimes and events 130–1, 138–9
  air shows 53
  clay pigeon shooting 72, 73, *73*
  concert 98
  culture shock and 97–9
  errors and 127
  hunting 10–11, 72–3, 124, 127–9
  marriages 131–2, 142
  motoring *133*
  parties and dances 13, 127
  rabbit shooting 105
  sports days *139*, 139–40, *141*
Somme (battle) 24, 35–6, 87

Sopwith, Phyllis 138–9
Sopwith, Thomas 138–9
Sopwith 1½-Strutter 34
Sopwith aircraft *70*, 138
Sopwith Camel 40, 79
Sopwith Pup 37
South African forces 125–6, 141
Spandau machine guns 20
Spittlegate aerodrome 48, 71–2, 96–7, 134–5
sports days *139*, 139–40, *141*
squadrons 18–19, 25, 32, 33, 52–3, 54, 67, 91, 93–5, 100, 108, 110–11, 183 n.1
  9th Aero 95
  50th Aero *93*, 94, 95–6
  85th Aero 94, 95–6
  165th Aero 94, 96–7
  638th Aero 95
  bombing 120
  casualty and 116–17
  discipline and 105
  drill 104–5
  experience and 115
  Jagdstaffeln 36, 37, 121–2
  journey to Harlaxton 102, 103
  mascot *109*
  mothballing and 134–5
  No. 26 47
  No. 44 47, 103
  No. 67 (Australian) 100
  No. 68 (Australian) 100, 102, 103–5, *104*, 108, 110–11, 115, 116–17, *117*, 120
  No. 69 (Australian) 100
  No. 71 (Australian) 121, 183 n.1
  numbers 16t., 17–18, 19, 33, 36–7, 47–8, 51, 118, 186 n.1
  one-day deployment 116–17
  rabbit shooting 105
  re-designated 47
  reconnaissance 18, 34
  rotation and 64–5
  Schlachtstaffeln 120–1
  school squadrons 93–4, 95–7
  strafing 105, 120, 121

INDEX

tactical fighting 25–6, 32, 77–9, 166 n.48
TDSs from 52, 118–19
welcome to 102, 103
see also offensive patrols
stalls 59, 88
Stewart, A.C. 87
stiff upper lip 71, 88–9
strafing 26–7, 70, 105, 119, 120–1
stunt flying 53, 61–2, 63, 85, 112
   confidence 67–8
   daring 85
   dogfighting 71–2, 72, 86, 108, 122
   Immelmann turn 20
   looping the loop 112–13
   low-altitude fighting 119–21
   manliness 86
   risk and 61, 64
   single and dual controls 64
   skill 85–6
   see also crashes; deaths and injuries
Sykes, Frederick, Air Vice-Marshal (CAS) 134

tailors 52
TDSs (Training Depot Stations) 52, 118–19
telegraphy 23–4
Thorne, Arthur, Lieutenant 79, 88
Townsend, Philip Brereton, Lieutenant 64
tractor design 16, 20, 34
training 45–6, 51, 54–5, 56, 62, 68–9, 74–5, 77, 143, 144, 175 n.29
   all-through 75
   autonomous methods 66–7
   controlled fear and 144–5
   cross-country 58–9
   encouragement and 75
   equality and 51
   experience and 5, 19, 38, 54, 65, 68
   graduation and 50–1, 52, 60
   hidden feelings 71
   inception 50
   limitations 16–17, 19, 34–5, 38, 53–4, 63–4, 66–7, 143

minimum hours 55–6
modernity and 143
replacement and 118
risk and 55, 79, 81
rotation and 64–5
schools of instruction 51, 68, 114–15, 178 n.44
single and dual controls 58
uniforms 51–2
wings 60, 176 n.78
Training Brigade 47–8
Trenchard, Hugh, Marshal (CAS) 4, 135
trenches 23

uniforms 51–2
US forces 92–9, 93, 96, 97, 98

V formation 78
Van der Riet, Lieutenant 126
Vickers machine guns 20–1, 26–7

Wallace, Howard, Lieutenant 10
Warburton, H.G., Lieutenant 125
Waterloo (station) 102
Watson, Howard, Lieutenant 79
Watt, Oswald, Major 102–3, 106, 112, 120
   death and 116
   on delayed participation 111–12
   on drill 104–5
   recognition 40
   on stunt flying 85, 86
Way, William 142
weather and climate 69, 104
Welby, Charles 13
Welby (later Portal), Joan 13, 131–2
wings (badge) 60, 176 n.78
wings (group) 18–19, 32, 69
WLMD (Women's Legion of Motor Drivers) 130
Women's Companies 130
Woolf, Virginia 123
Work and Training (RFC) 44
WRAF (Women's Royal Air Force) 127, 130–1